I0812728

IMAGES
of America

EASTERN POCONOS

DELAWARE WATER GAP TO BUSHKILL

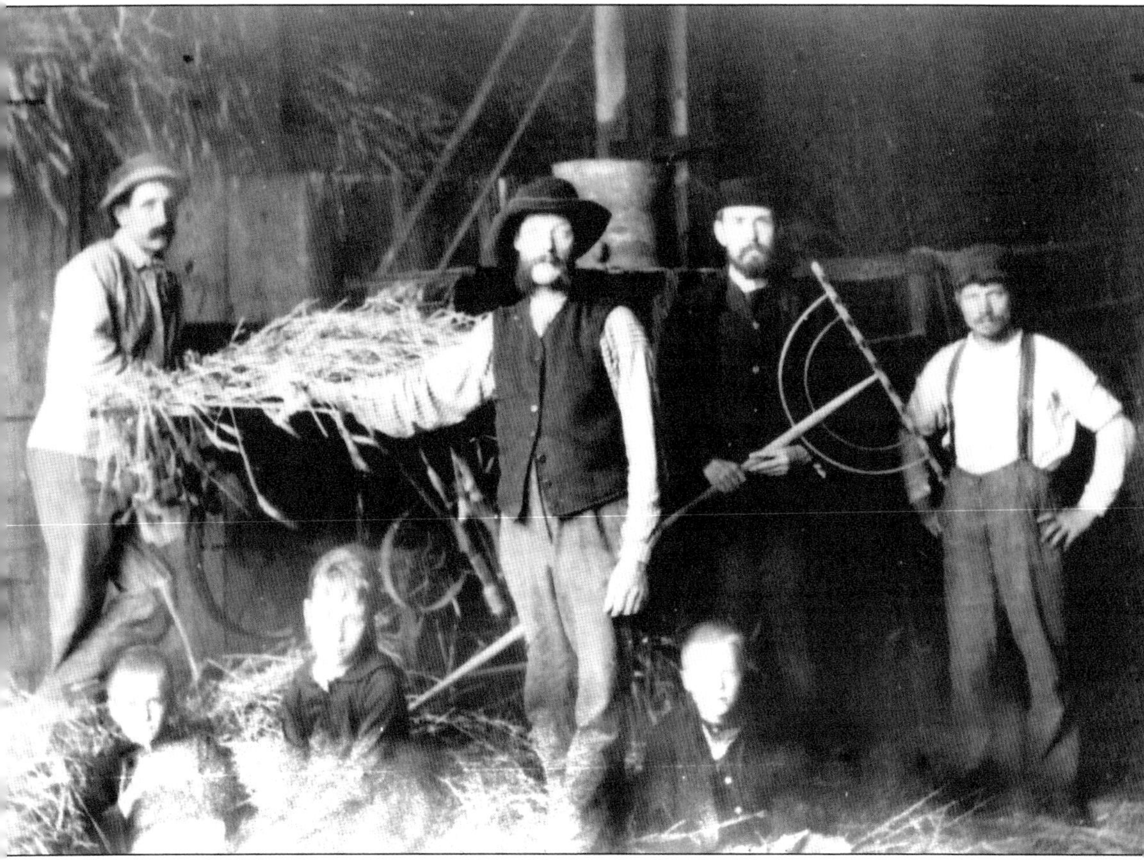

This Bushkill threshing crew worked without benefit of modern machinery, using only hand tools to separate the grain from the chaff. Posing for the camera most likely offered them a welcome relief from their labor.

IMAGES
of America

EASTERN POCONOS

DELAWARE WATER GAP TO BUSHKILL

Marie J. Summa, Frank D. Summa,
and Arthur Garris Jr.

ARCADIA
PUBLISHING

ISBN 978-0-7385-3848-8

Published by Arcadia Publishing
Charleston, South Carolina

Printed in the United States of America

Library of Congress Catalog Card Number: 2005925441

For all general information contact Arcadia Publishing at:
Telephone 843-853-2070
Fax 843-853-0044
E-mail sales@arcadiapublishing.com
For customer service and orders:
Toll-Free 1-888-313-2665

Visit us on the Internet at www.arcadiapublishing.com

Contents

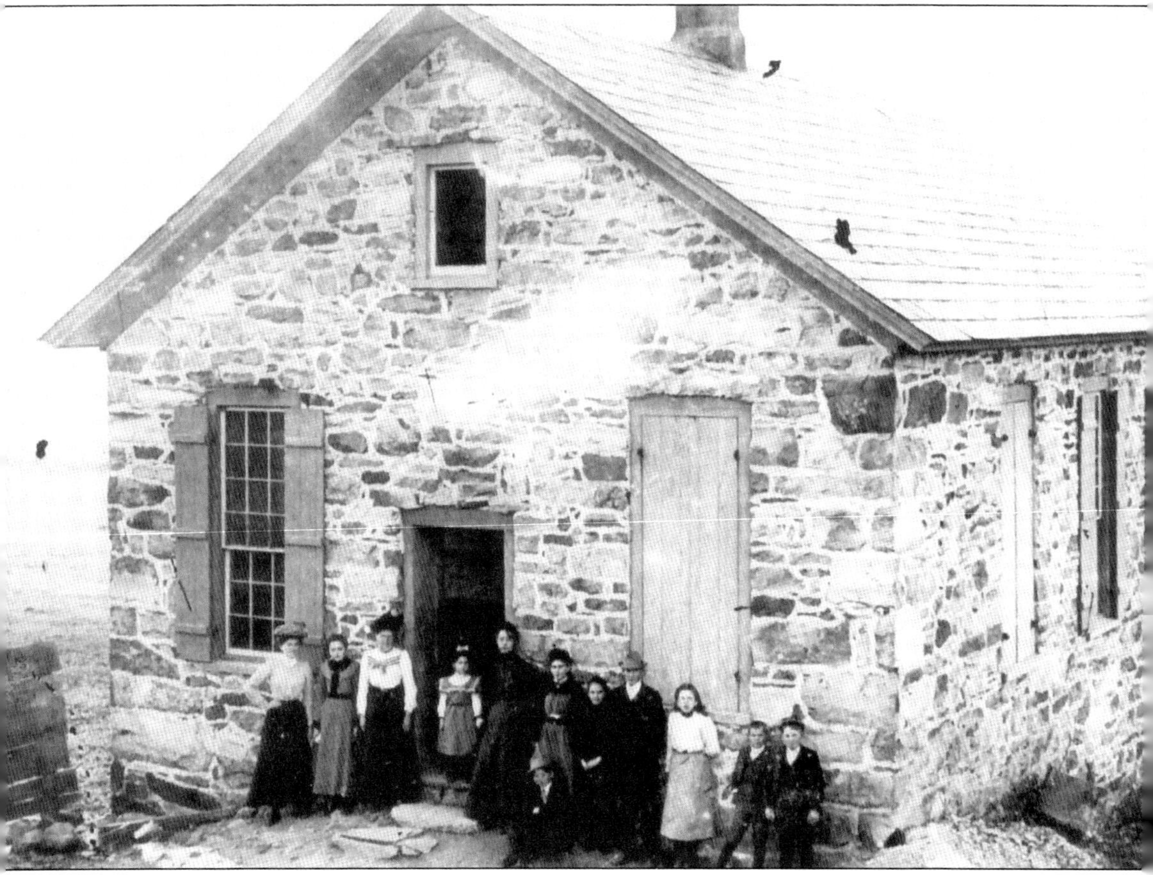

Before the era of modern transportation, one-room schools such as this one dotted the landscape. This is the Hollow or Eilenberger School, situated on Hollow Road in Shawnee. Its stone structure was a rarity, for most of the schools were wood-frame buildings. The building still stands today as a private residence.

INTRODUCTION

Long before European settlers arrived, the area now known as the Eastern Poconos was part of a vast, sparsely populated region inhabited by the Native Americans. These were the Minsi, or "Wolf," clan of the Lenni-Lenape nation of Native Americans. Their name means "the Original People," and over 20 Indian nations, including the Wyandottes, Shawnees, and Miamis confirmed their antiquity by calling them "the Grandfathers." They were a peaceful tribe who fished, hunted, and planted their crops where they could find rich soil. The land was known in early days as the Minisink, a Native American term with its most common interpretation being "where there are Minsis."

Nicholas Depue, who made a large purchase of land from the Minsis in 1727, is the first documented white settler. According to historical accounts, he brought his family down the old copper mine road from Esopus (now Kingston), New York, and crossed the New Jersey side of the Delaware River to Shawnee. There he chose the lush river land in and around the current village of Shawnee as his home. His presence was unknown to the provincial authorities until rumors reached Philadelphia that a white settlement existed north of the Blue Mountains, or Delaware Water Gap. Depue later had to repurchase his lands from the provincial government.

Other settlers moved to the area and lived amicably with their Native American neighbors until 1737. Two sons of William Penn, Thomas and John, along with land speculators William Allen and James Allen, produced a copy of a deed dated 1686 that conveyed to William Penn "lands as far as a man could walk in a day and a half." Lenape sachems had no memory of the deed, and the chiefs who had allegedly signed the deed had died, as had William Penn. James Logan recruited 10 Iroquois chiefs, considered overlords of the Lenape nation, in order to put pressure on the Lenapes. With these forces against them, the tribe agreed to the walk. At sunrise on September 19, 1737, Edwin Marshall, Solomon Jennings, and Edmund Yeates set out on the walk, starting at Wrightstown, Pennsylvania. Marshall was the only one of the three to complete the course, ending his rapid journey a few miles east of present Lehighton in Carbon County. He had performed an amazing feat, covering an amazing 65 miles in 18 hours. The terms of the old deed were indefinite, stating merely that a line should be drawn to the Delaware River. To gain maximum advantage, the proprietors had the line drawn in a northeast angle instead of a line straight to the Delaware. This took away the treasured Minisink hunting grounds of the Lenapes. Their northern neighbors, the Iroquois, did not stand with them but instead ordered them to leave the area. Bitterness over the matter festered and culminated with the bloody Indian uprisings beginning in 1755 that resulted in the massacre of many white settlers.

Although not the first settler to arrive in Delaware Water Gap, Antoine Dutot made perhaps the biggest impression. A rebellion of slaves had erupted in St. Domingo (now Haiti), and as a wealthy plantation owner and slave owner, he was forced to leave. He left in 1793 and arrived in Delaware Water Gap with the dream of founding a utopian city and naming it for himself. With the help of Thomas Armat, a planning consultant from Philadelphia, he mapped the town of Dutotsburg, sold lots, and built about a dozen houses. Additionally, he opened a sawmill, boat landing, and a toll road. The road did not work well financially due to friction with neighbor Ulrick Hauser and riders who passed through the gate without paying tolls. He started building the Kittatinny House in 1829 but ran out of money, partly as a result of the toll road venture. Although his dream of a city evaporated, the name Dutotsburg lasted for over 50 years. The town had become so important that when Monroe County was formed in 1836, it became a leading contender for the location of the county seat. Stroudsburg won the vote over Dutotsburg and Kellersville. As the railroad arrived, numerous resorts and boardinghouses burgeoned throughout the entire region. In the golden age of tourism, Delaware Water Gap initially became the brightest star.

Minisink Hills claims the distinction of being the most frequently named area in the Eastern Poconos. Early settler George Zimmerman arrived there and settled along a branch stream of the Delaware River, and so the area was called Branchville. When a post office was opened in 1829 at the Bell House, the official name became Experiment Mills. It was named so for the innovative manner in which the flour was produced at the mill on the property. By 1892, both towns united to become Minsi. In 1902, the name officially changed to North Water Gap. That name lasted until 1931, when it was renamed Minisink Hills. Sub-areas existed with various names. The area of the road leading from Minisink Hills to Buttermilk Falls was called California, facetiously named so for two men who had gone to California during the 1849 gold rush and had returned. Another little settlement was dubbed Tinkertown, for the area where immigrants building the Delaware, Lackawanna and Western Railroad lived in small shacks provided by the railroad line. Hauserville, or Houserville, was another small area named for the family who settled there.

The area from Marshalls Creek to Bushkill was situated along the way of the Easton to Milford Road, a stagecoach route that opened in 1810. The road made travel easier between these villages and the little hamlets lying along this route. Later, the Delaware Valley Railroad followed roughly the same course, creating the opportunity for the many boardinghouses to cater to the summer visitors who flocked to the area.

The flood of 1955 brought about an ill-conceived project called the Flood Control Project of 1962. The act called for a 37-mile-long lake and a 72,000-acre park surrounding it. A group of power companies made plans to utilize the reservoir to generate electricity, and they lobbied heavily for the dam. This began a decades-long struggle between government forces and local individuals. As eminent domain proceedings began, local opposition grew. Citizens banded together in a David and Goliath–like struggle, finally succeeding in having the dam project deauthorized. In the interim, however, entire villages were eradicated. Bushkill residents, for instance, moved up into the hills surrounding the former village. Others moved away from the area. Today, the Delaware Water Gap National Recreation Area remains where these lands were seized. With the rapid growth the area has experienced, some consider this a mixed blessing, for it provides "clean-and-green" space and the bonus of recreational activities. The park service that operates the recreation area has helped to dispel some of the past bitterness by acknowledging and helping to re-create some of the area's lost history.

Today, only a handful of resorts remain, and the leisurely days of yesteryear are gone. The northern lake resorts of Unity House and Tamiment no longer exist. Unity House has become the Mountain Laurel Center for the Arts, and Tamiment's buildings were recently razed to create a housing development. The area is now coping with a population explosion as residents of neighboring states have fled to the region. Local and state officials are dealing with the problems of traffic congestion and the ever increasing burden of property taxes. Hopefully, they will succeed.

One

Through the Gap

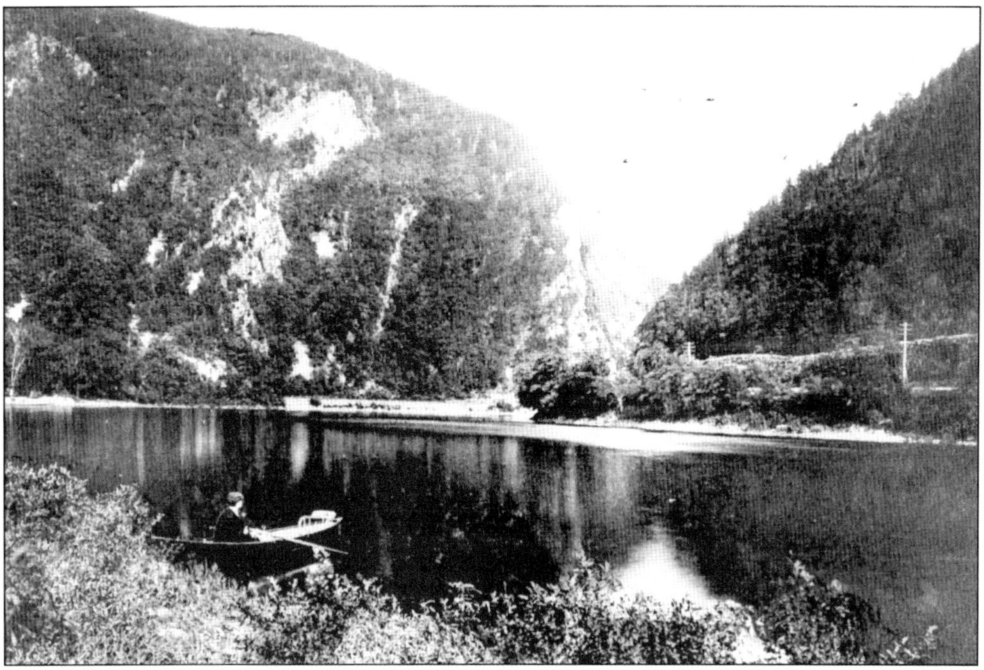

The Delaware River courses almost 120 miles from its origin until it reaches Delaware Water Gap. Often dubbed the eighth natural wonder of the world, the gap has lured visitors since time immemorial. Mount Tammany is seen on the left side of the river and Mount Minsi across the river on the right. The geographical feature shares its name with the town sheltered on the Mount Minsi side of the range. The beauty of the gap attracted many visitors to the area. After the Civil War, the town, first called Dutotsburg, was considered to be the second largest inland resort town in the United States, ranking after Saratoga Springs, New York, with its clientele consisting mainly of the upper classes of Philadelphia and New York.

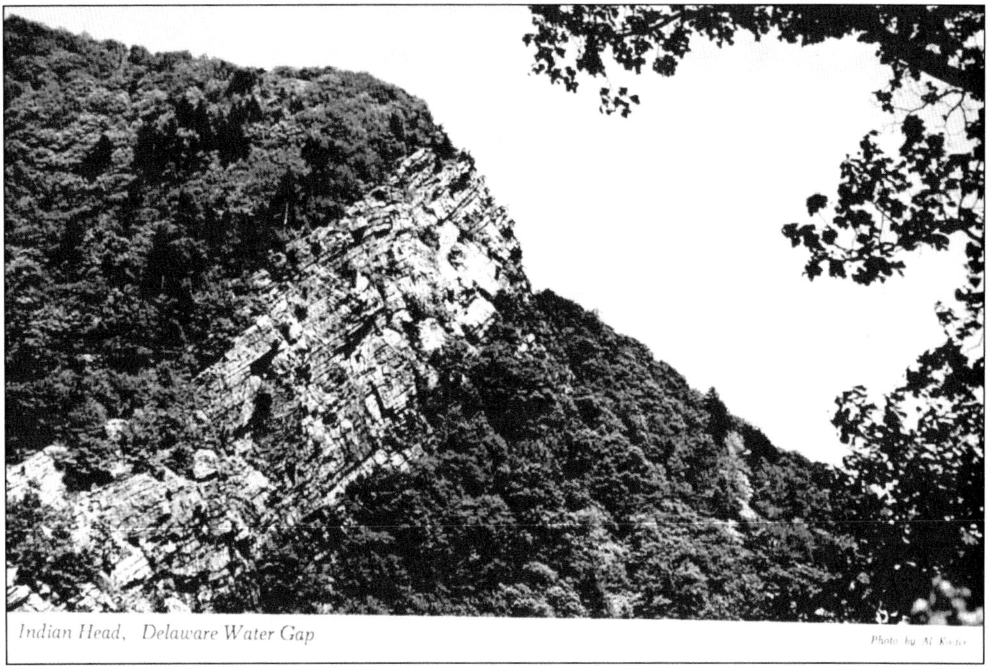

Carved by nature, the Indian Head on Mount Tammany seems symbolic of the first inhabitants of the area. Named for Tamenend, the leading chief of the Lenape tribe with whom William Penn made a treaty at Shackamaxon, Pennsylvania, this range is situated on the New Jersey side of the Delaware River. At the time of the American Revolution, Tamenend (or Tammany) was so revered that May 1 was designated as St. Tammany Day.

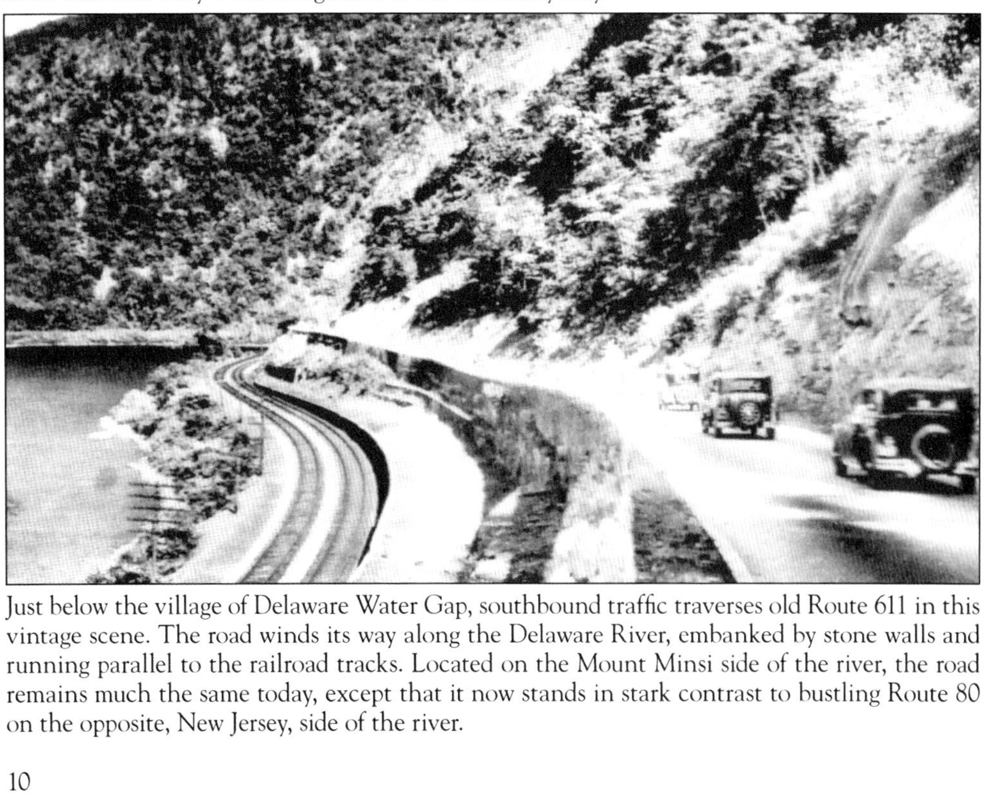

Just below the village of Delaware Water Gap, southbound traffic traverses old Route 611 in this vintage scene. The road winds its way along the Delaware River, embanked by stone walls and running parallel to the railroad tracks. Located on the Mount Minsi side of the river, the road remains much the same today, except that it now stands in stark contrast to bustling Route 80 on the opposite, New Jersey, side of the river.

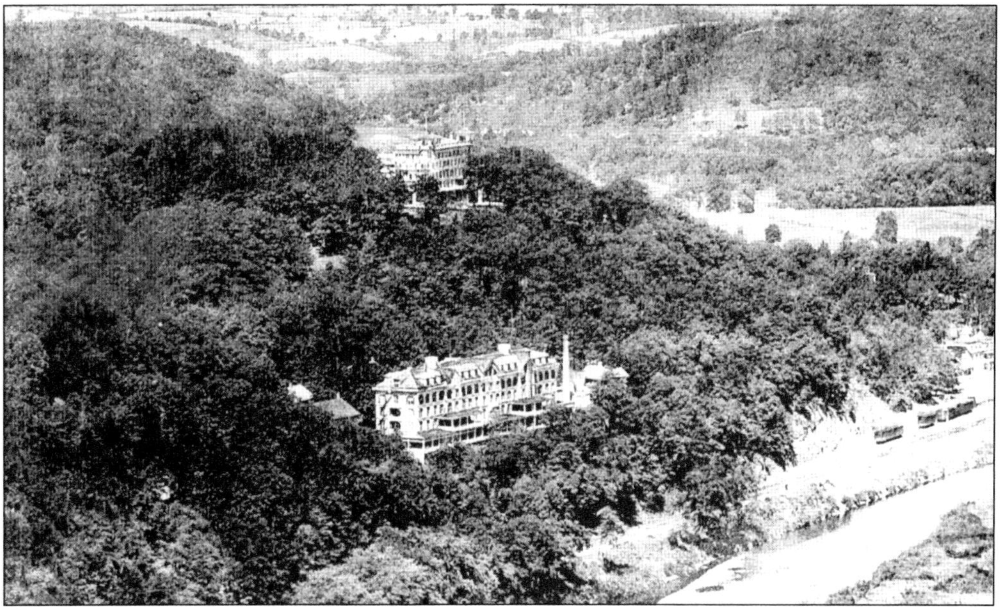

The Kittatinny House is seen in the lower middle section of this picture, with the Water Gap House perched higher above it. The Delaware River and the Delaware Water Gap railroad station are shown to the lower right. Today, a portion of the foundation of the Kittatinny remains at the right corner of the Resort Overlook on Route 611 South where the Kittatinny once stood.

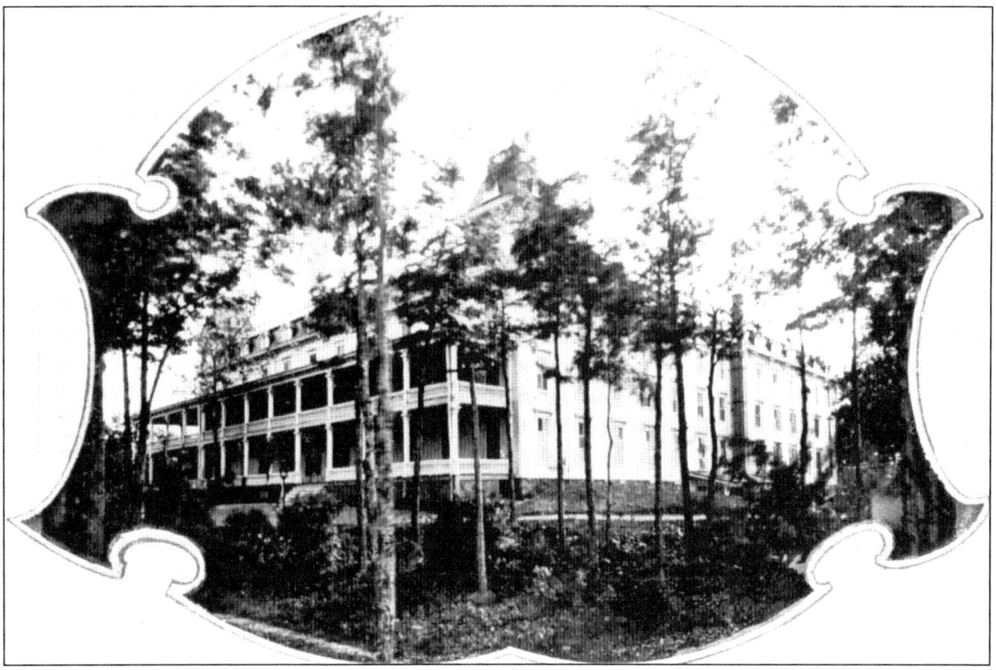

The Water Gap House, built in 1872, rose about 400 feet above the Delaware River and 200 feet above the Kittatiny, providing magnificent views of its surroundings. Originally built to accommodate 275 guests, it later expanded to five stories that could lodge 300 to 400. The hotel catered to many prominent and wealthy guests. A November 12, 1915, fire destroyed the magnificent hotel.

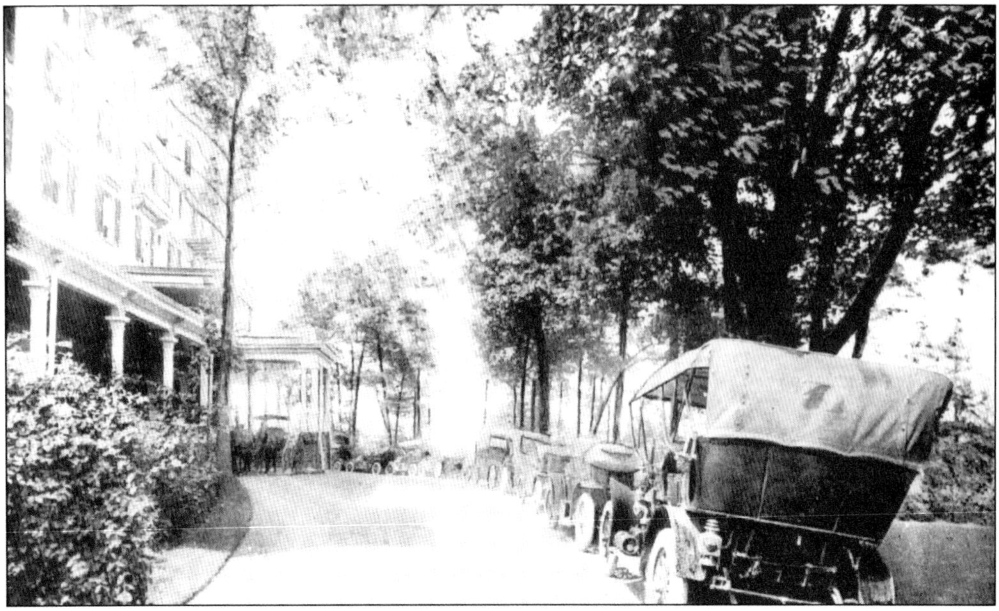

This is an early-1900s view of the Water Gap House. By that time, J. Purdy Cope, who also owned the Albemarle Hotel in Atlantic City, owned it, having purchased it in 1904. Luke Brodhead had died in 1902, and the property had been taken over by his heirs until Cope bought it.

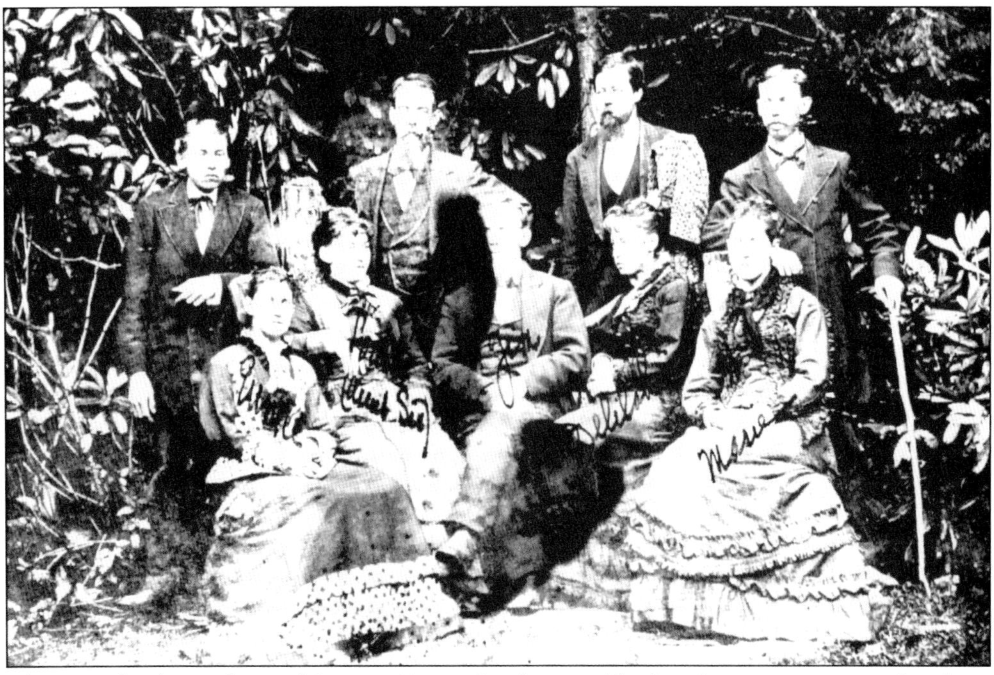

These are the descendants of Antoine Dutot. It is lamentable that there is no picture, sketch, or painting of Dutot, whose vision helped to bring prosperity and a great deal of concrete history to Delaware Water Gap. However, this picture of his descendants remains as a reminder of his legacy. (Photograph courtesy of Dutot Museum.)

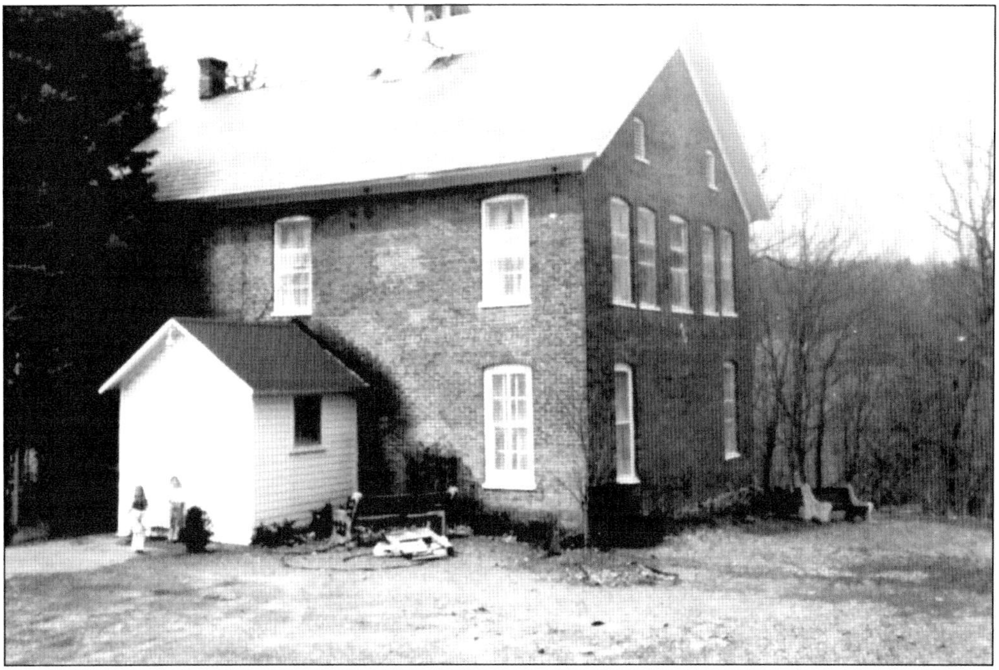

The Dutot School and Museum, used first as the Laurel Hill School, was rebuilt in 1874, replacing an earlier structure. It is situated behind the Trail's End Café in Delaware Water Gap and is open to visitors. (Photograph courtesy of Lucy Kosmerl.)

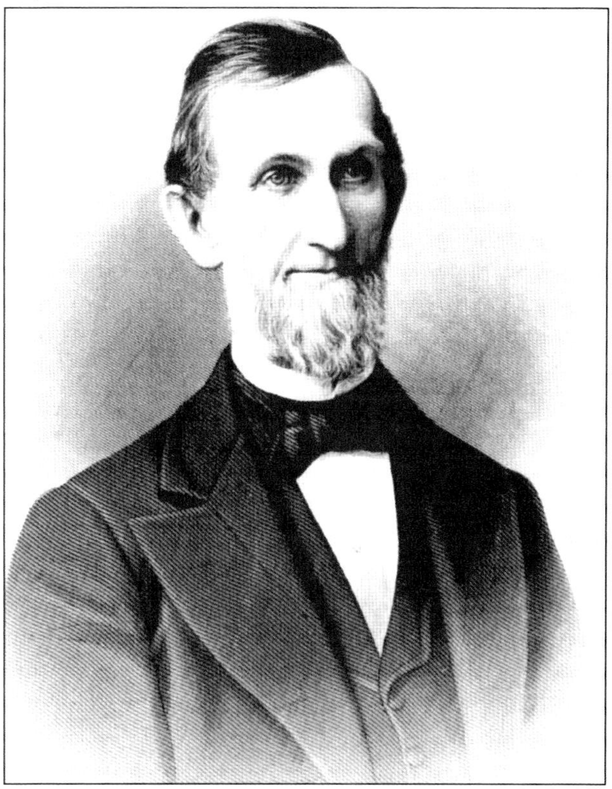

Luke Wills Brodhead managed the Kittatinny Hotel for a time and opened the Water Gap House. He built the Water Gap House without a bar and managed the hotel to attract the most distinguished clientele of any in the gap. Luke was one of eight sons and one daughter born to Luke and Elizabeth Wills Brodhead. All the boys were over six feet tall, a fact that led their mother to comment that she had "48 feet of sons."

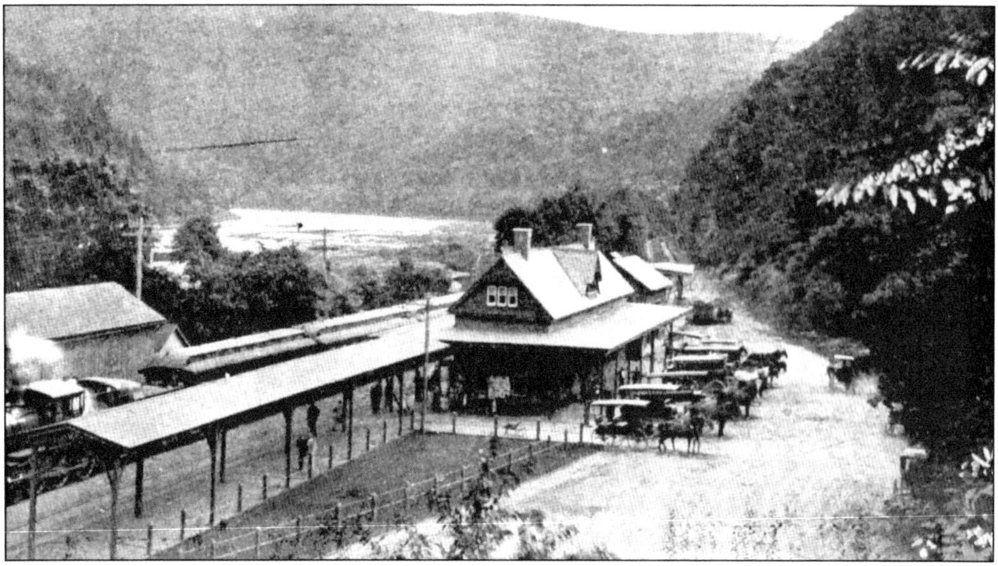

Pictured in 1897, this was the first Delaware Water Gap railroad station. It served as a depot for the main line of the Delaware, Lackawanna and Western Railroad. A March 2, 1902, explosion of unknown origin created a huge fire in the depot and damaged other nearby buildings.

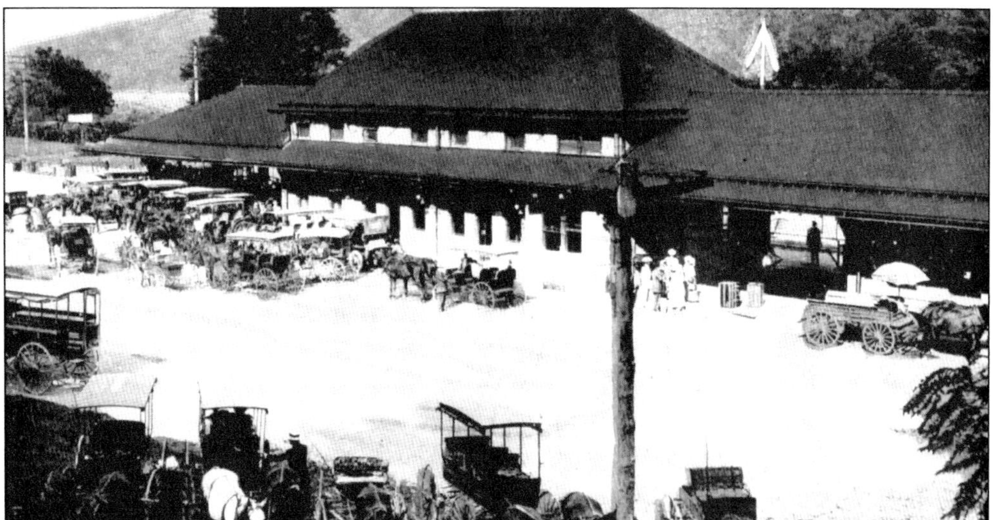

Commissioned by Lackawanna Railroad president William Truesdale to rebuild the burned depot, company engineer Frank Nies designed a new station for the "Gateway to the Poconos." The new depot was built shortly thereafter, the only one of brick construction in Monroe County. High ceilings and terrazzo floors highlighted its interior. It served as a railroad stop until the mid-1950s, when the East Stroudsburg station became the major terminal for eastern Monroe County.

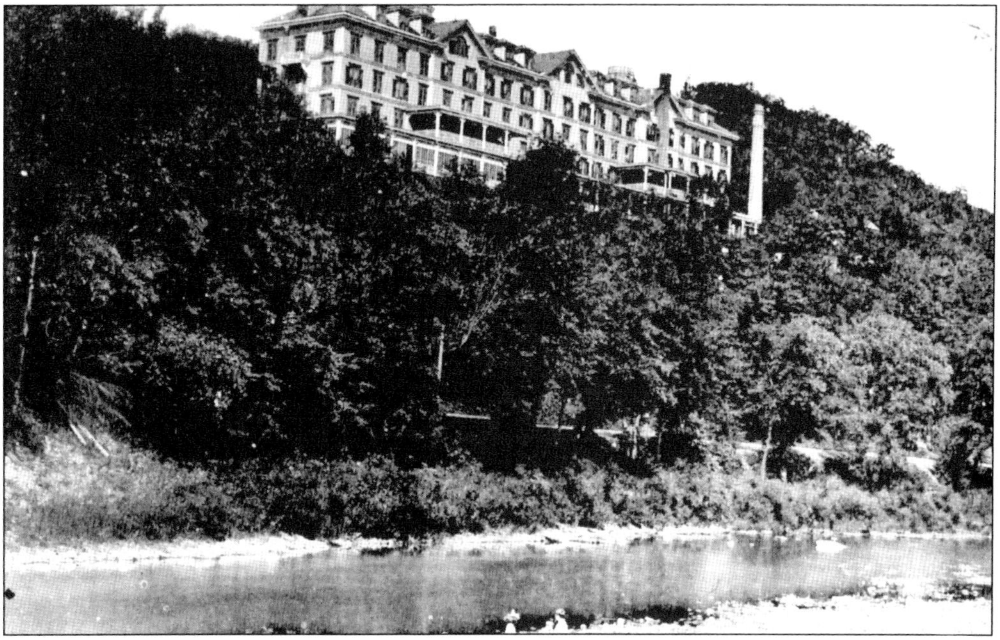

Antoine Dutot, considered by many to be the founder of Delaware Water Gap, began construction on the Kittatinny House in 1829 but did not complete it. Samuel Snyder purchased it in 1832, followed by a succession of proprietors who continued to expand it. By 1866, the hotel could accommodate 275 guests. The years 1891 and 1892 brought major structural changes with an elevator, gas, electric bell, and steam heat. The venerable old hotel burned to the ground on October 30, 1931.

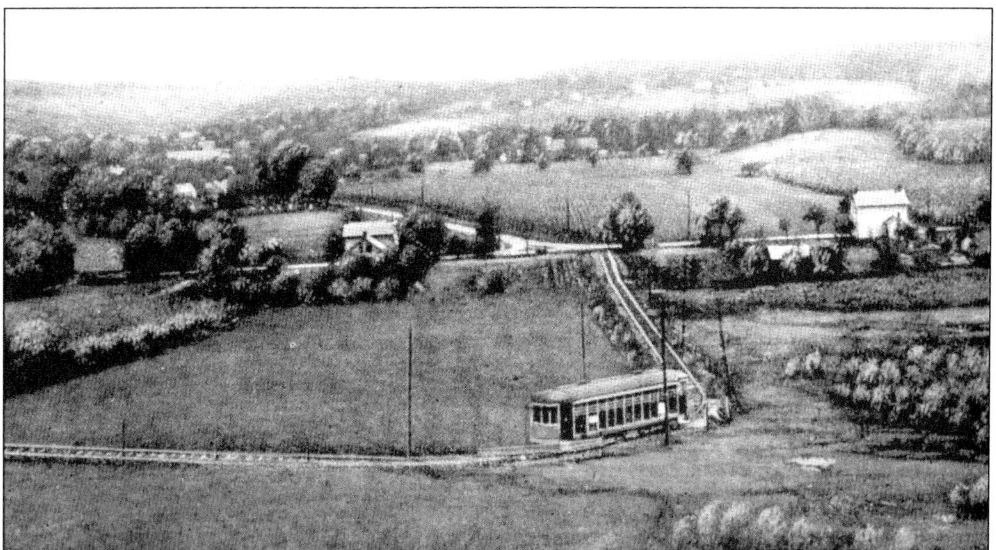

Mountain View Trolley began operations in 1905, connecting the boroughs of Stroudsburg and Delaware Water Gap. It ran from Seventh Street in Stroudsburg to the trolley terminal in the gap. A 1912 merger extended the line to Portland, Pennsylvania. By subsequently linking up with the Liberty Bell Limited of Lehigh Valley, it made possible travel by trolley from Stroudsburg all the way to Philadelphia. The trolley line closed down in 1928.

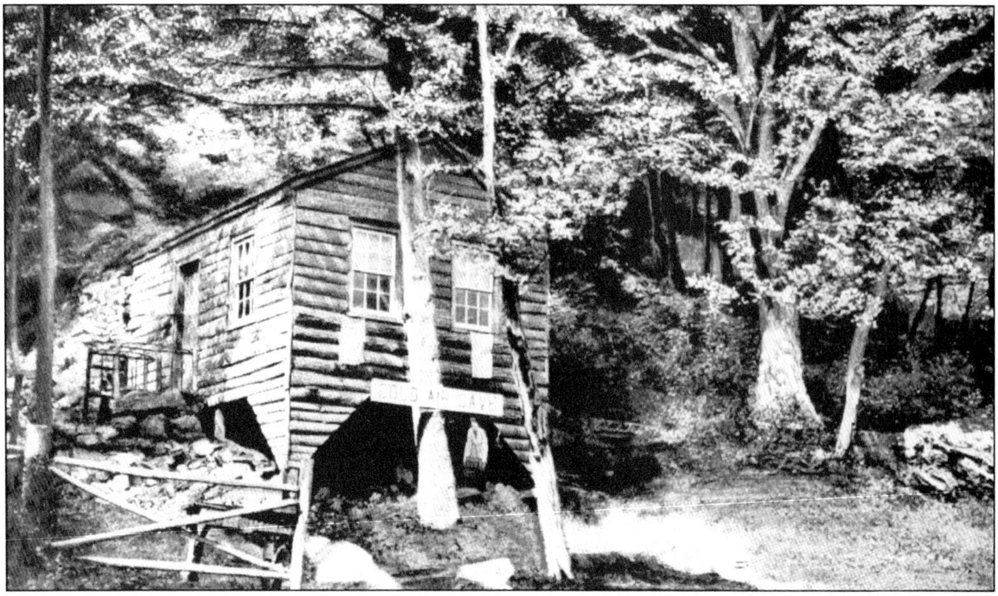

The Cold Air Cave presented a really "cool" attraction to the many tourists who flooded the area. Myrtle Williams and her family owned and operated the site for over for over 60 years. While average cave temperatures are 50 to 60 degrees Fahrenheit, this cave was a chilly 38 degrees. Myrtle retired, and the old building was abandoned. In 1967, the Army Corps of Engineers purchased the property. Today, a gravel parking lot covers the former site.

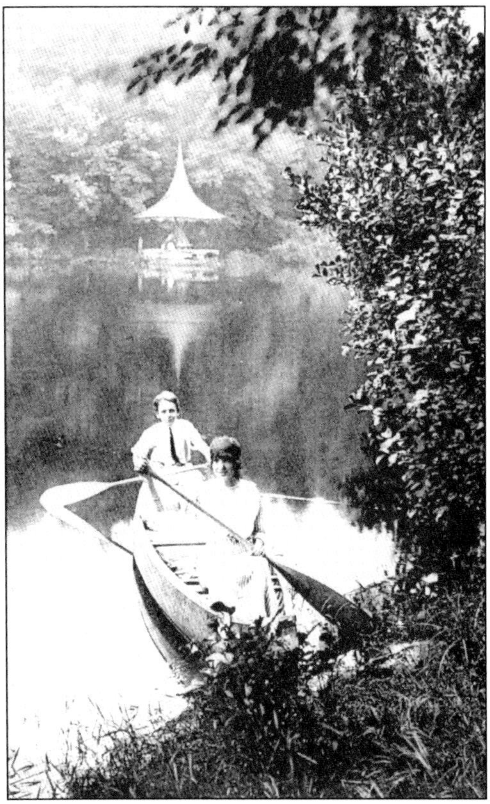

Teenager Fred Astaire and his sister Adele canoe the waters of Lake Lenape, whose charming gazebo sits on the opposite shore. The future famous dance team and their mother spent summers at the gap from 1911 to 1914.

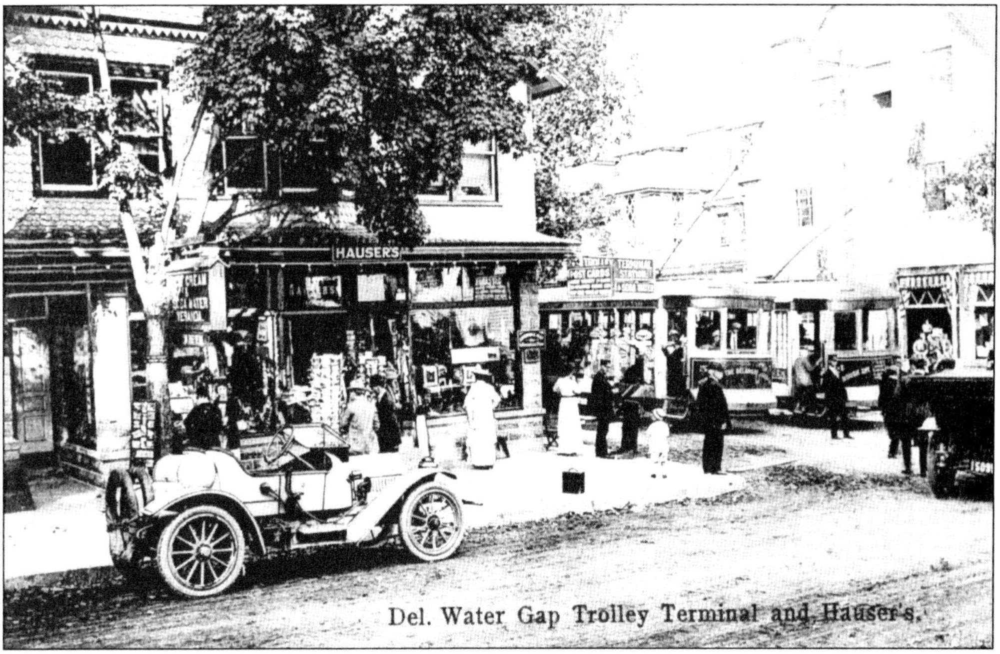

During the heyday of tourism, Hauser's was indeed a busy place. The store stood across from the Castle Inn, and its proximity to the trolley made it convenient to tourists and trolley travelers alike. In addition to running its busy soda fountain and souvenir business, Hauser's published numerous postcards. This postcard image is an example of one of the store's productions.

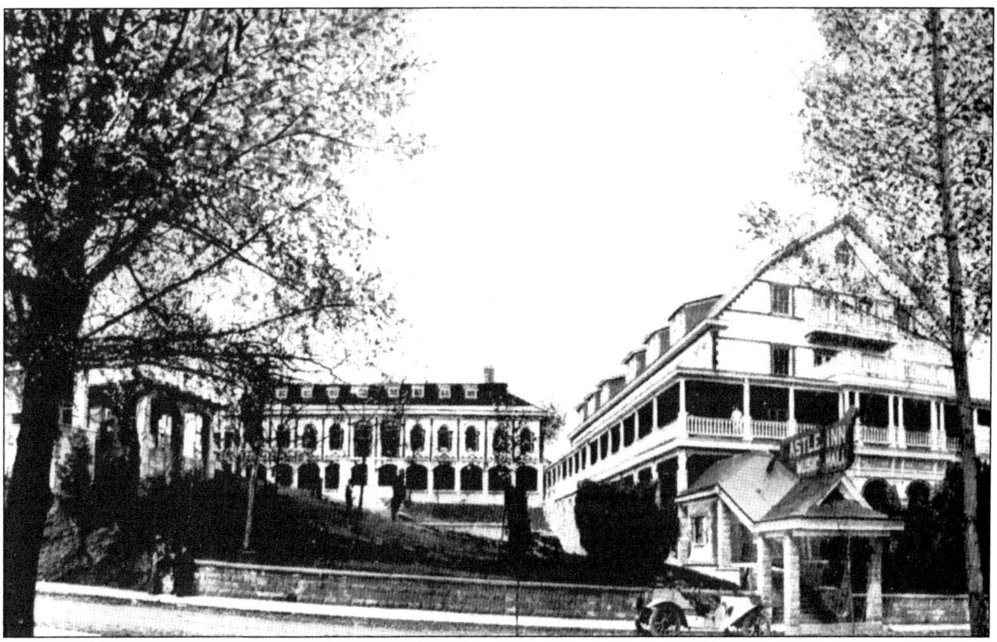

Castle Inn, the pride of Delaware Water Gap, provided a renowned cultural center. Built by Dimmick Drake in the early 1900s, its music hall included luminaries John Philip Sousa, Fanny Brice, and Enrico Caruso. Joseph H. Graves operated it for about four years. Later in the century, Fred Waring Enterprises bought the property. The inn burned down in 1985.

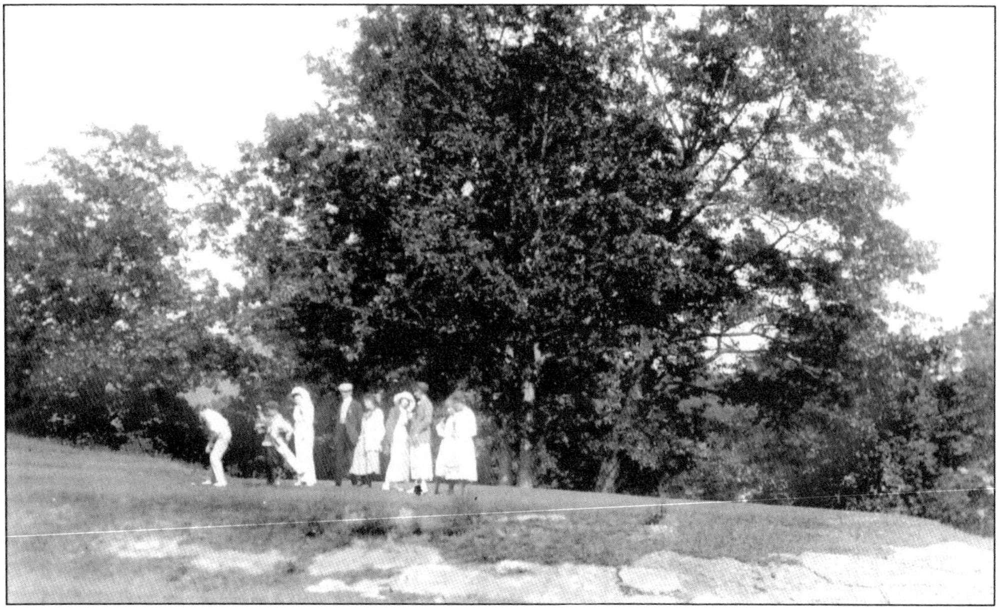

Charles C. Worthington constructed the Caldeno Golf Course in the 1880s. Located near the current courses of Water Gap Country Club, this nine-hole course was one of the first in the area. In the 1920s, it was replaced by the 18-hole Wolf Hollow Golf Course, now the Water Gap Country Club course. Charles Worthington later built a golf course at his Buckwood Inn in Shawnee.

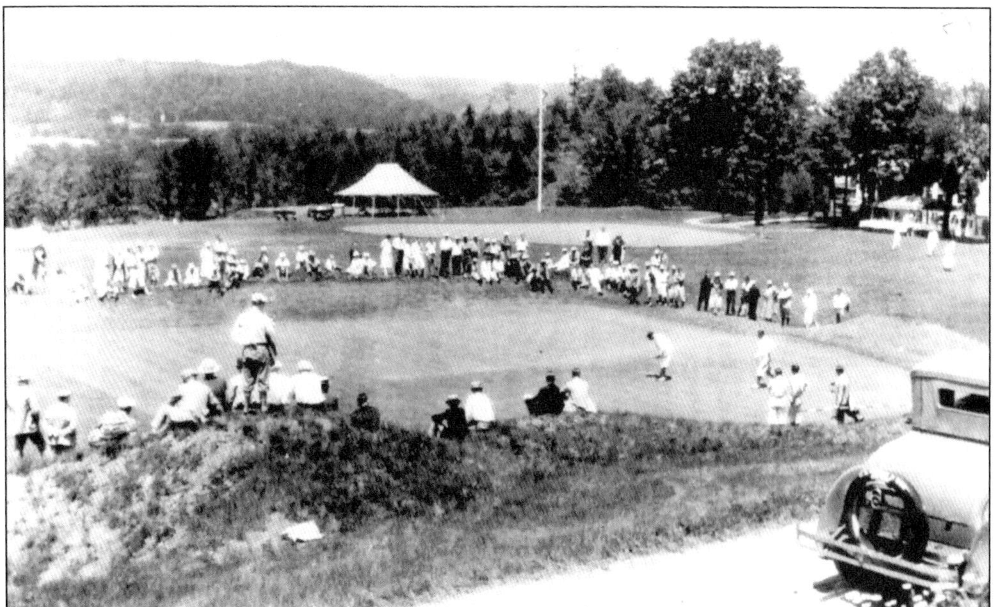

This is a view of renowned golfer Walter Hagen at Wolf Hollow Golf Course. A group of investors formed a company, naming it the Wolf Hollow Country Club, and built its first clubhouse in 1925. The Eastern U.S. Open tournament was held here initially in 1929 and continued for three years. This later became the Water Gap Country Club. (Courtesy of Water Gap Country Club.)

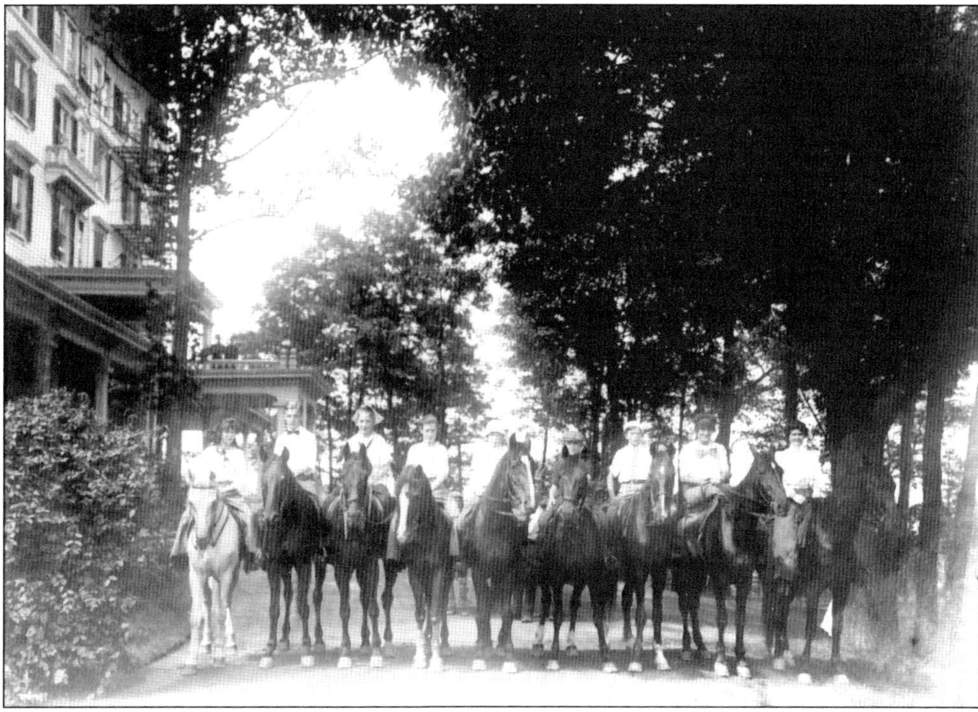

Fred Astaire is pictured among these equestrians passing in front of the Water Gap House. The Water Gap House had a riding stable, and the neighboring Kittatinny House had a riding academy, the only hotel in the gap to possess one.

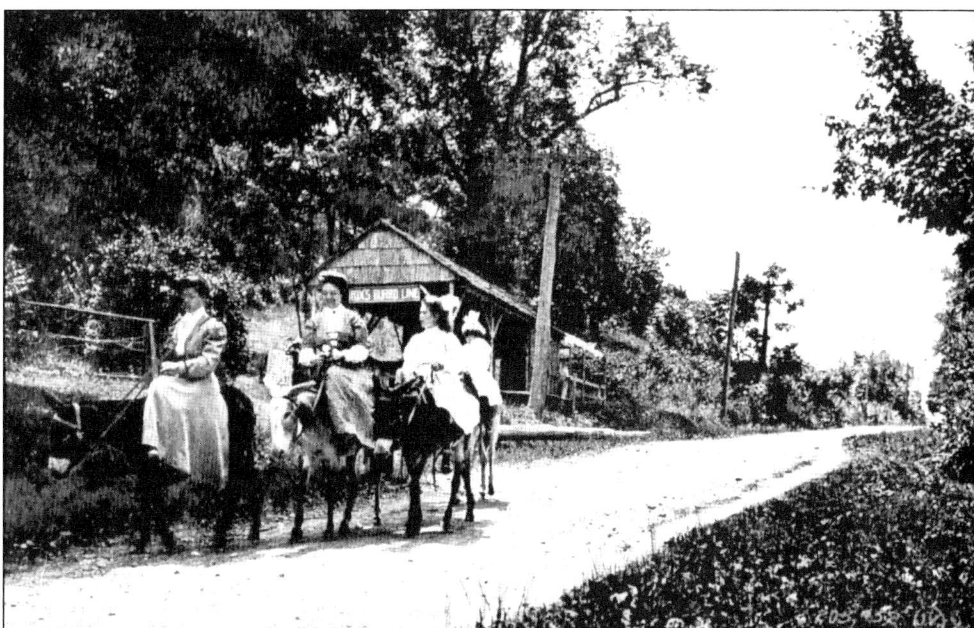

The terrain in the area was rough, and hiking would have been difficult for ladies in their long dresses. The Burro Stand provided a less elegant but more sure-footed means for them to enjoy the spectacular scenery of the gap. It was located near the site of the present post office.

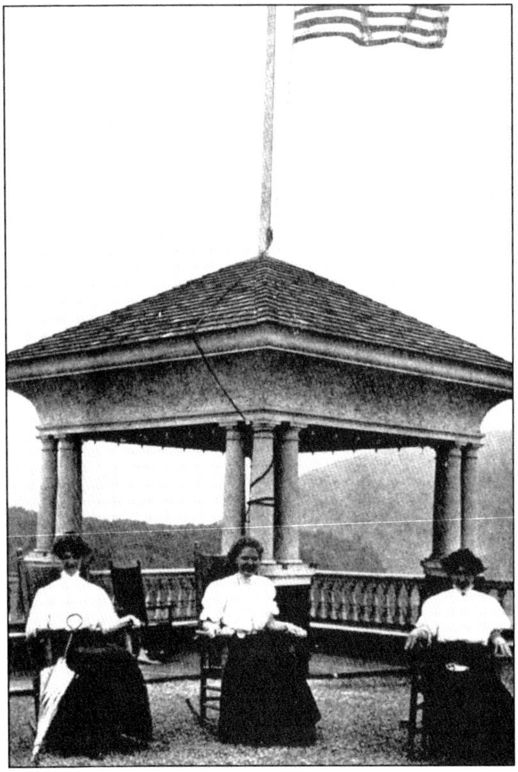

Seated at the top of the Water Gap House, these ladies enjoy a magnificent view. Looking toward the gap, one could see its majestic spectacle of the mountains and river, while another aspect revealed the islands in the river, the farmlands beyond, and the rolling hills of Shawnee.

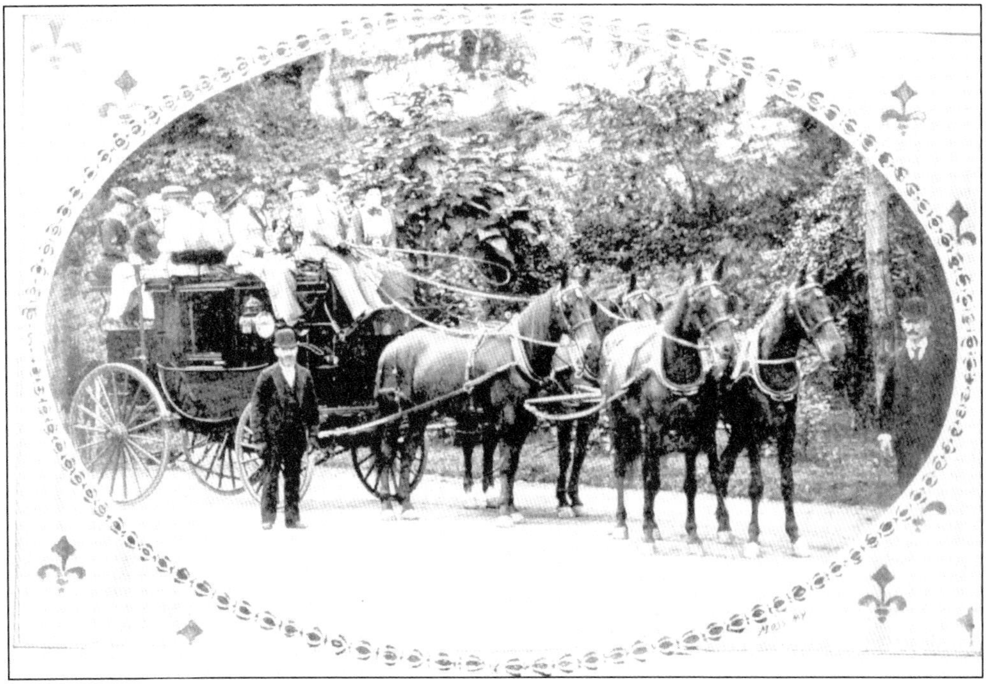

This 1896 view of a stagecoach in the gap shows passengers out either for a jaunt or on their way to one of the many hotels that once dotted the area. Although the roads were bumpy and dusty, the stage provided a convenient and principal means of travel to various destinations.

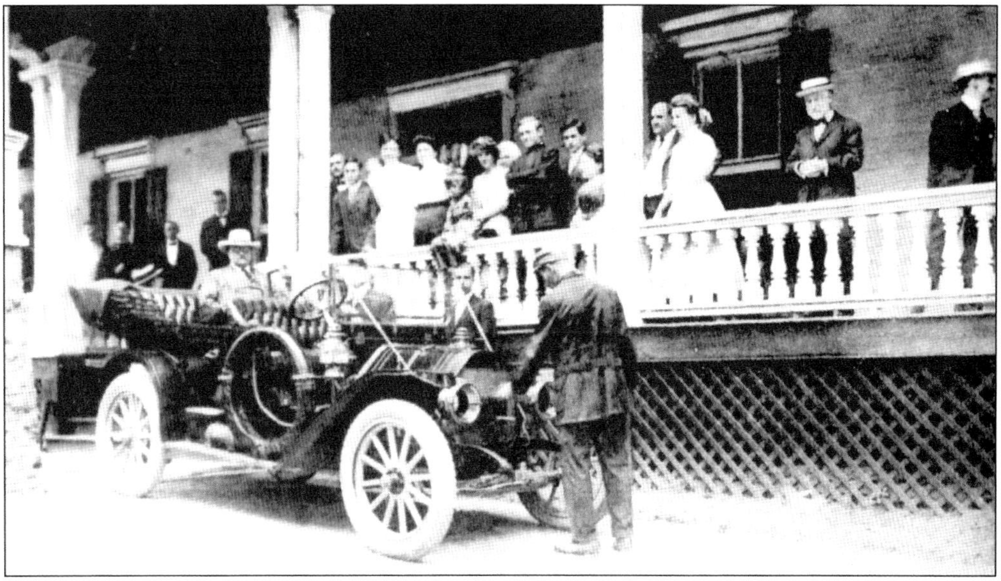

Here we have an August 10, 1910, image of Theodore Roosevelt sitting in his auto in front of the Water Gap House. He was preparing for a motor tour of the Poconos. During his stay at the hotel, he visited the roof observatory, attended a reception held for him in the music room, and sat in on a musicale held in his honor by the hotel's orchestra.

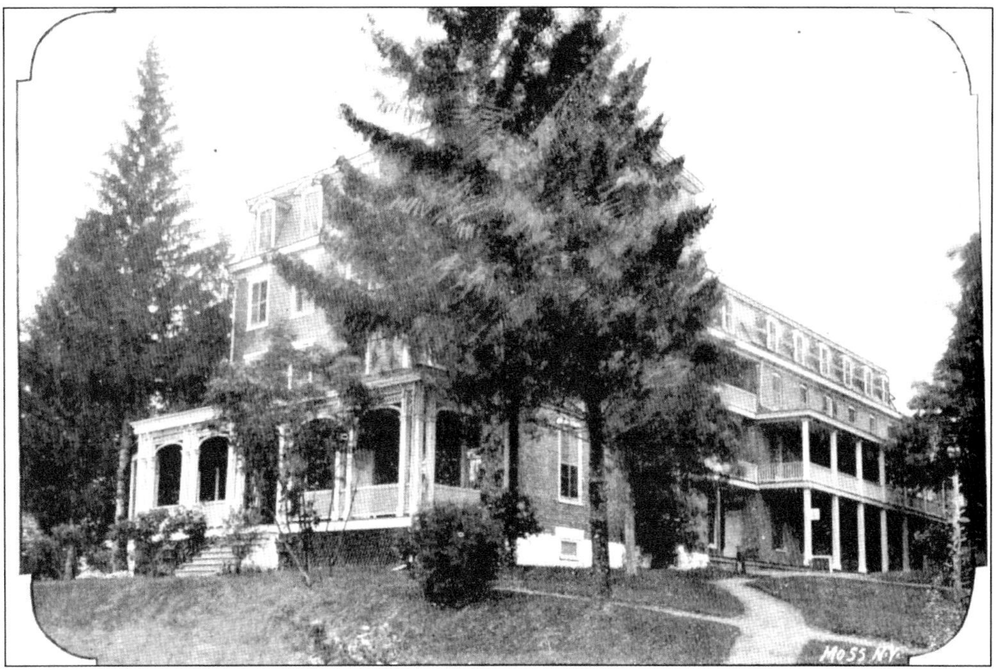

The Glenwood, originally built in 1855 by Rev. Horatio Howell, was started as a school for boys called the Delaware Water Gap Classical School. Unfortunately, Howell was killed at Gettysburg while serving as a Civil War chaplain. The academy lasted only a few more years before being enlarged and converted to a hotel. The hotel remains today as the last of the great era of resort hotels.

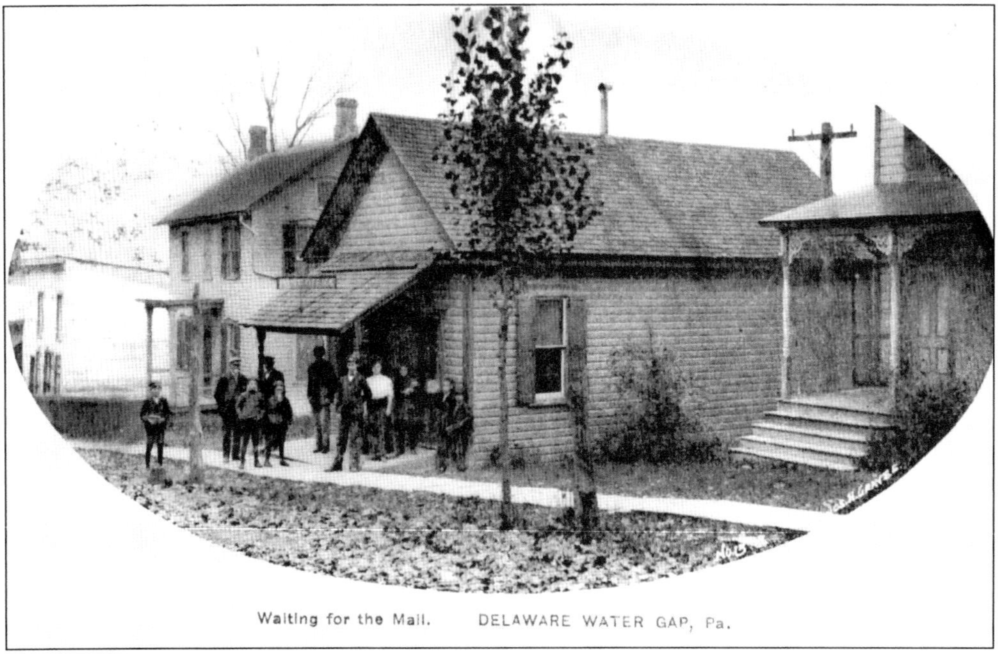

Photographer Joseph Graves snapped this scene of the old post office in Delaware Water Gap. It stood on Main Street where the Marketplace is located. It was razed in 1916 to make way for the Castle Inn's tile and brick garage, later turned into the Marketplace. A new post office was erected in 1966 and formally dedicated on September 10 of that year.

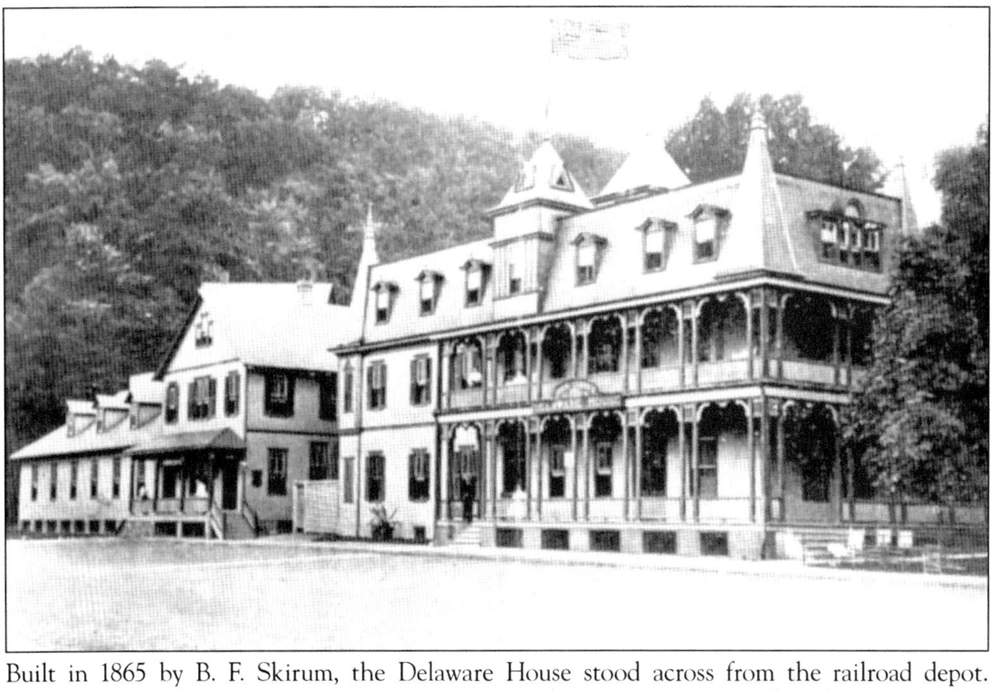

Built in 1865 by B. F. Skirum, the Delaware House stood across from the railroad depot. In later years, it was known as Ma's Hof Brau. The Delaware River Joint Toll Bridge Commission acquired the property on October 10, 1951, and proceeded to have the hotel demolished. All that remains is a concrete curb that marks the position of the former building.

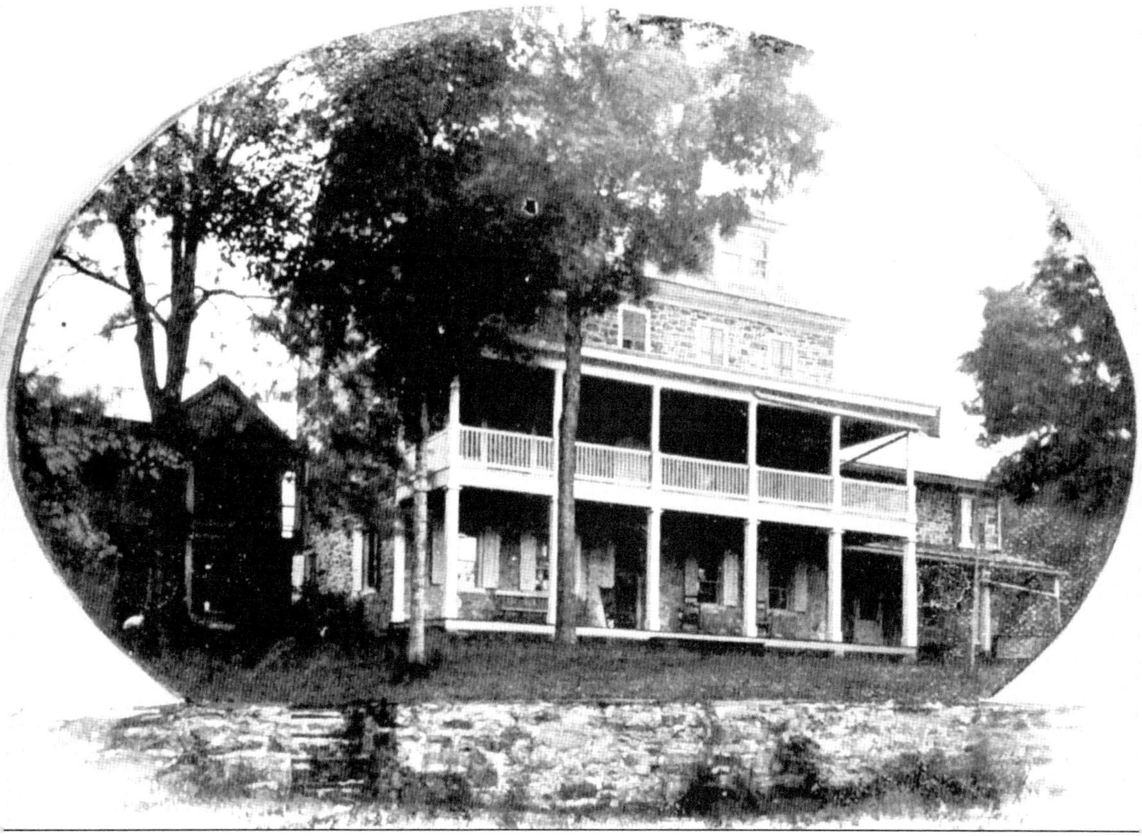

The River Farm House was most likely the oldest stone building in Monroe County. Aaron Depui purchased the land, called John Smith's Farm, from his father, Nicholas, in 1745. The farmhouse was built shortly thereafter. To date, no deed giving ownership to John Smith has ever been located. However, there is convincing evidence that that the origin of the naming of Smithfield Township began with the original owner of this property. It is generally believed that subsequent title papers referring to the property as Smith's Fields and a 1747 land transfer of Aaron Depui's land speaking of his property as Smithfield make this a strong probability.

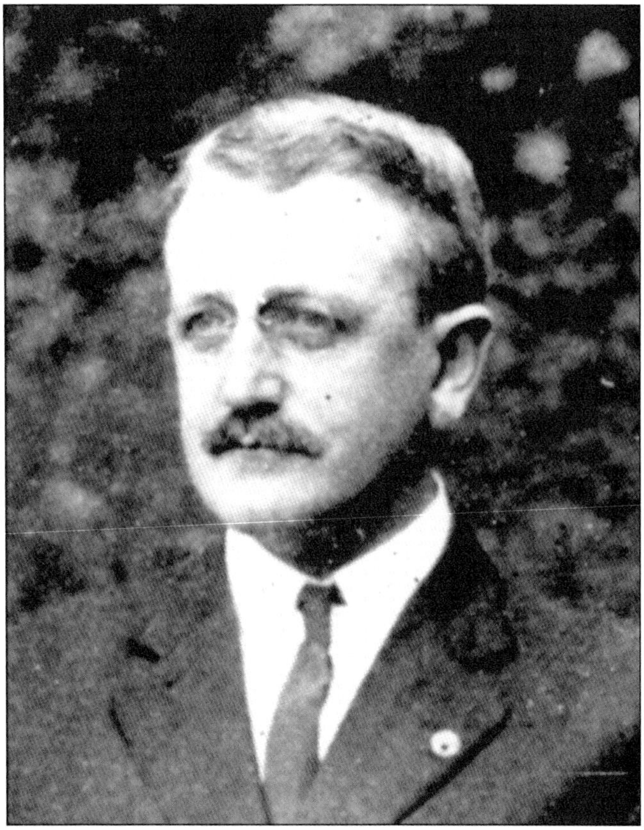

Joseph H. Graves was a photographer and producer of hand-colored postcards that pictured primarily the Delaware Water Gap. His postcards are highly collectible today. Joseph was the son of Jesse Graves, who produced the *Mountain Echo*, a local newspaper that did much to promote tourism in the gap. He also served as associate judge of Monroe County.

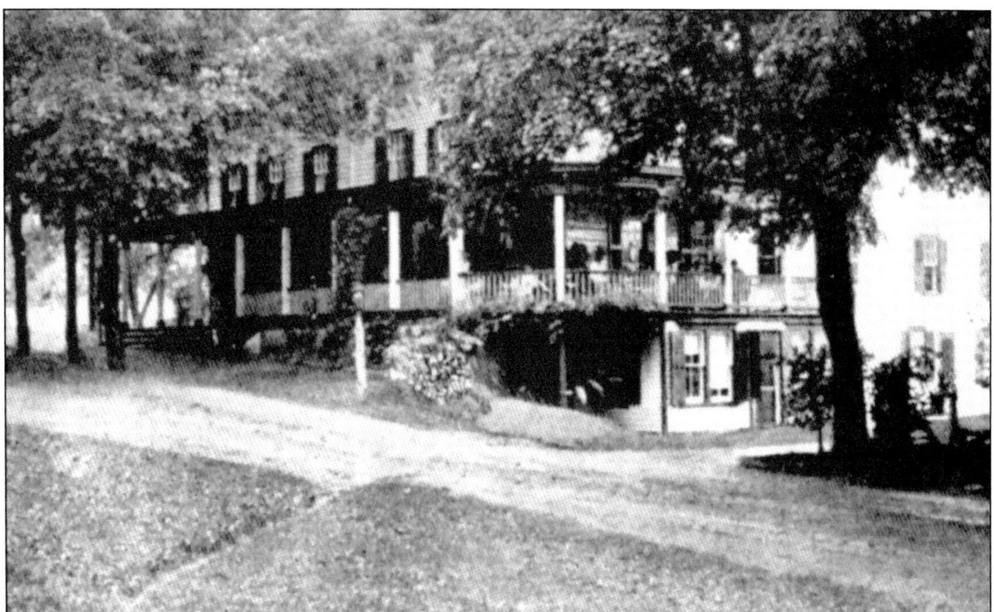

Theodore Hauser built the Mountain House, opening it for guests in 1871. Like many of the hotels in the gap, it hosted its share of celebrities. The hotel remained in the family until Frank Brown bought it in 1982. It was destroyed by fire on June 1, 1987.

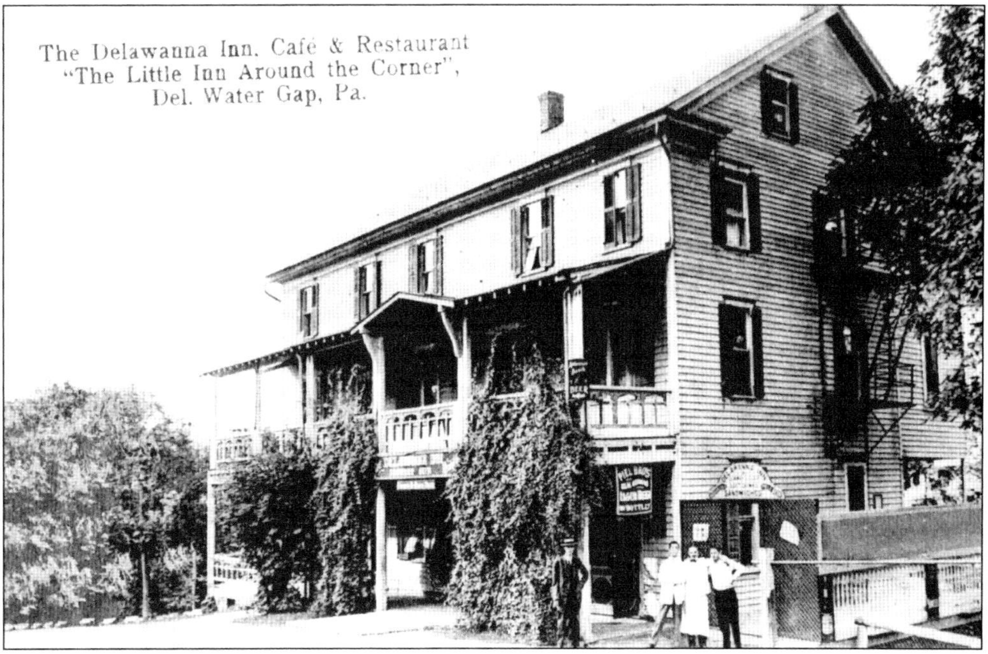

The three-story Delawanna Inn was located on a hill next to the Forest House, with its front facing Main Street. Early in the 1900s, Harvey Blair and Eugene Conway owned and operated both the Delawanna and the Bellevue Inns. The Delawanna operated principally as a tavern in later years. It was acquired by the Delaware Water Gap National Recreation Area and razed in 1968.

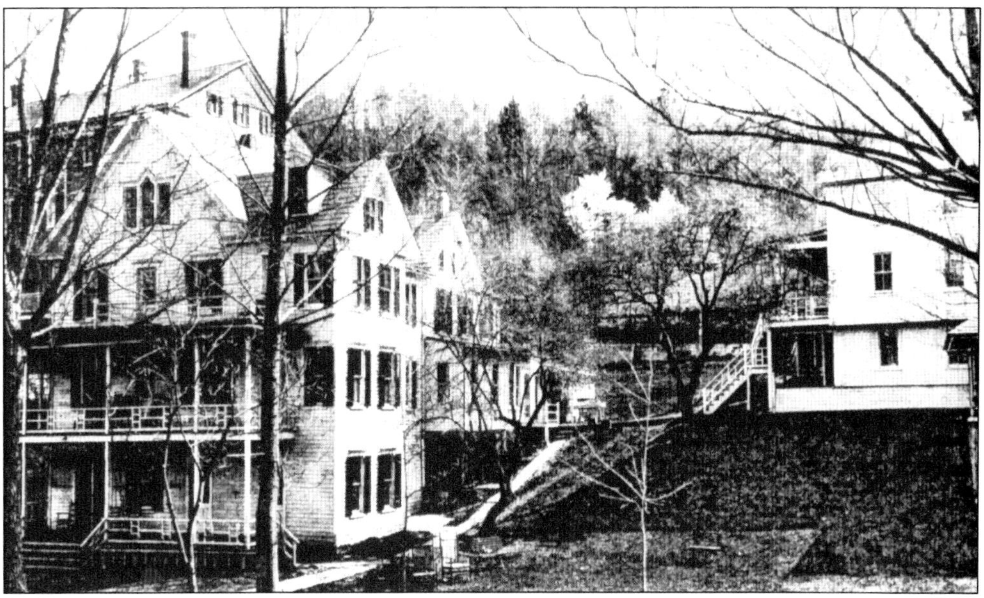

The Forest House stood on Delaware Street with its main entrance facing Castle Inn's Music Hall entrance. Abram Marsh owned and operated the Forest House. It was demolished for the Delaware Water Gap National Recreation project.

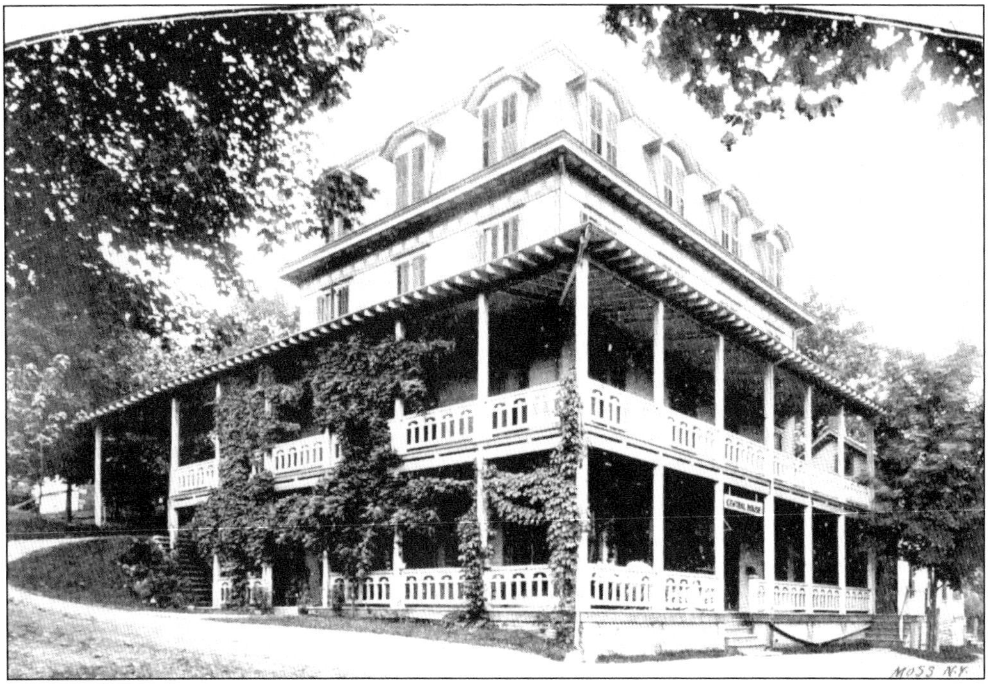

Samuel Overfield built the Central House, later known as the Deerhead. A Victorian building reaching stories high with a mansard roof, it still stands at the corner of Route 611 and Waring Drive. Its carriage house was originally located in the rear, reached by an alleyway adjacent to the Presbyterian church.

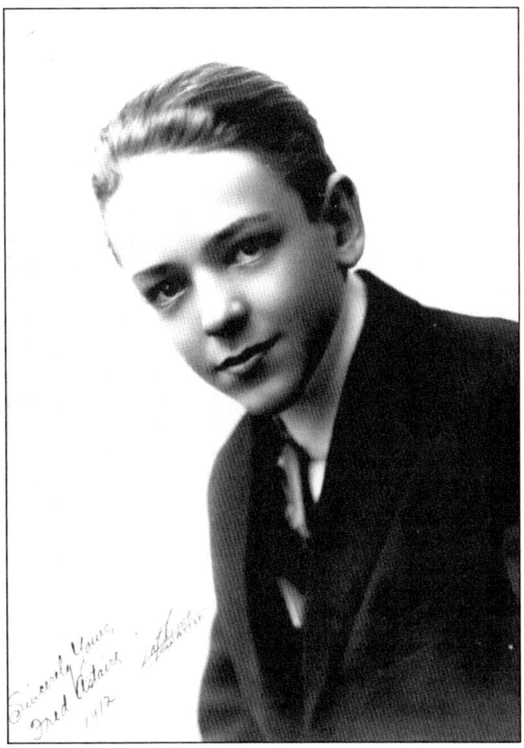

Fred Astaire (1899–1987) autographed this 1912 photograph for his Delaware Water Gap friend while vacationing in the gap. By all accounts, Fred thoroughly enjoyed his four summers spent in the gap. It was here that he acquired his lifelong love of golfing while playing on the Caldeno Golf Course links. His early years of horseback riding here also engendered his fondness for horses.

Autographed, also, to her Delaware Water Gap friend is this picture of Adele Astaire in 1912. Although lesser known in later years than her brother, she was earlier considered to be the more talented one of the brother-sister dancing duet. The family escaped the heat of the city in the summer and took a break from the New York City dance lessons that honed the children's talent.

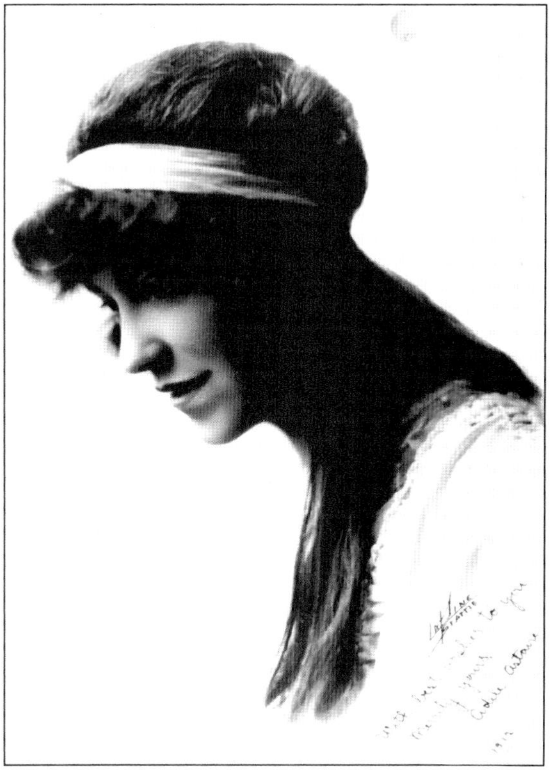

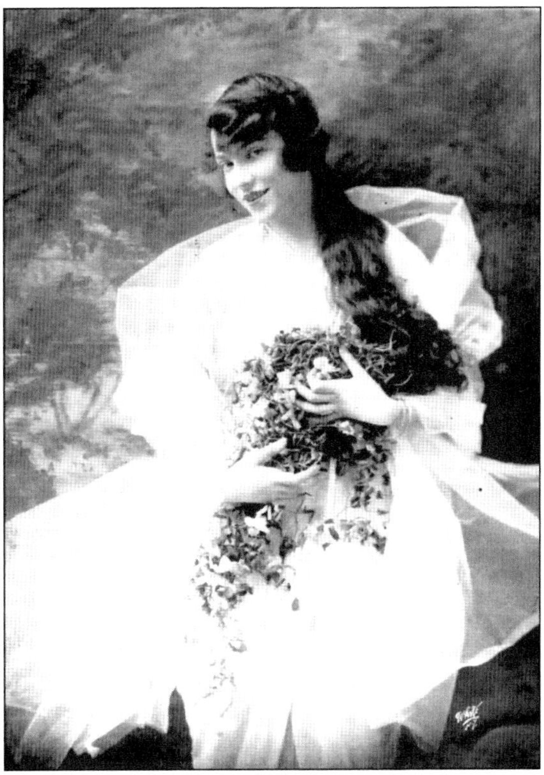

In this picture, Adele Astaire presents an almost ethereal appearance with her gauzy dress and delicate bouquet. Her career with Fred lasted from 1924 to 1932, when she married Lord Charles Francis Cavendish, the second son of the Duke of Devonshire. Brother Fred left Broadway and went on to a successful Hollywood career.

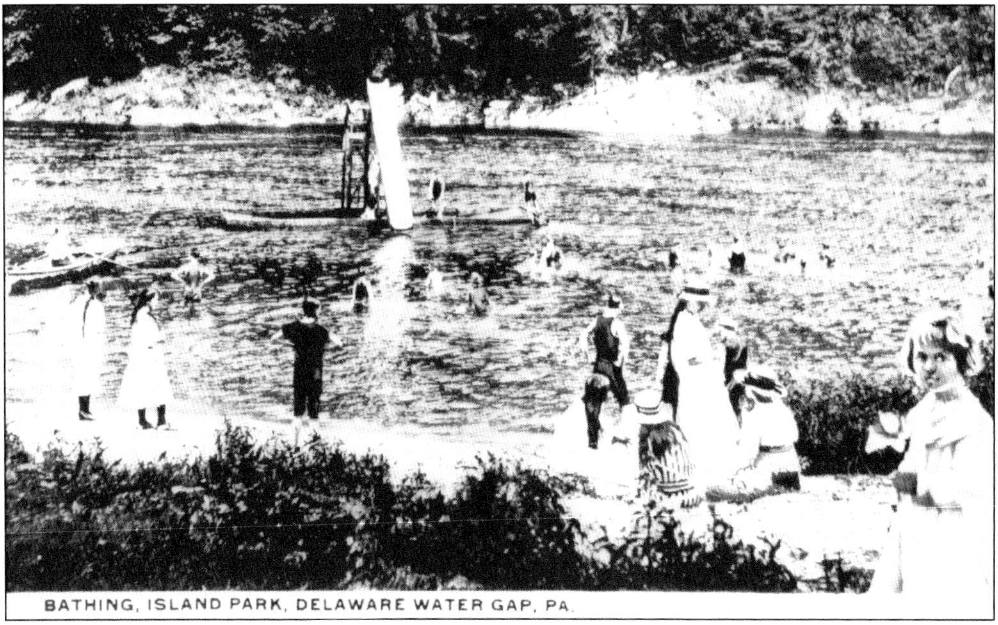

Island Park was once a huge attraction for tourists and locals alike. Thomas Carson owned and developed his one-third share of the island, putting in a bathing beach, covered pavilion, bath houses, and a refreshment stand. Group excursions traveled from Philadelphia, the Scranton and Wilkes-Barre area, and many other regions to picnic and enjoy the beach. Later known as Shellenberger Island, the park was subsequently swept away by a flood.

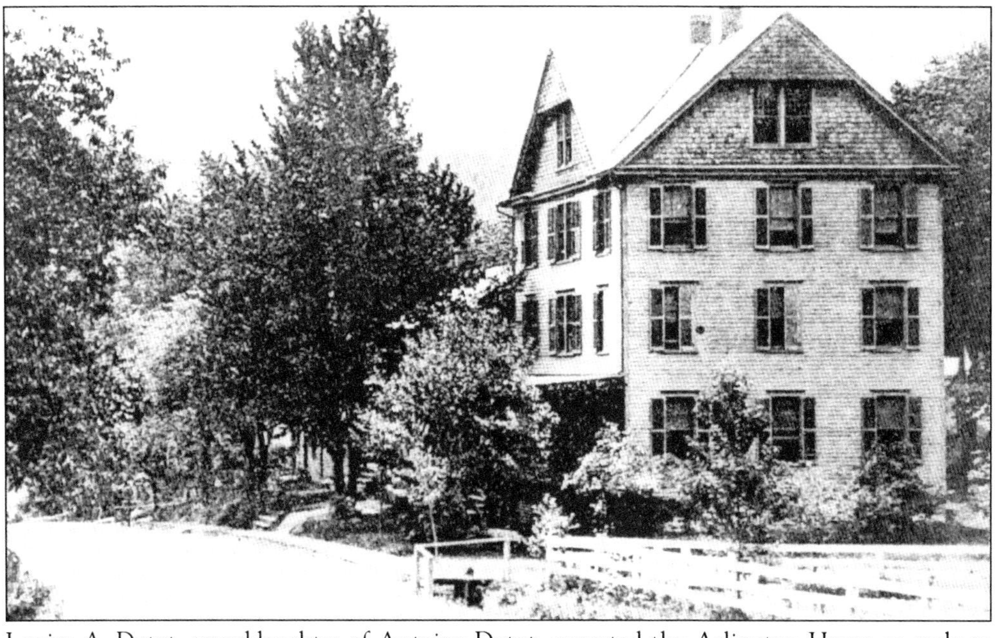

Louisa A. Dutot, granddaughter of Antoine Dutot, operated the Arlington House as early as 1901. In the early 1900s, Harvey Blair and Eugene Conway purchased the property and enlarged the building to three stories with room for 40 guest rooms and a larger dining room. The hotel, later called the Bellevue, located on Delaware Street, passed through several owners until it was acquired by the bridge commission and demolished.

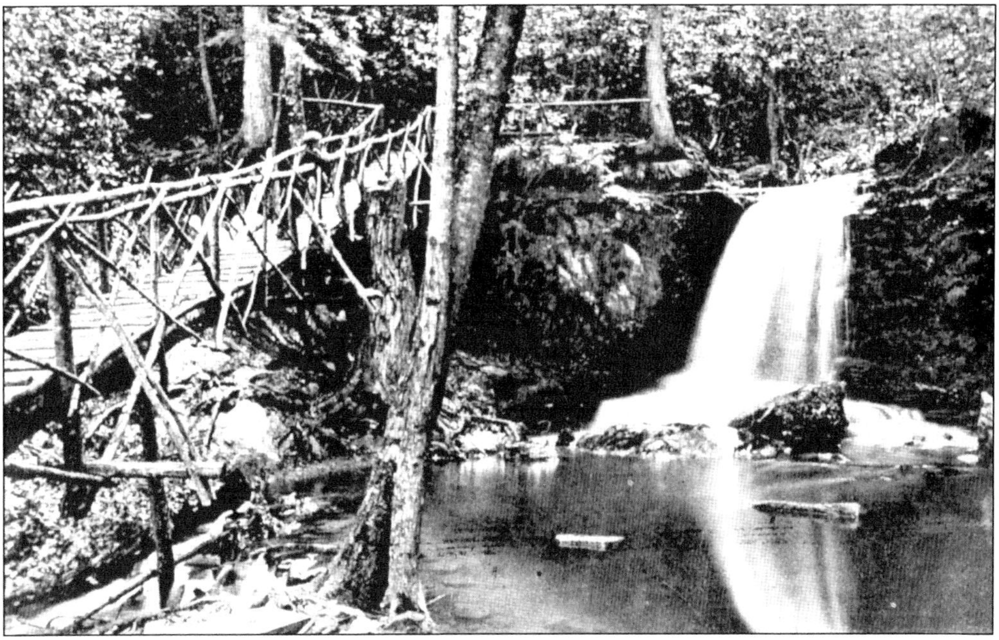

Located on Mount Minsi and close to many of the mountain resorts, Caldeno Falls became a big attraction for tourists. While locals took for granted the many sights and waterfalls, not giving them names, it was a big thrill for visitors to title them. In 1851, three Philadelphians named the falls by taking letters from their surnames: Pas**cal**, Og**den**, and McD**o**ud.

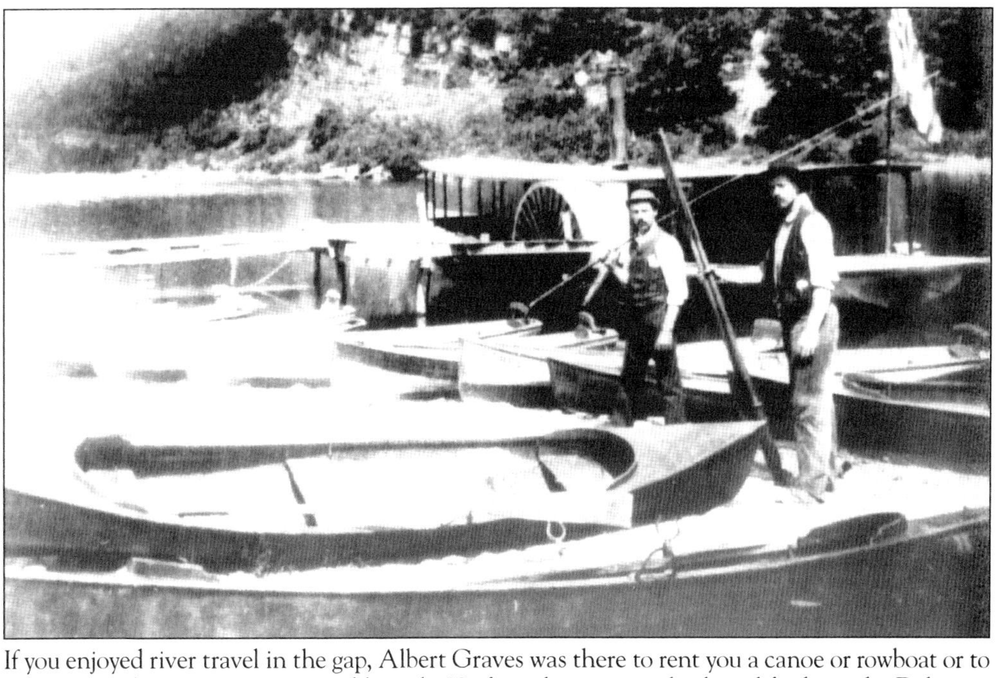

If you enjoyed river travel in the gap, Albert Graves was there to rent you a canoe or rowboat or to give you a ride on a steam-powered launch. He ferried passengers back and forth on the Delaware River to the Karamac Hotel on the New Jersey side. Always versatile, he sold bait to fisherman and furs of animals he had trapped to furriers. (Photograph courtesy of National Park Service.)

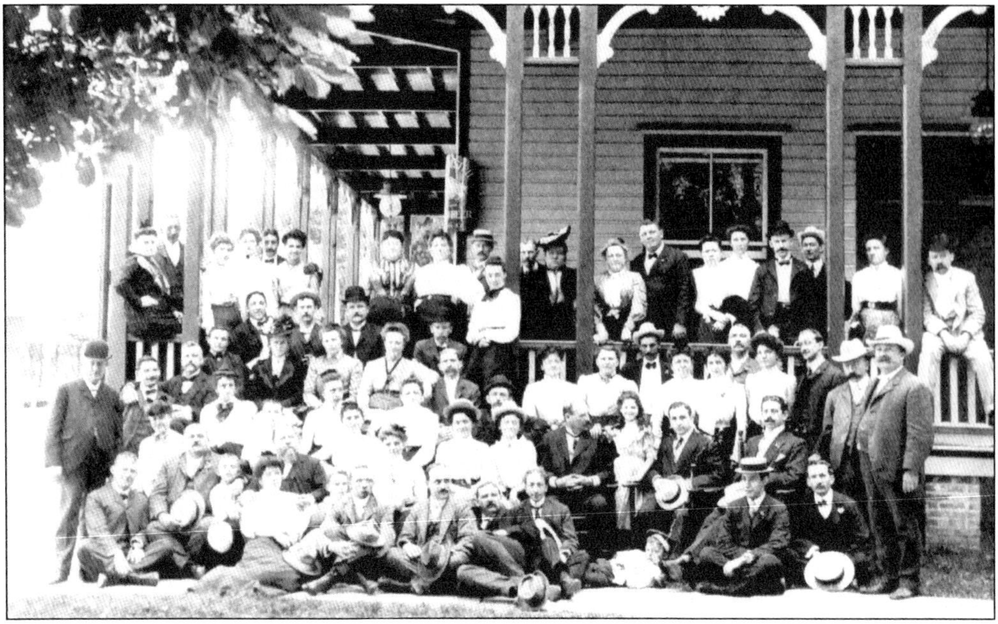

A tour group poses in front of the Water Gap Hotel in 1902. During the summer months, the exquisite hotel was solidly booked, so these guests most likely made their reservations far in advance. (Photograph from private collection.)

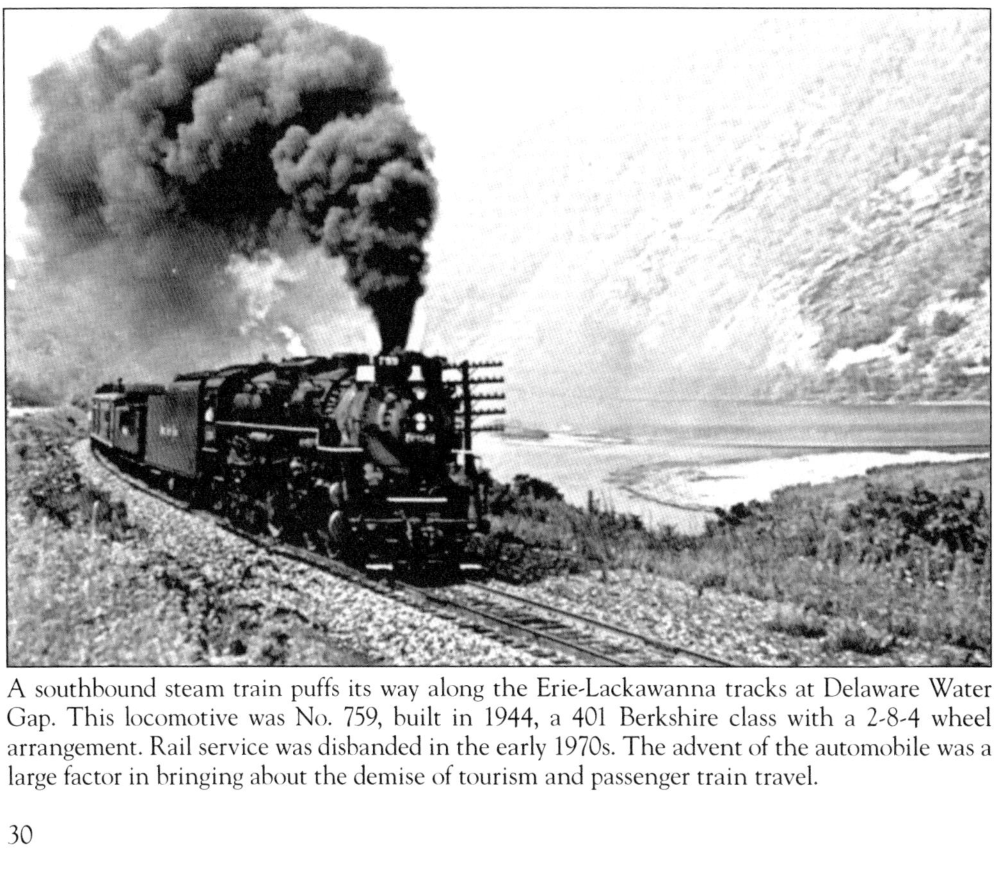

A southbound steam train puffs its way along the Erie-Lackawanna tracks at Delaware Water Gap. This locomotive was No. 759, built in 1944, a 401 Berkshire class with a 2-8-4 wheel arrangement. Rail service was disbanded in the early 1970s. The advent of the automobile was a large factor in bringing about the demise of tourism and passenger train travel.

Two

MINISINK HILLS

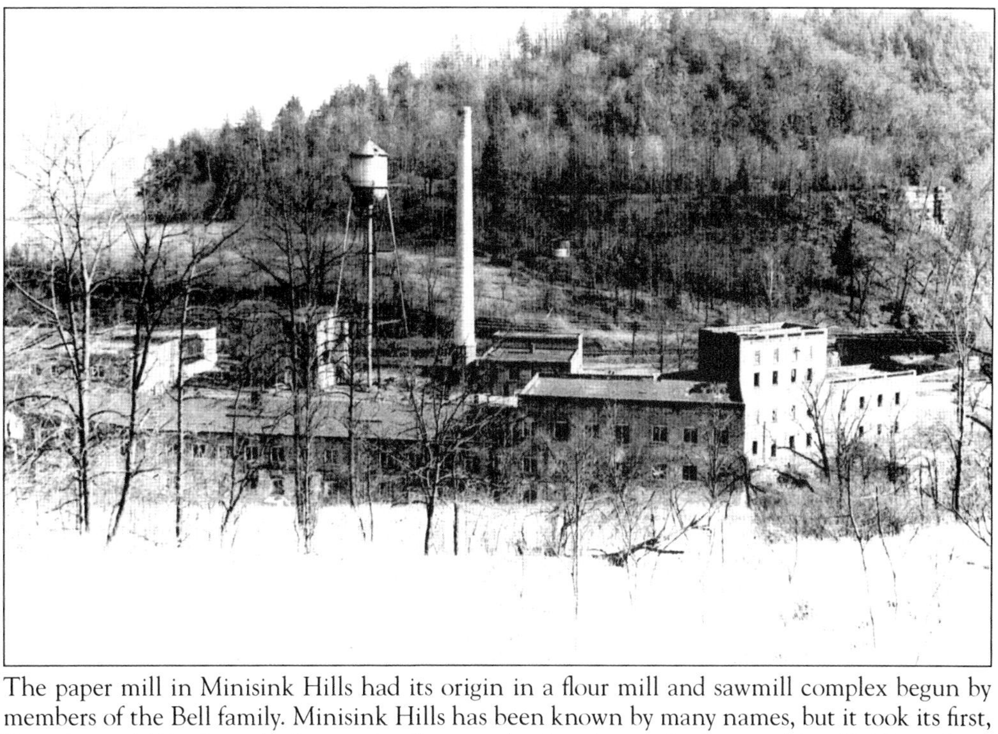

The paper mill in Minisink Hills had its origin in a flour mill and sawmill complex begun by members of the Bell family. Minisink Hills has been known by many names, but it took its first, Experiment Mills, from the innovative flour production that took place at this mill. Since then, the surrounding area has changed its name several times, becoming known as Minsi and North Water Gap, before it was finally designated Minisink Hills. This is a 1930s view of the paper mill before the Bell House was removed from the property. After many changes of name and ownership, the company exists today as Rock Tenn. (Photograph courtesy of Rock Tenn.)

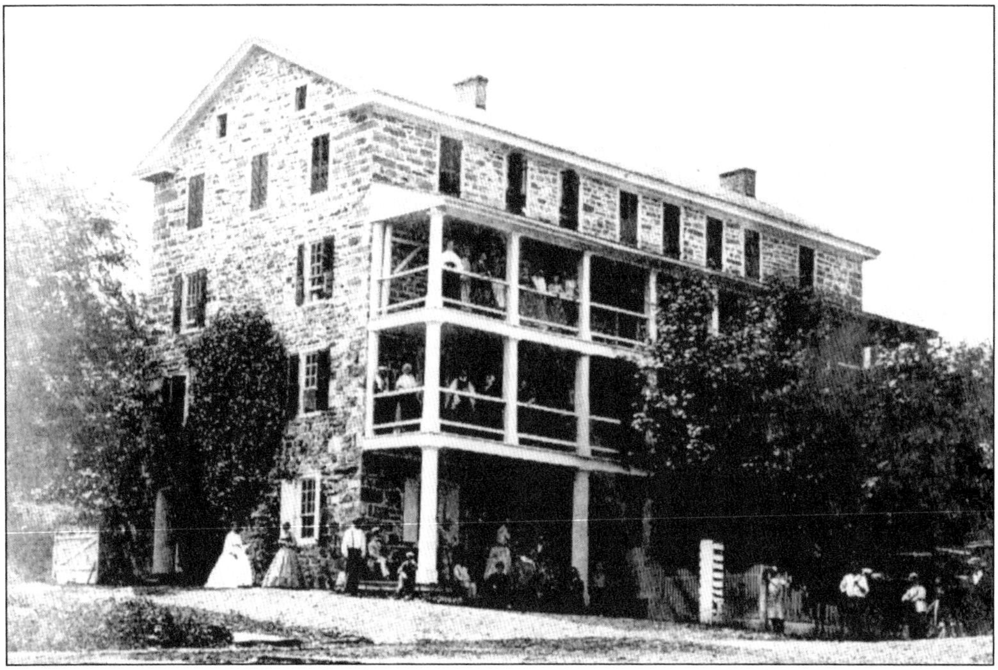

James and Thomas Bell built this house in 1829 on their property, which also included a flour mill, store, and sawmill. The building initially housed a post office and general store. The house was torn down in 1936 when the mill closed for a while. (Photograph from private collection.)

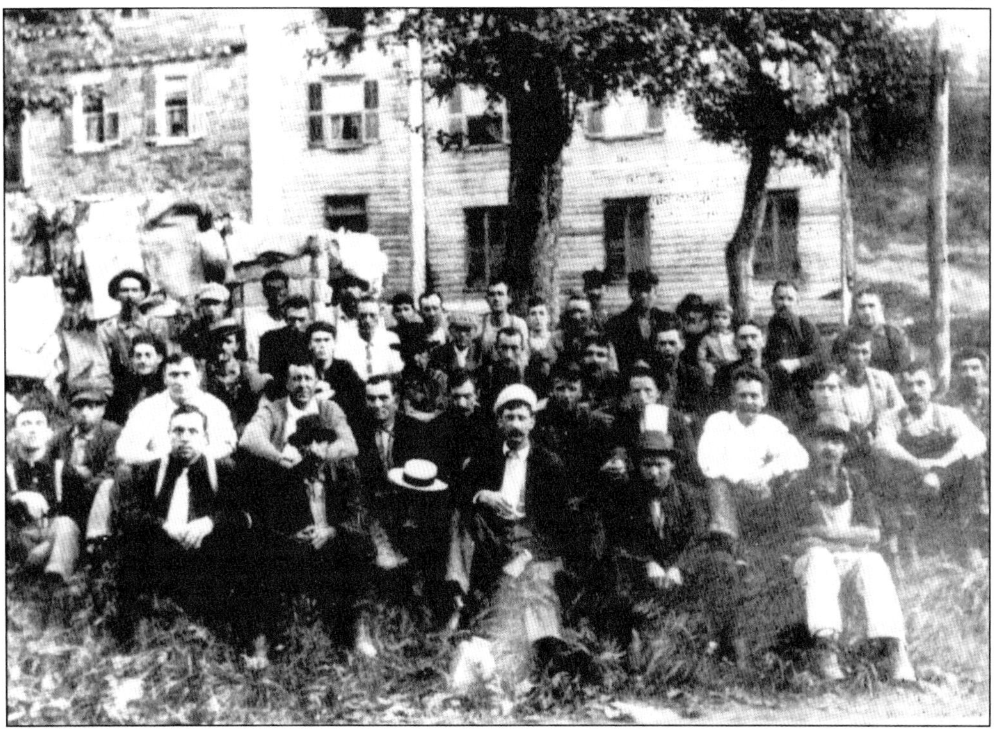

This is a 1906 photograph of employees in front of the Bell House, which housed many of the employees. By then, the mill had been renamed Minsi Pulp and Paper Company.

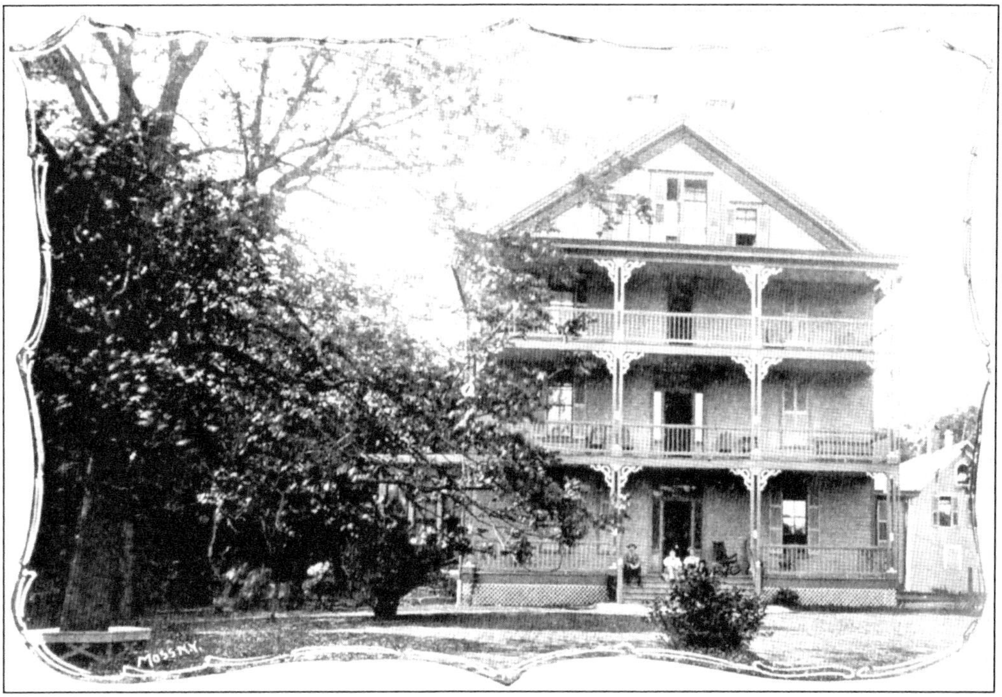

The Water Gap Sanitarium opened in 1873 on what is now near the junction of Route 447 and Route 209 before where the latter meets Route 80. Many traveled to the health center, known for its Wesley Water Cure, a regimen of treatment that involved a strict diet and water and massage therapy. It was destroyed by fire in 1911 and was never rebuilt. The Shannon Inn now stands on its former grounds.

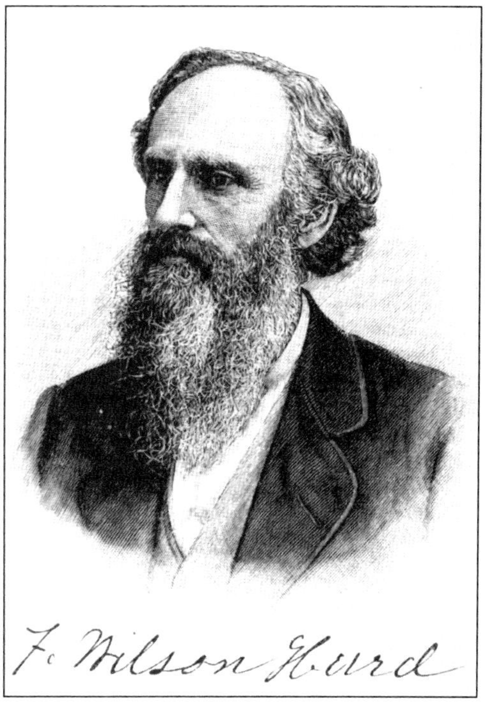

F. Wilson Hurd graduated in 1860 from the hydropathic school known as the Hygeio-Therapeutic College of New York City and attended lectures at Bellevue Medical College in New York. In 1871, impressed by the location, he purchased the Taylor farm of 200 acres at the foot of Minisink Hills, where he built his sanitarium. His daughter, Fanny H. Brown, joined him in his practice.

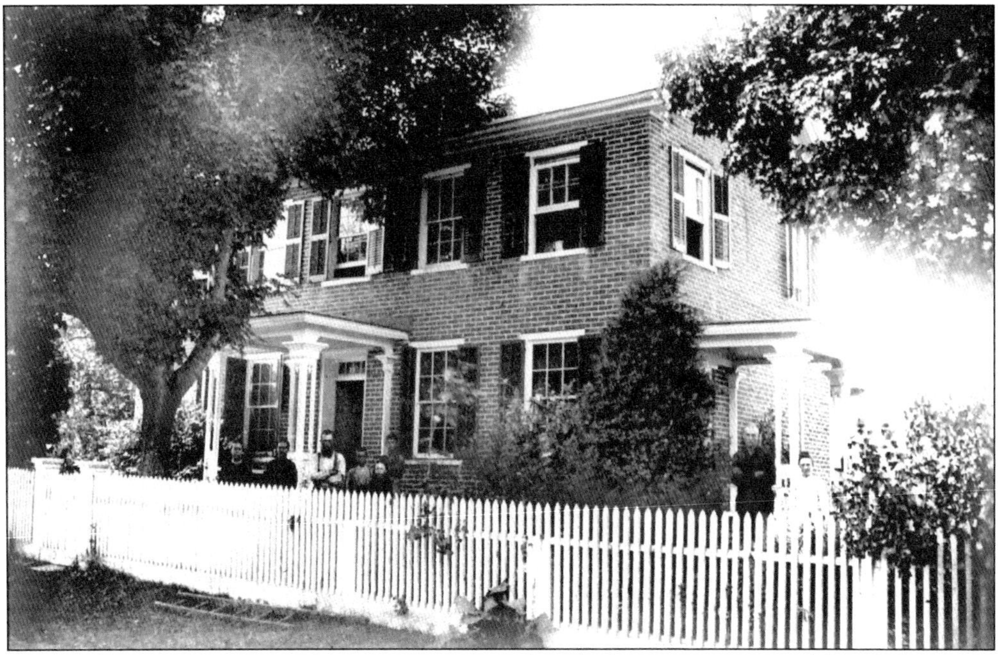

The Brick House at Mosier's Farm was constructed in the late 1800s. Pictured from left to right are Annie Dennis (adopted daughter of James and Martha Armitage), Martha Armitage, James Armitage, and unidentified boys. The couple at the end might be James Carson Mosier and Mary Ellen Armitage. (Photograph courtesy of the Mosier family.)

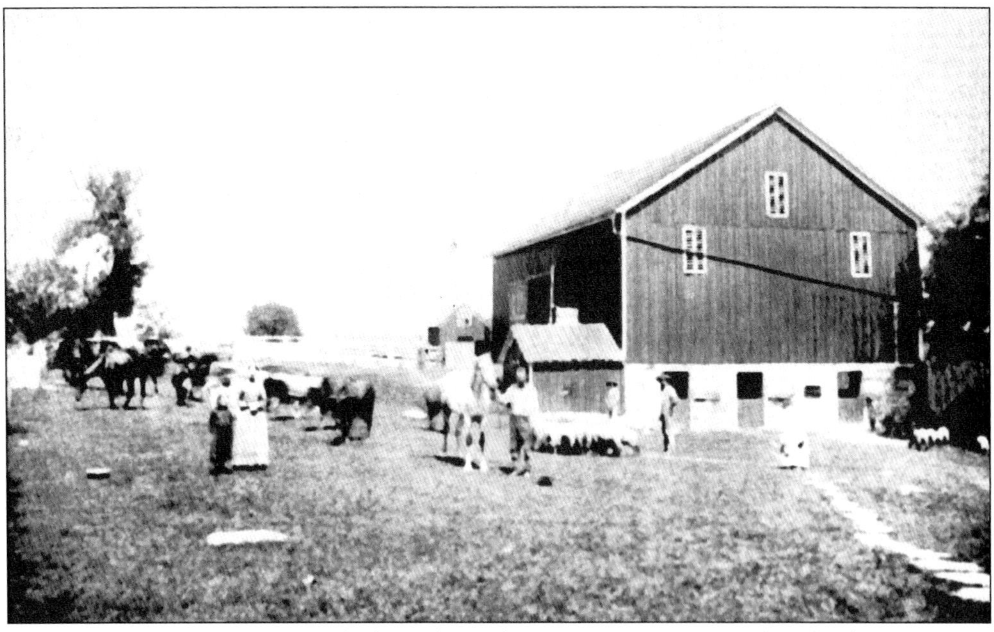

The barn on Mosier's Farm was built in the mid-1800s. James Armitage bought the farm at an auction in 1898, becoming its third owner. The woman on the left with the young girl is Martha (McCune-McEwing) Armitage, and the man with the horse is James Armitage. Others in the picture are unidentified. Seven generations of the family have lived on the farm. (Photograph courtesy of the Mosier family.)

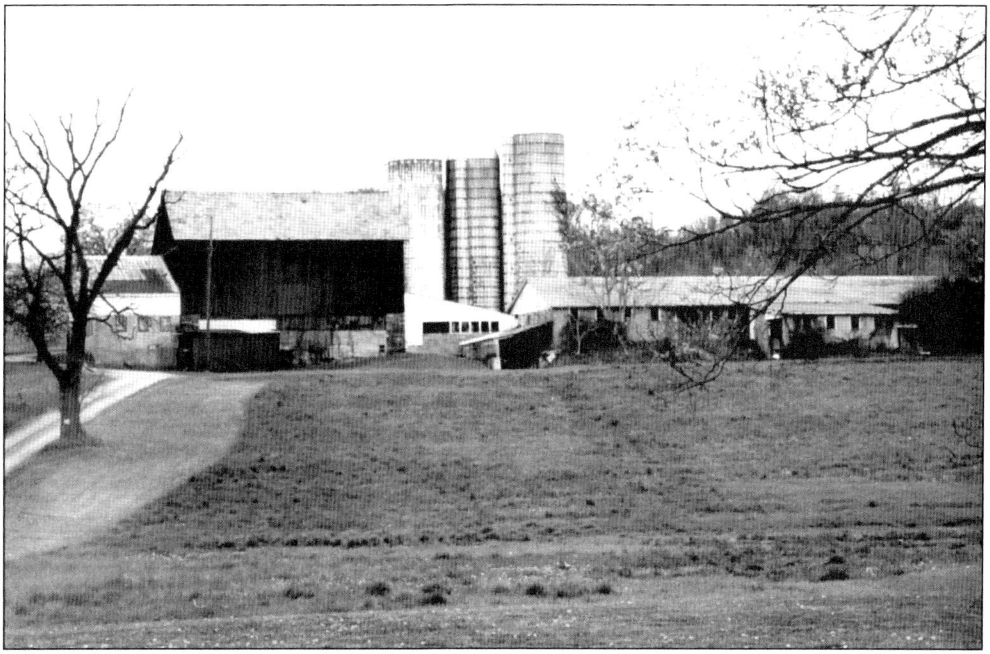

In later years, the Mosier family refurbished the barn, complete with silo, and opened up a nearby store, Mosier's Dairy, where they sold their bottled milk and other dairy products. The farm was a favored spot for many years to take schoolchildren on field trips. (Photograph from private collection.)

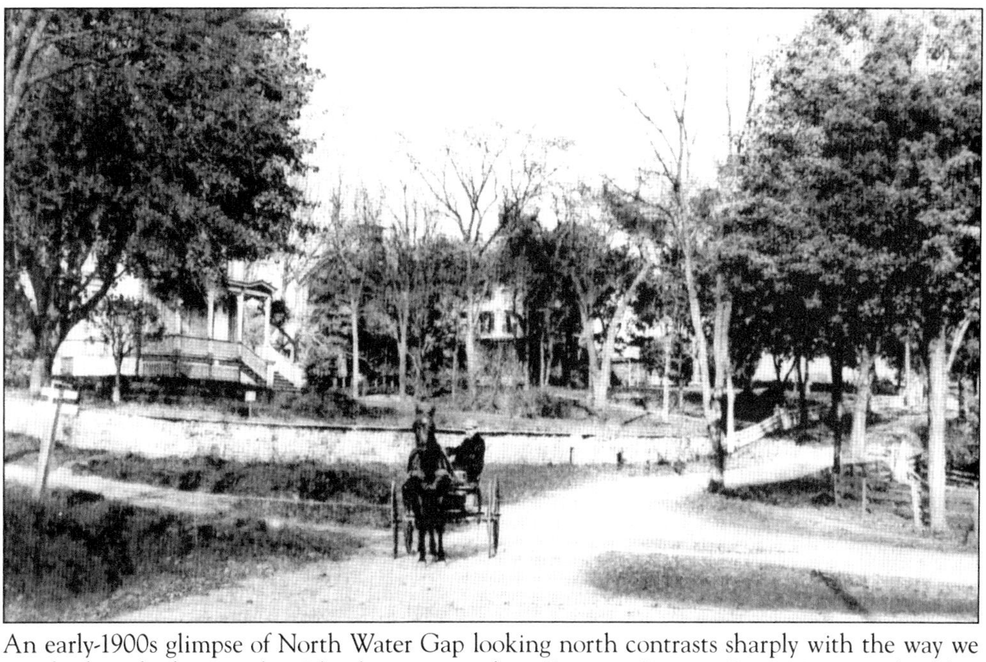

An early-1900s glimpse of North Water Gap looking north contrasts sharply with the way we see the busy highway today. This location is where Route 447 meets Route 209 North today. Back then, the Hurd Sanitarium building was situated on the left, where the Shannon Inn now stands. Dirt road has succumbed to a small concrete highway that does little to contain a massive commuter population.

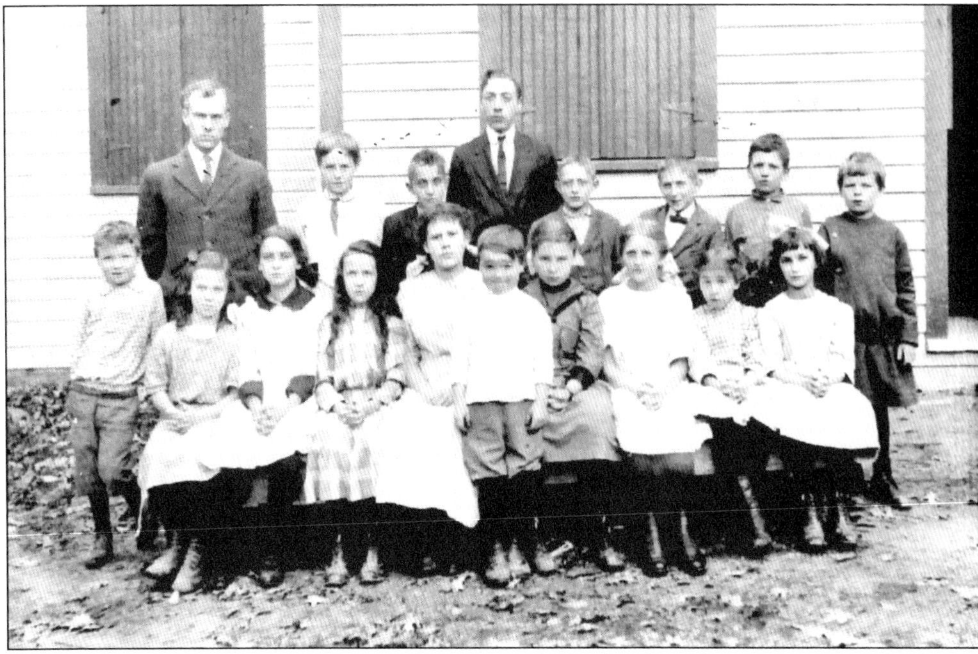

Houserville School was named for Jacob Houser, who built a large house in 1833 at the foot of Minisink Hills, located a little farther up the road from the Hurd Sanitarium. An engineering firm has its office there today. Some of the students pictured in front of the school are identified as Clarence Strunk (first row, far left), Sarah Eilenberger (first row, 4th from left), Clarence Strunk (first row, 6th from left), and Margaret Eilenberger (first row, 10th from left). (Photograph courtesy of Michelle Kintner.)

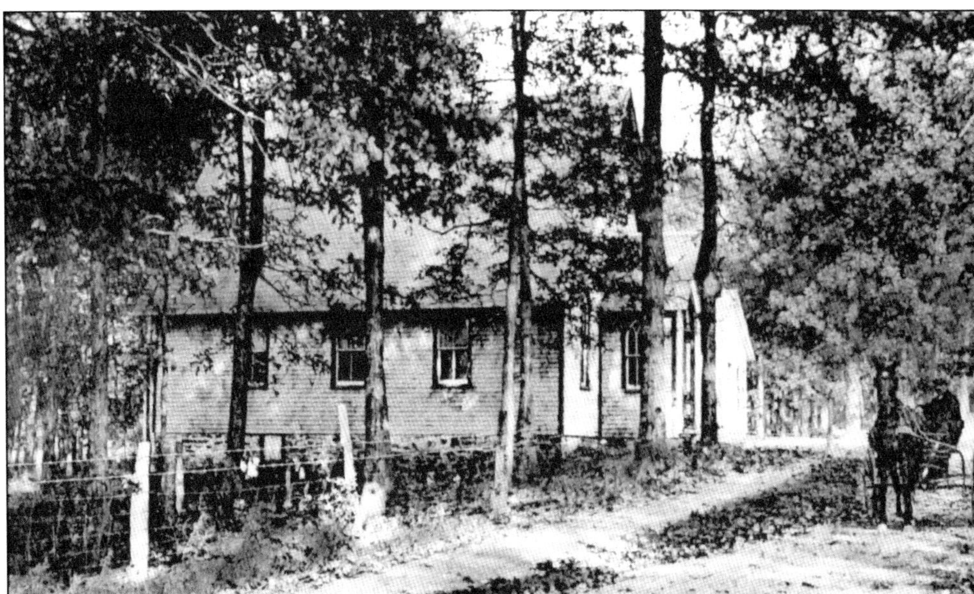

This is an early-1900s view of the Houserville Church and meeting grounds, located just north of what was then the Hurd Sanitarium. The church building is now a chiropractor's office.

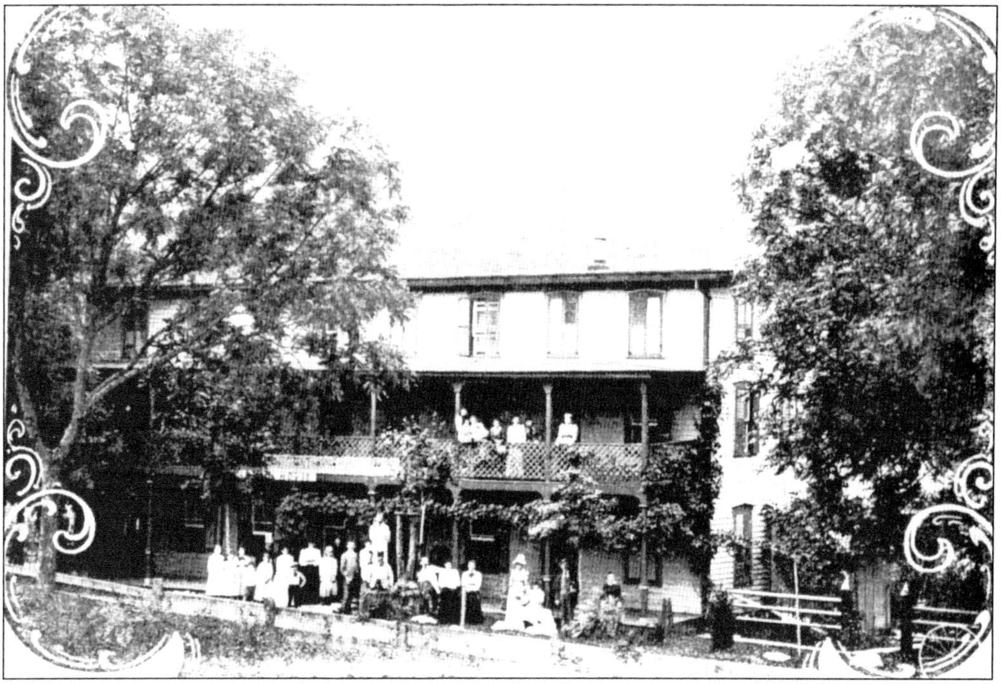

This is an 1897 view of the Cataract House, originally built by Daniel Zimmerman and operated in this time period by Lewis M. Tucker. The boardinghouse could hold up to 100 guests. It stood on Route 209 on the property known in later years as the Pococabana. Remnants of the old hotel's foundation still remain, situated close to the highway.

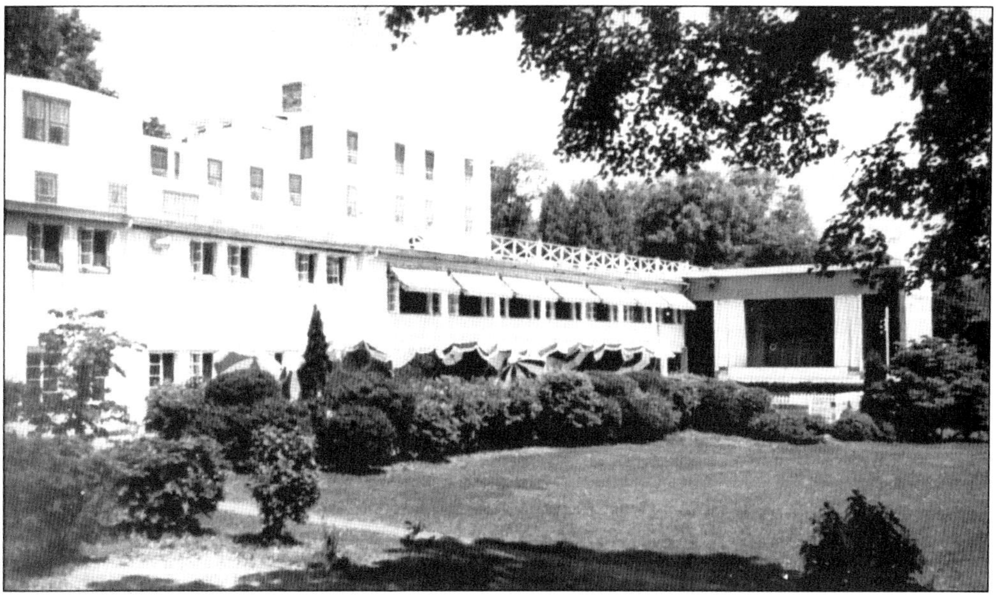

Walter Giseland took over the Cataract House in 1937 and operated it until 1972. He renamed it the Pococabana and turned the property into a small resort by enlarging the building and adding a swimming pool and tennis court. A fire on April 13, 1973, destroyed the main building. The swimming pool and tennis courts were later removed, and the property now contains rental units.

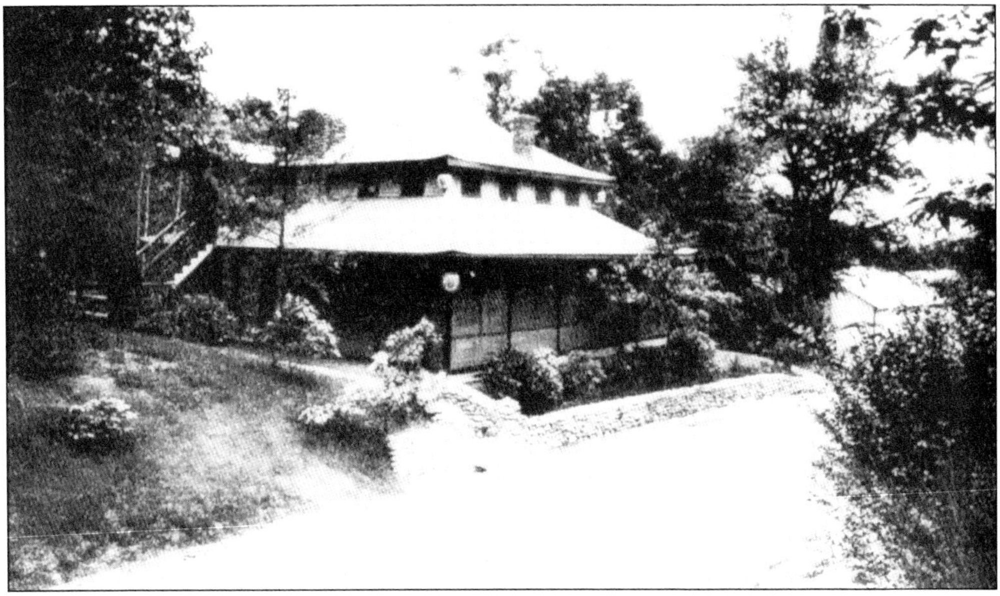

Mrs. Ernest Hogg spent several years in China. Upon her return in 1924, she directed the construction of this teahouse, a miniature reproduction of the Empress Dowager's summer palace in China. The former Yin Hoo Cha Yuan Tea House on Silver Lake is now a private home.

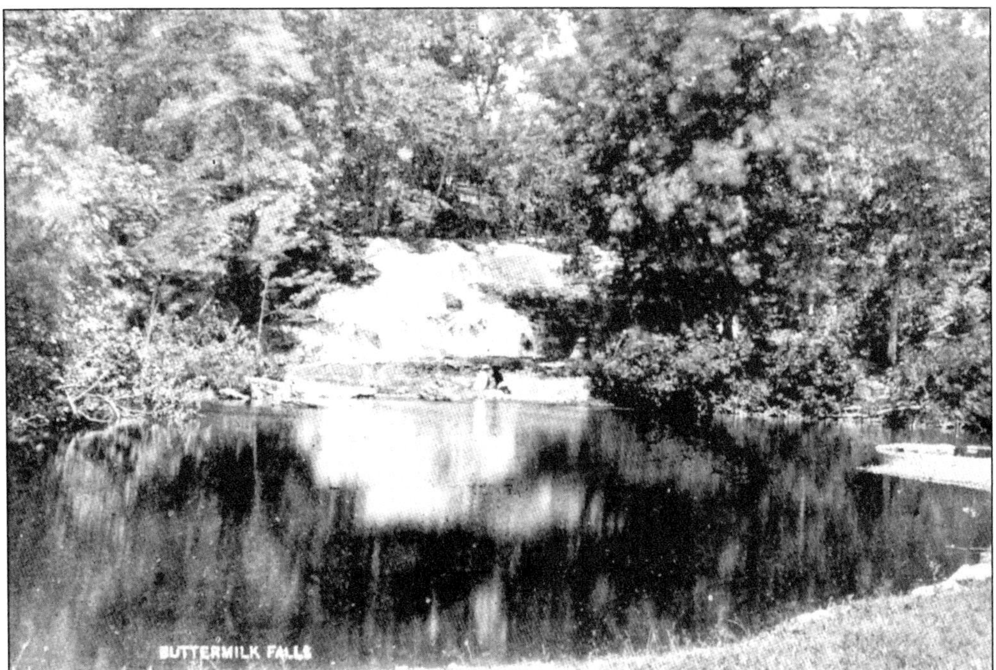

In rainy seasons, water spills over the rock table of Buttermilk Falls, churning and creating a frothy, creamy appearance like freshly made buttermilk. Buttermilk Falls lies on Marshalls Creek as its third falls. At one time, the waterfall was also known as Cataract Falls. It has presented the background for many wedding photographs of newlyweds who have held their wedding receptions at nearby Shawnee Inn.

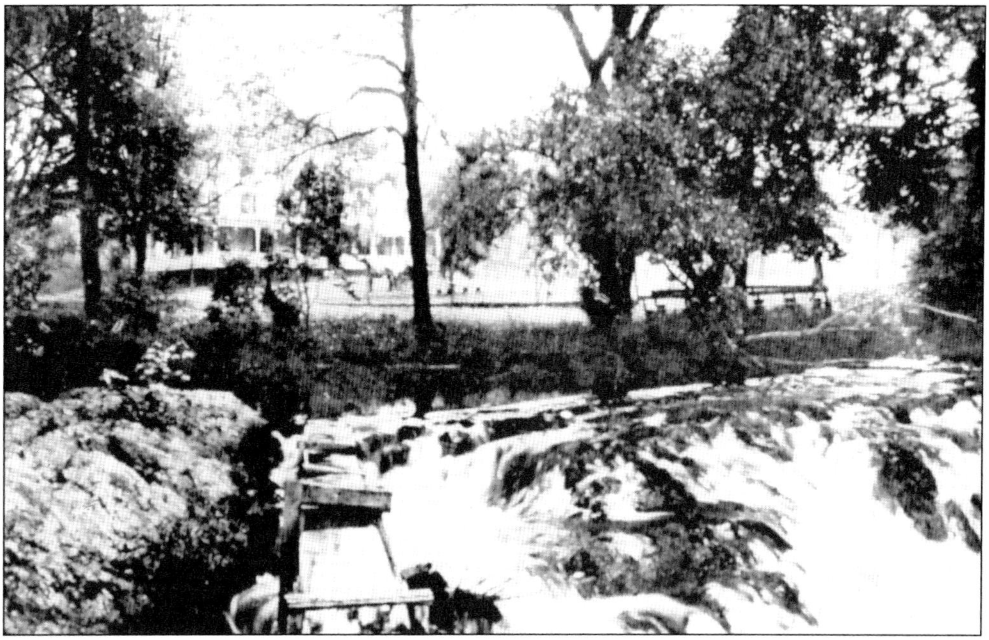

The Willow Dell opened in the 1850s as the Maple Cottage Boarding House, a small frame building with a log structure built at its side. At the dawn of the 20th century, it was replaced by the larger frame building. In 1911, Mrs. L. S. Van Nort ran the hotel, which by then could accommodate 60 guests. It currently houses Shawnee Development's office.

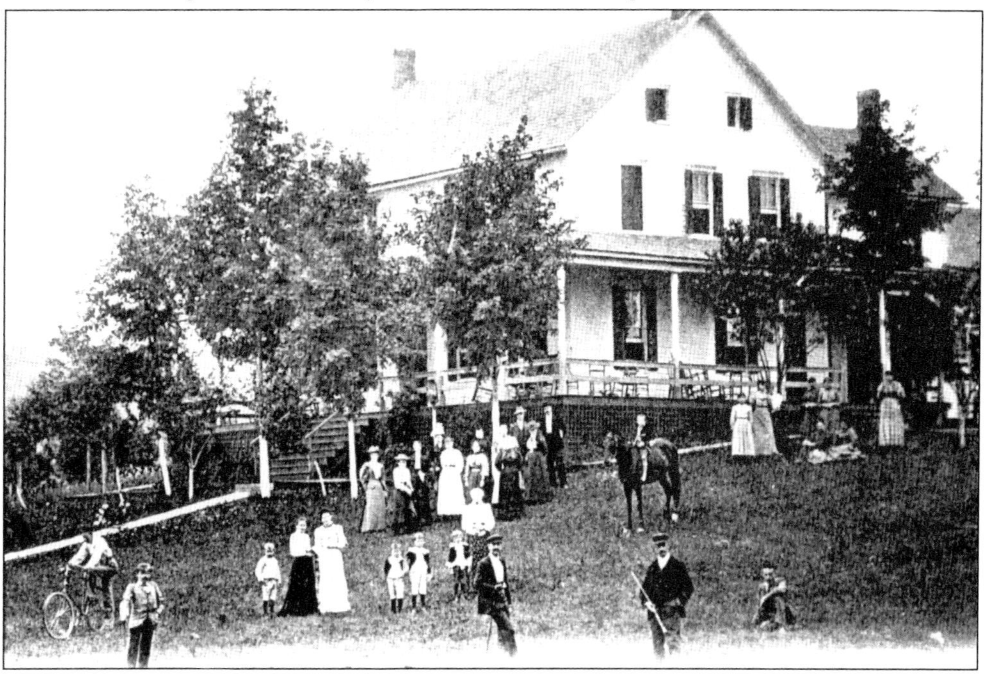

The Gap View House, pictured in 1896, was situated at the top of Shawnee Hill. According to 1897 historian Jackson Lantz, it commanded "a beautiful and extended view, one of the loveliest of the Gap and the Shawnee portion of the Delaware Valley." Samuel Overfield was its proprietor, and "Red Ann" Overfield later operated it.

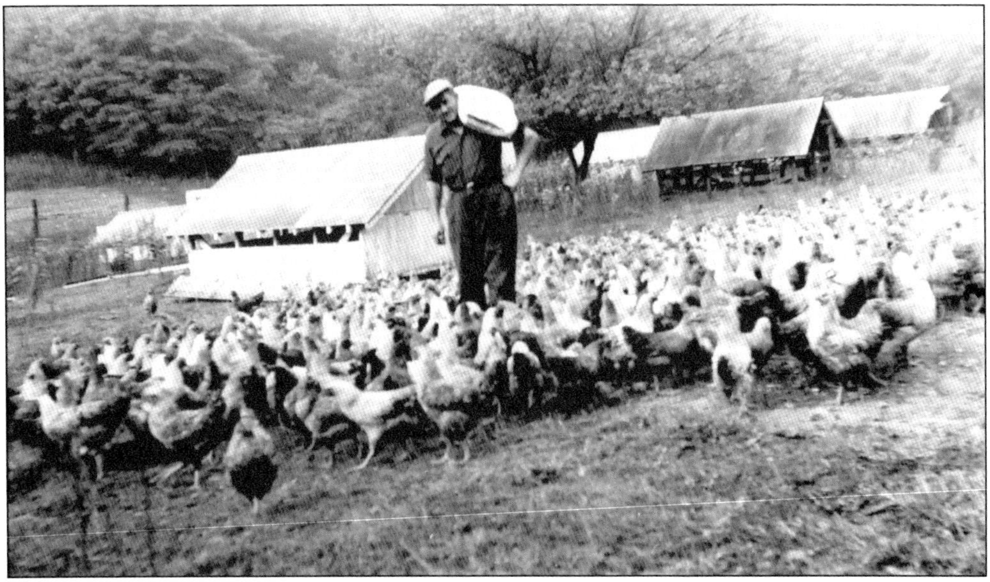

Herbert Hoover promised "a chicken in every pot" in his 1928 campaign as he paraphrased Henry IV. Ray Hartmann must have remembered this and did his best to provide the poultry. Here he stands among his flock of 2,000 chickens, trying to keep the population fed.

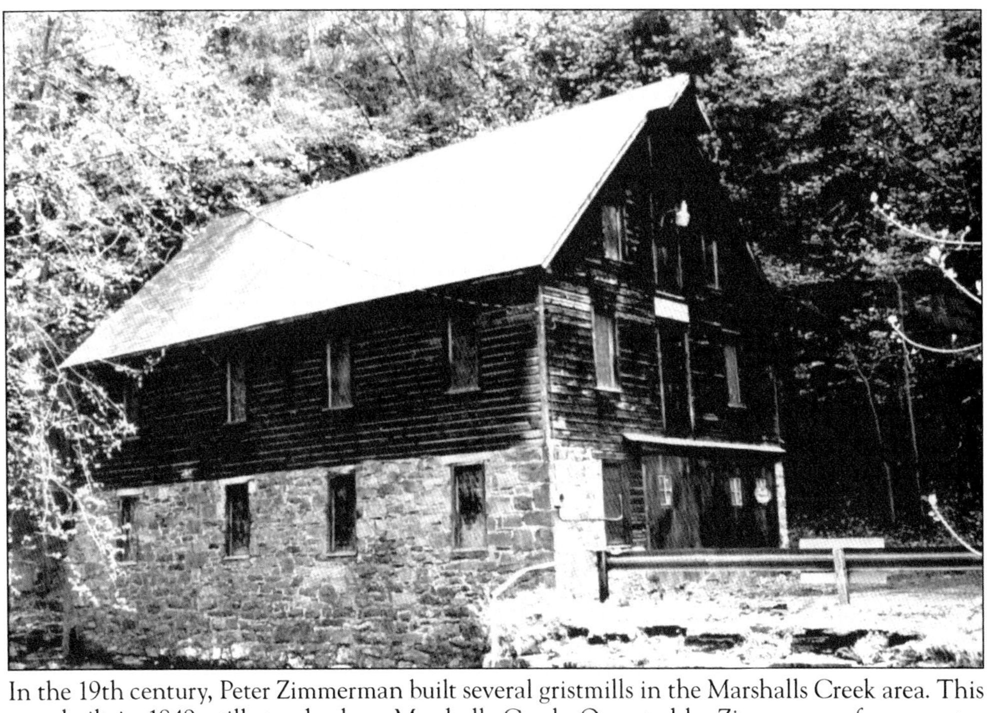

In the 19th century, Peter Zimmerman built several gristmills in the Marshalls Creek area. This one, built in 1849, still stands along Marshalls Creek. Operated by Zimmerman for a quarter of a century, it was later sold and continued to operate as a working mill until the 1920s. A restoration project has kept the mill looking much the same as it did in its original condition.

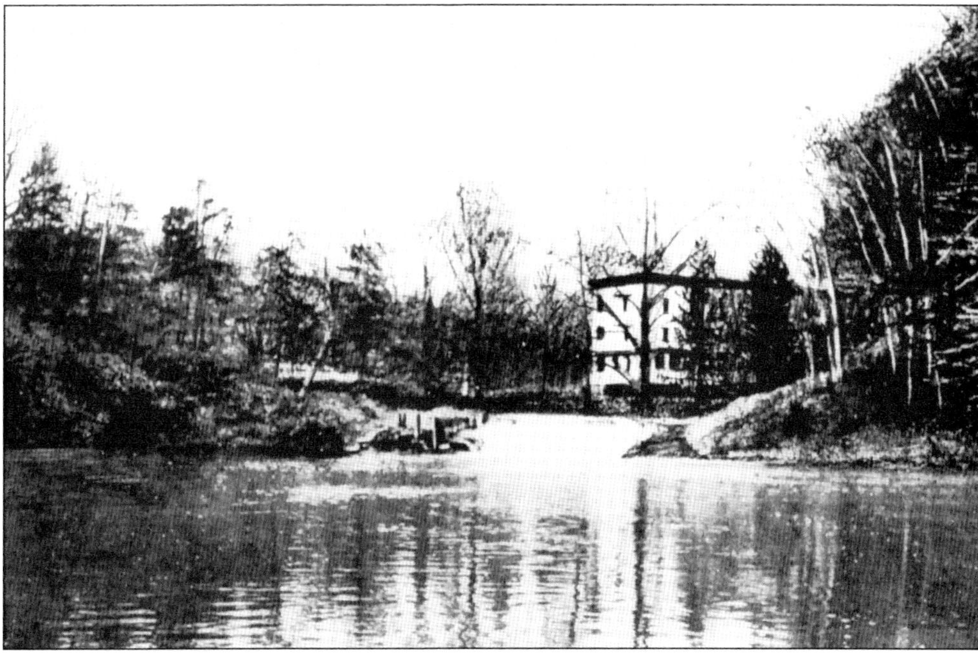

Silver Lake, fed by Marshalls Creek, was located just below Buttermilk Falls. It once covered an area about half a mile long and one-eighth of a mile wide. At the beginning of the 20th century, its brilliant waters supported a variety of recreational and business opportunities. In the late 1890s, P. J. Pipher, who owned a flouring mill at its foot, rented boats for rowing and fishing on the lake.

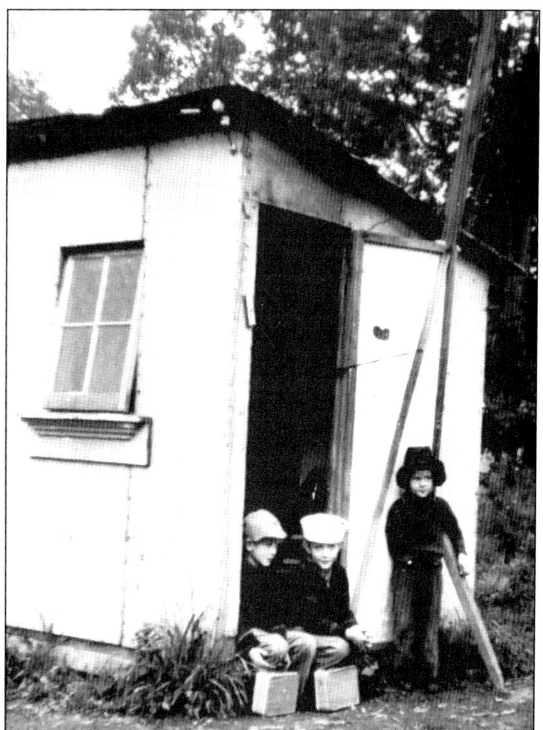

During World War II, Ray Hartmann and family, as civil defense volunteers, used this lookout shed to watch for enemy planes. It was located across from where the Pococabana stood. Pictured, from left to right, are Ben, Roger, and Phyllis Hartmann. (Photograph courtesy of Roger Hartmann.)

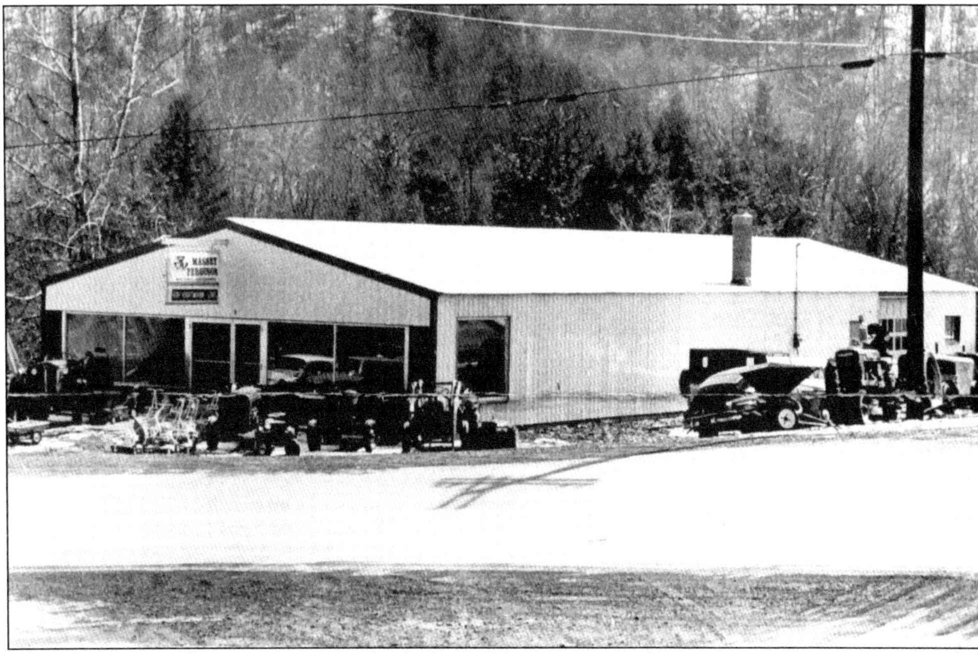

Ray Hartmann and Sons initially opened their business in 1952, operating first from a cellar at their house. They subsequently built this store, where they sold and serviced lawn mowers and chain saws. The business evolved into a large center that sold loaders, bulldozers, and snowmobiles. It closed in 1990. Bargain Hunters Gift Shop stands there today. (Photograph courtesy of Roger Hartmann.)

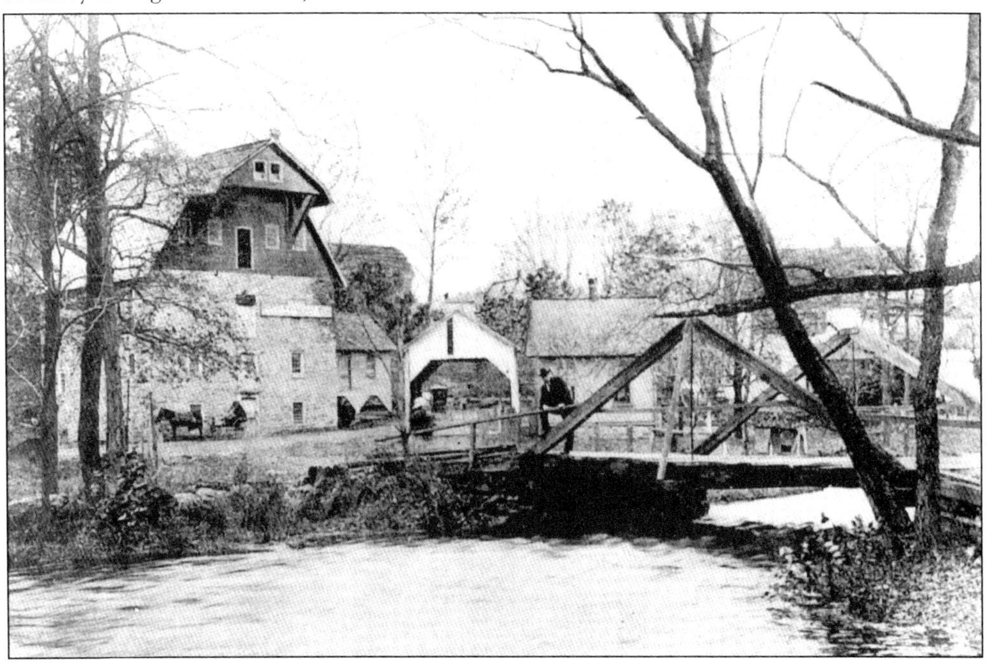

Eilenberger Mills, owned by Fred W. Eilenberger, was located in Minisink Hills, near the building once known as the Carmen Roller Skating Rink and the present Minisink Hotel. It encompassed the lumbermill and all the Eilenberger manufacturing interests.

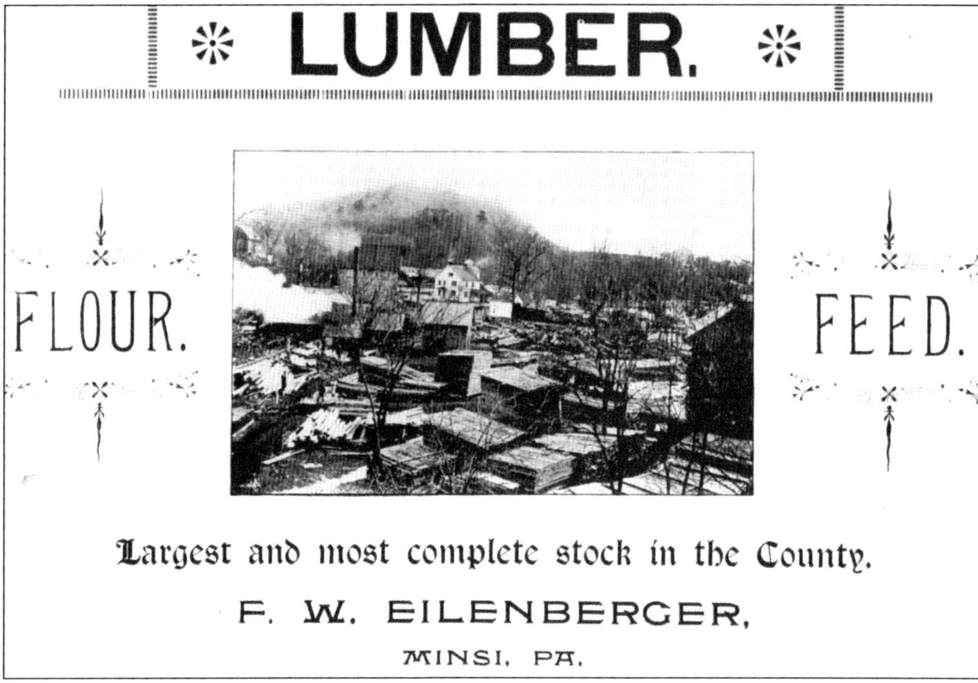

Frederick W. Eilenberger began manufacturing lumber with his father-in-law, Melchoir Heller, and later went into business with Frank Heller. In 1892, he bought his partner's interest in the grist- and sawmill and opened Eilenberger Lumber Company. To this he added a planing mill and steam cider mill on the old Heller property and became one of the largest grain and lumber dealers in the area.

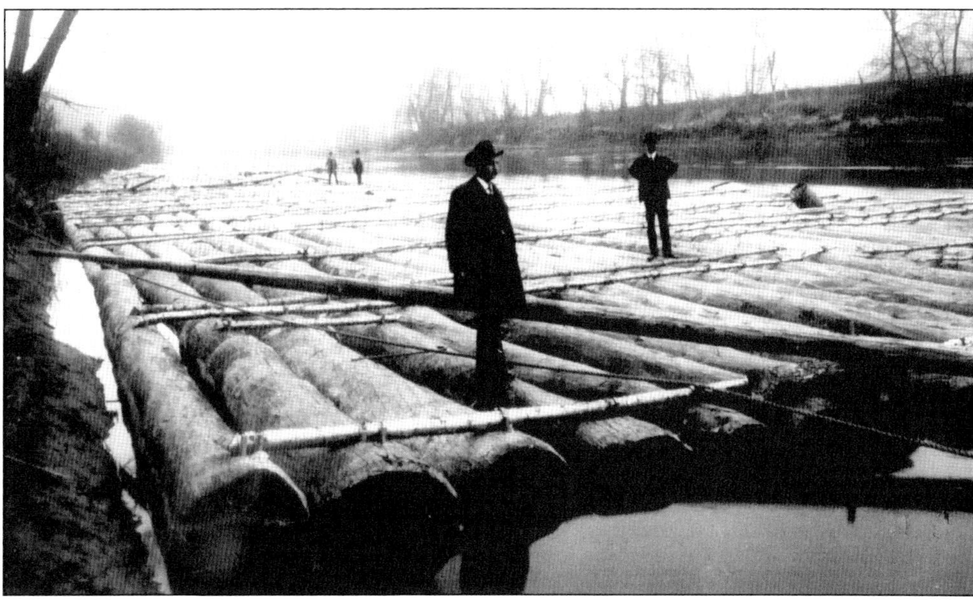

The timber rafting industry prospered from around 1760 until more than a century later. The raftsmen who steered the lumber down the Delaware River must have indeed been a skilled but daring and adventurous lot. Numerous hazards lay along the waterway. Fred Eilenberger is pictured in the foreground.

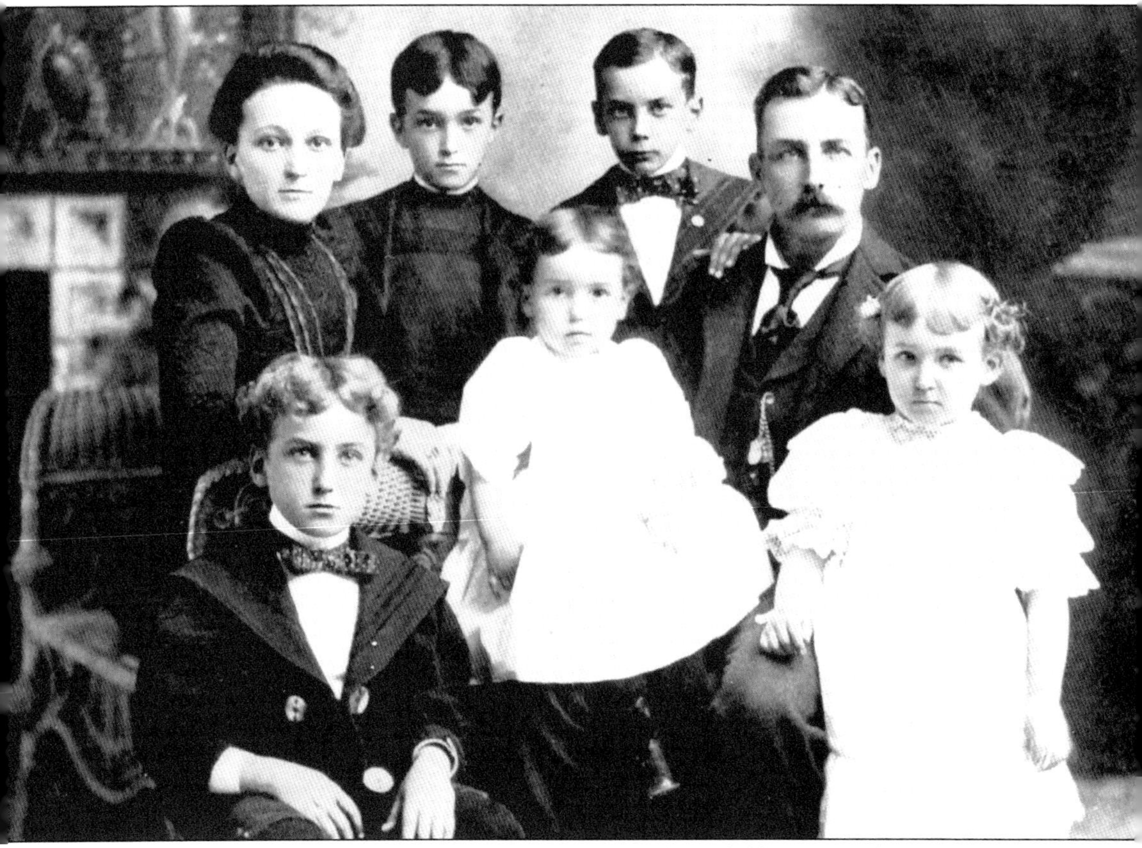

Pictured are Fred and Amy Eilenberger with five of their children. From left to right are (first row) Melchoir, Vera, and Cleo; (second row) Amy, Frank, Willard, and Fred Eilenberger. Fred was born February 25, 1866, in Middle Smithfield Township, the son of John and Katie V. Bush Eilenberger. His great-grandfather Andrew Eilenberger was one of the first settlers of Middle Smithfield Township. Frederick's wife, Amy, was the daughter of Melchoir and Sarah Heller. Amy Eilenberger graduated from the Moravian Ladies Seminary, Bethlehem, and before her marriage, taught at what was known as the Houserville School near the Hurd Sanitarium. Three daughters, Sara, Margaret, and Amy H., were born after the photograph was taken. The family has many descendants in the region.

Three

SHAWNEE

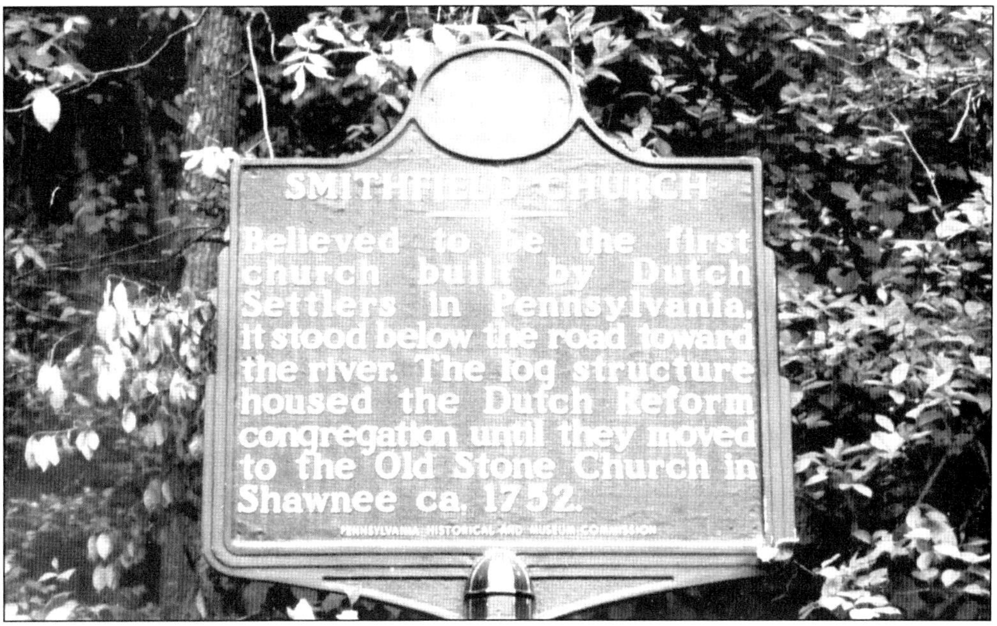

As the marker indicates, an ancient church stood near this location on River Road. This log building was situated about two miles from the 1750 Stone Church and present Presbyterian church. Its precise date of organization is unknown, but early church records give some indication. In 1741, Johan Casper Freyenmoet served as its first regular pastor. Records published in the "Smithfield Church" section of the *New York Genealogical and Biographical Society* collection show that settlers from many outlying areas attended services and had their children baptized there. Some of these came from as far away as Esopus, New York (now Kingston), as well as others from across the river in Sussex County, New Jersey. To be sure, the Depuy (Depue) family of Shawnee is prominently mentioned in the earliest of records. By 1752, the congregation had evolved largely to Presbyterianism. There are several possibilities for this. The most likely possibility is that there was a shortage of qualified Dutch Reformed ministers to serve the area, and more Scotch-Irish and others of that faith had settled in the region.

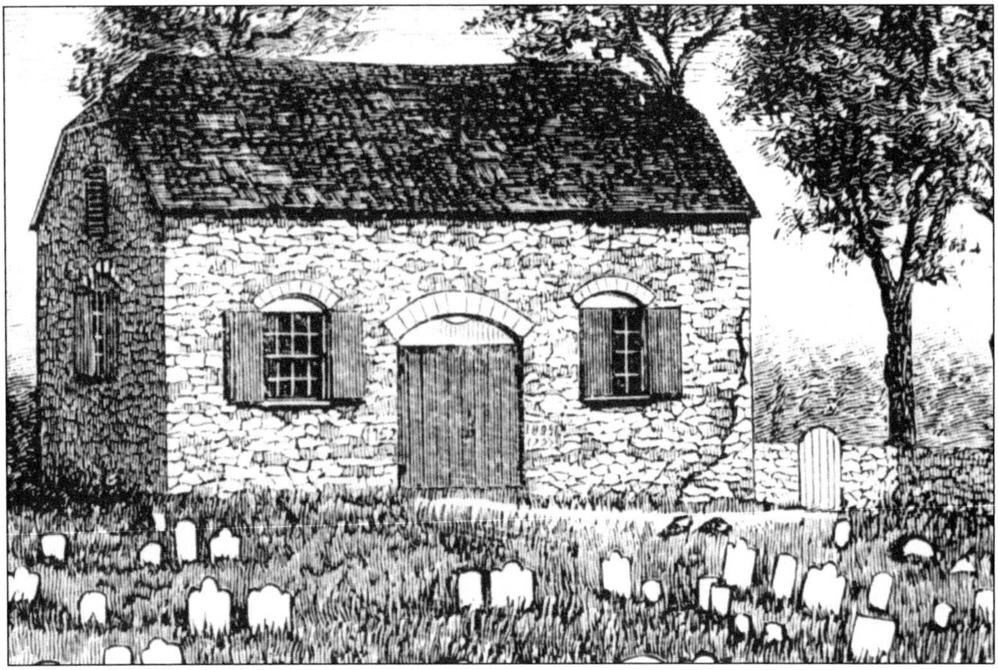

In 1750, William Allen, land agent of Pennsylvania, granted five acres in Shawnee for use as a "Presbyterian Meeting House." Two years later, the stone church in Shawnee was built under the direction of Nicholas Depui, Samuel Depui, and Abraham Van Campen. It was open to all denominations. Presbyterian, Dutch Reformed, Lutheran, and Reformed congregations worshiped there.

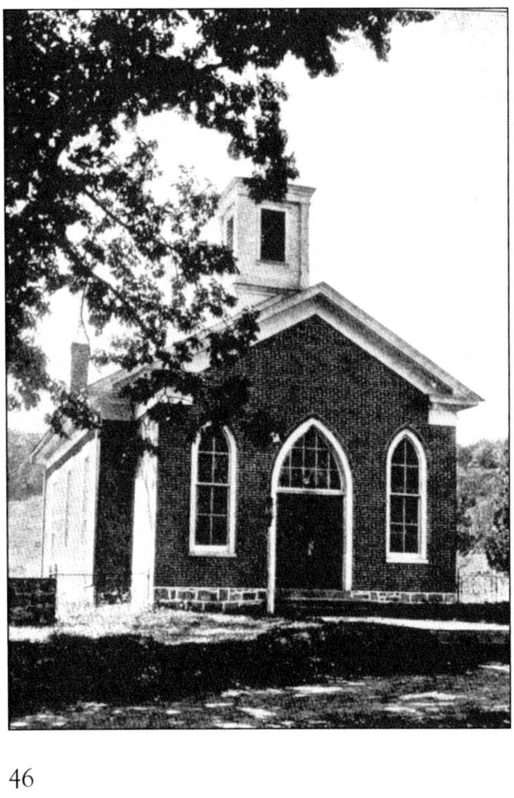

In 1853, the present Shawnee Presbyterian Church replaced the old stone church. Rev. Kirby Davis served as its first pastor. In addition to serving the church's religious needs, he also ran a private school for boys in the nearby schoolhouse. Initials of the founders—N. D. P. (Nicholas DePuy), S. D. P. (Samuel DePuy), and A. V. K. (Abraham Van Kampen)—are located on the foundation of the present building.

This is the front of the Presbyterian church in Shawnee. The c. 1950 photograph shows the christening group for baby Lillian George's baptism. The child's older sister, April, is pictured in front. From left to right are an unidentified man, Melinda George, Sarah Booth, Lillian Garris (holding baby Lillian), and Al Garris. (Photograph courtesy of April George Duganieri.)

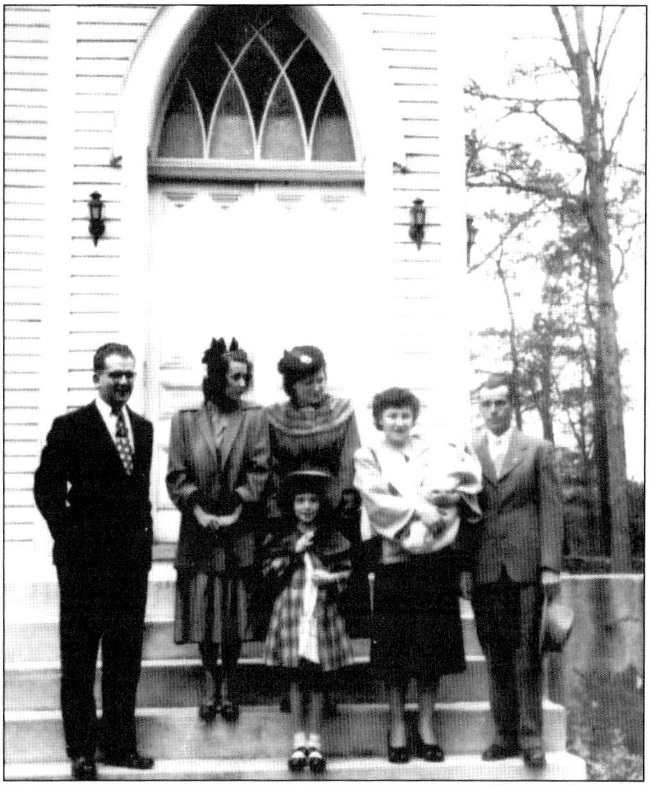

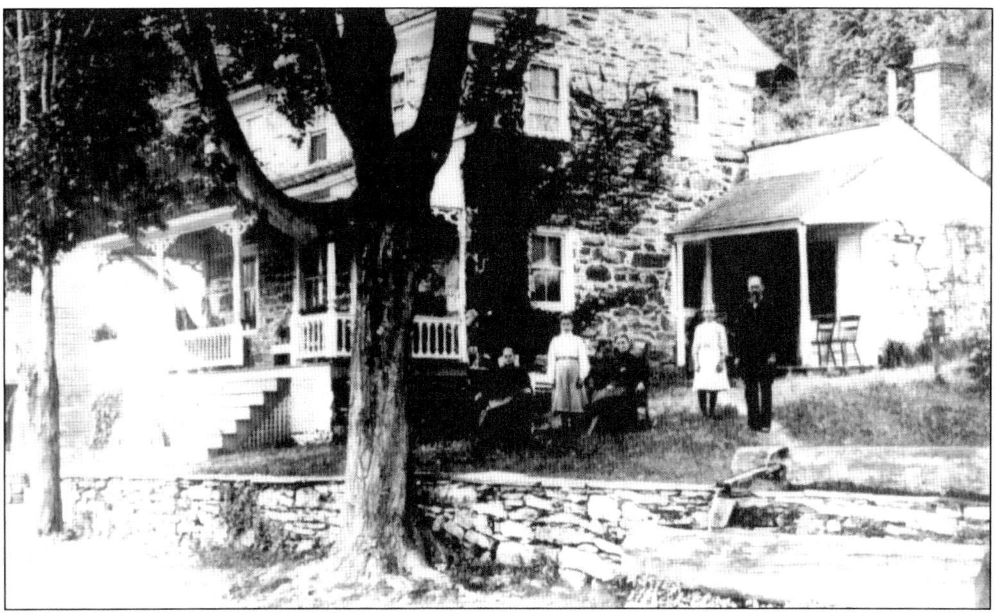

Pictured on the Christian Kautz Farm on River Road are, from left to right, Mrs. Christian Kautz, Bertha Kautz (daughter), unidentified, unidentified, and Christian Kautz. The water trough was placed for the convenience of passing teams and drivers. The old Dutch Reformed Church, a log building, was located on the property across from the house. (Photograph courtesy of National Park Service.)

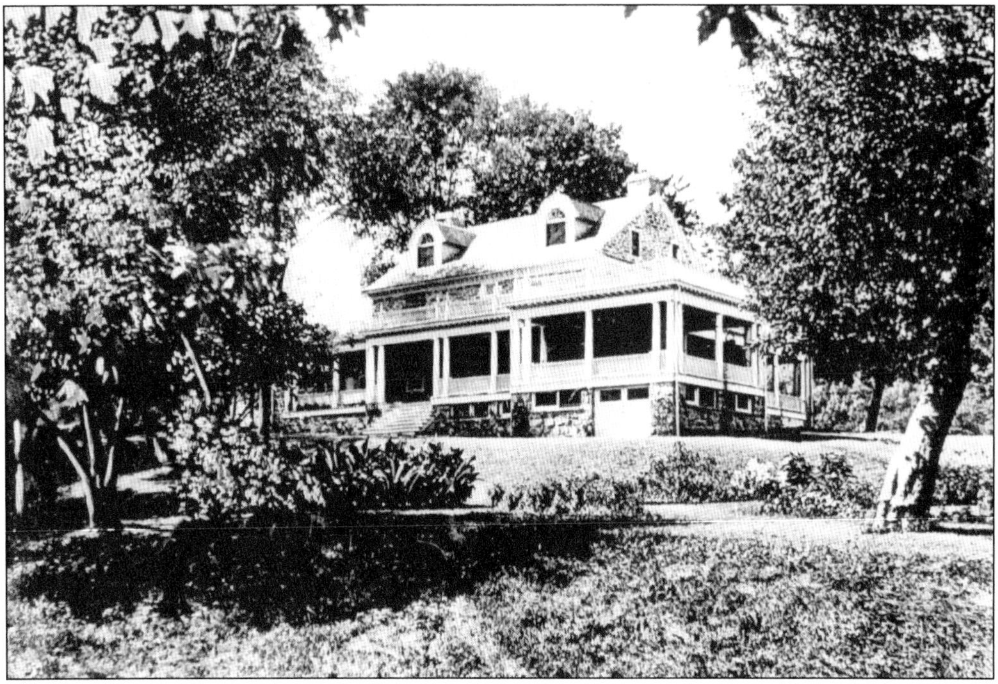

Manwalamink, the stone house built by the Depuy family, stands by the Delaware River. It was used for a time as a country club until Charles Worthington built the Buckwood Inn. William Walter occupied the house at the dawn of the 20th century and farmed the upper island, called Manwalamink, or Depue, Island.

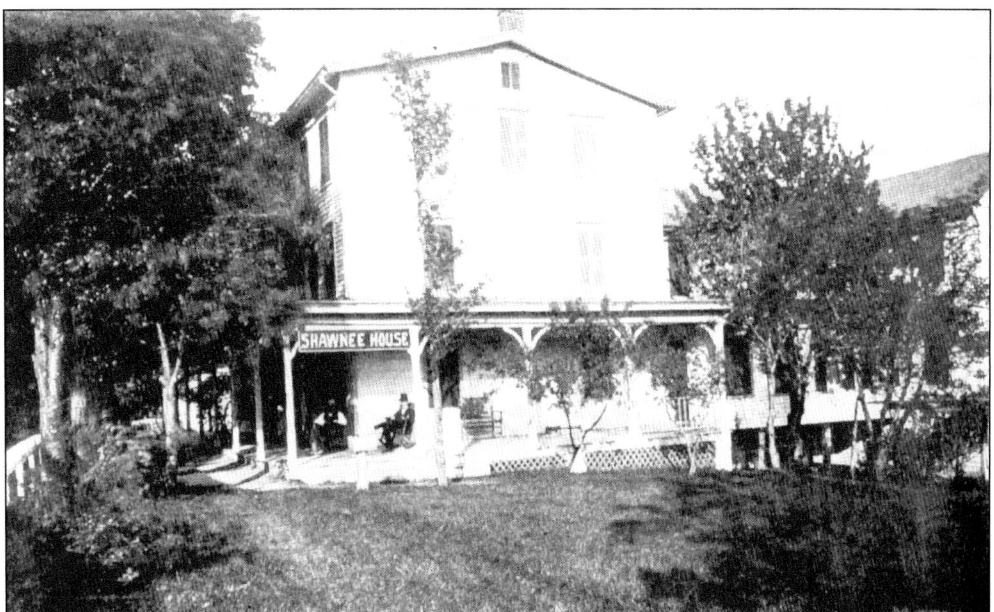

For many years, the Shawnee House, located on River Road, was the principal resort of the village. Isaac R. Transue built and operated it, and according to author and photographer Jackson Lantz in 1889, it was "long owned and maintained" by Mr. Transue. In the 1880s, advertisements claimed that the hotel could accommodate 100 guests.

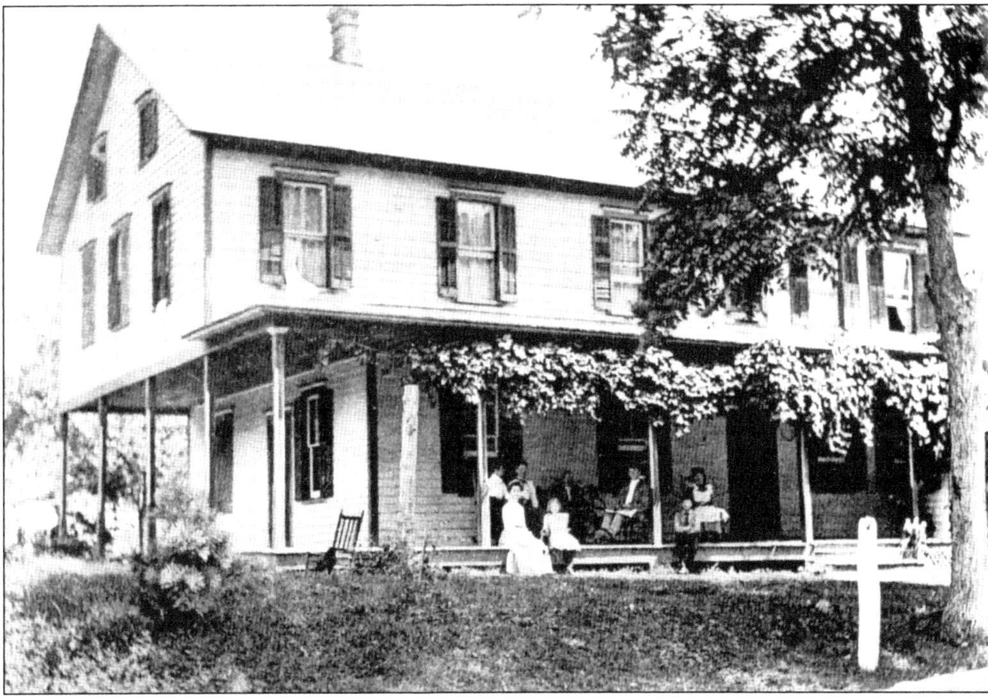

The Lenwood House, located on what is now Hollow Road in Shawnee, was another early-1900s boardinghouse. For a time, George Detrick managed it, with Hattie Sandt as its proprietress. Al and Dixie (Waring) Wilson later purchased the house.

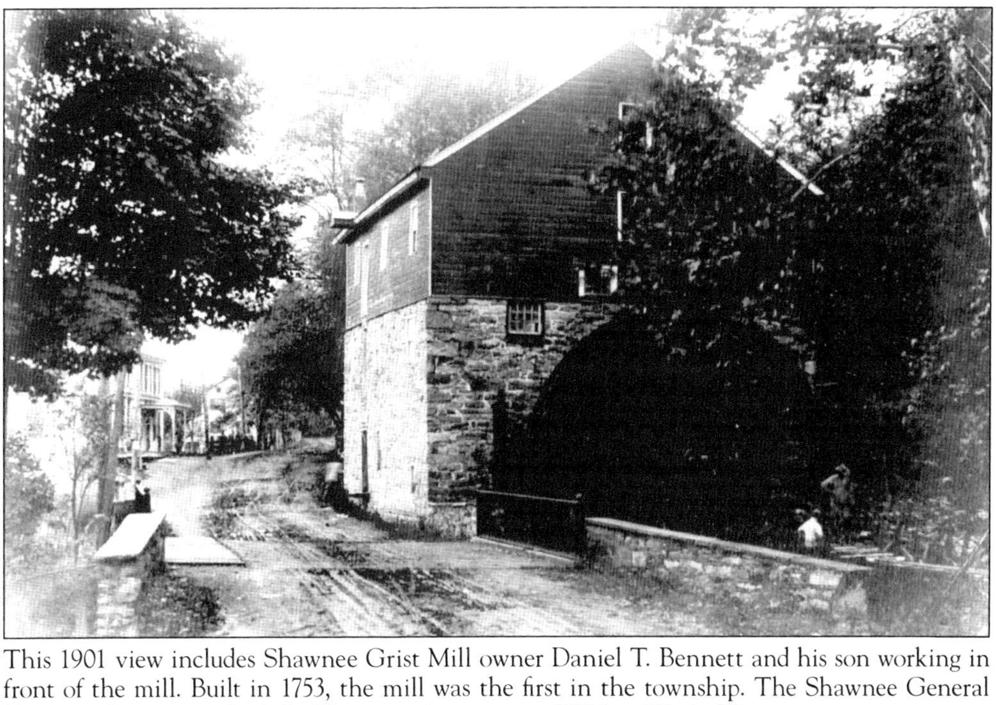

This 1901 view includes Shawnee Grist Mill owner Daniel T. Bennett and his son working in front of the mill. Built in 1753, the mill was the first in the township. The Shawnee General Store can be seen to the left. (Photograph courtesy of Walter Wyckoff.)

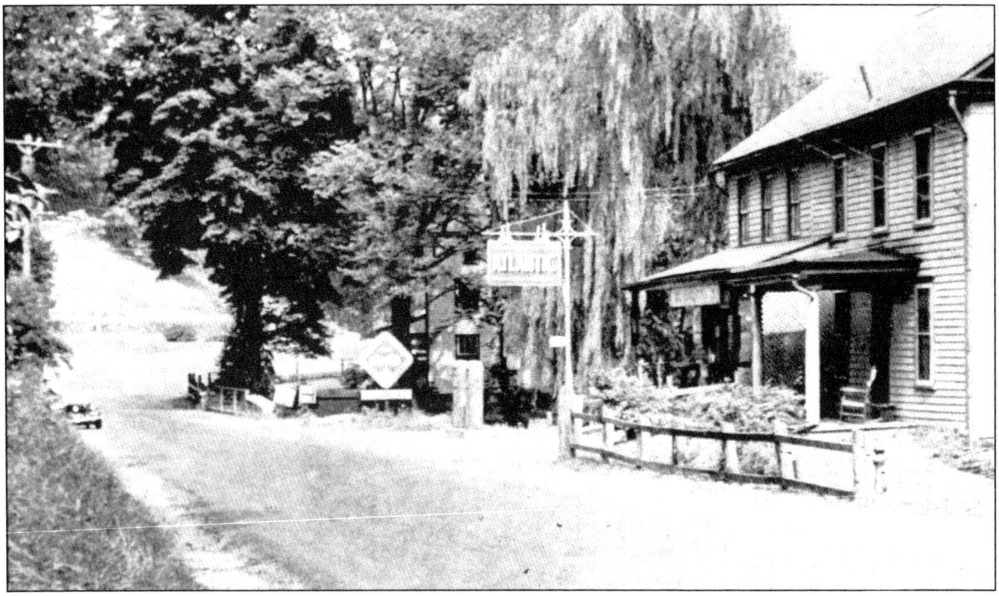

J. Depue LaBar owned and operated the Shawnee General Store from 1859 to 1893. His son Hiram took over the one-room store and soon after built an addition to provide more merchandise. The store also served as the village post office. Hiram operated the business until 1903. Bill and Theresa Rooth currently own the store.

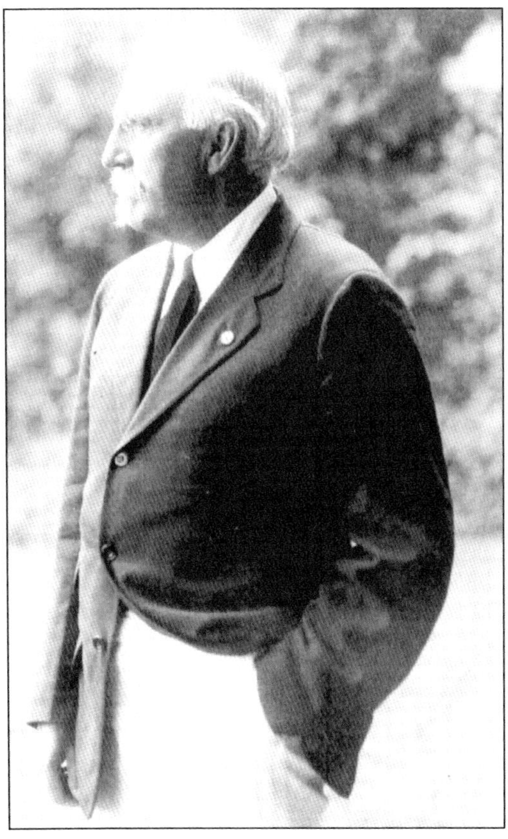

After Nicholas Depui, Charles C. Worthington (1854–1944) could be considered the next most important figure to affect Shawnee. In 1899, he sold his interest in the Worthington Pump and Machinery Corporation and soon thereafter purchased thousands of acres in the Shawnee area on both sides of the river. Among his many achievements, he brought the game of golf to the area and invented the Worthington gang mower, resulting in the formation of Worthington Mower Company, later based in Stroudsburg.

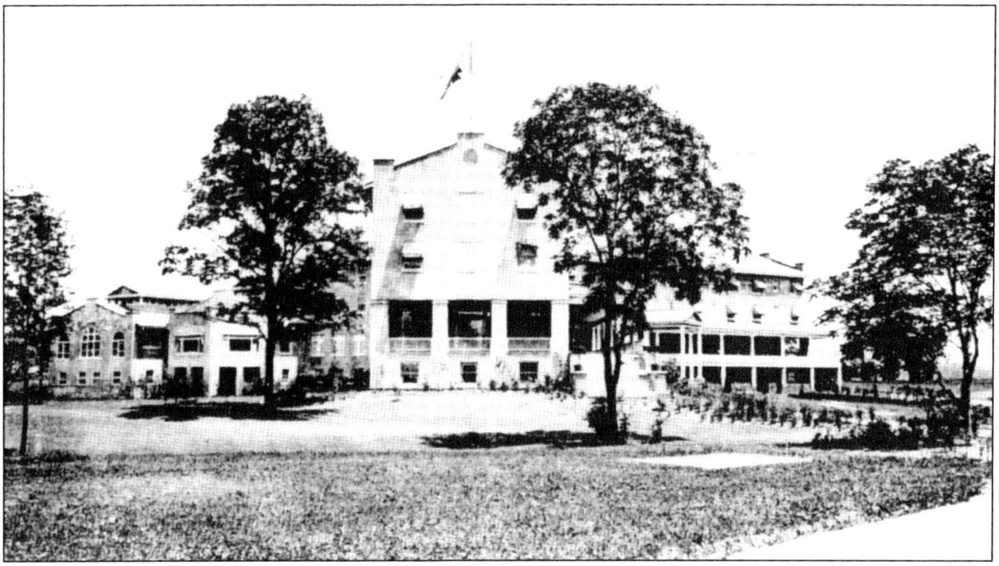

In 1911, Charles C. Worthington built the Spanish-style Buckwood Inn of tile and concrete, one of the first fireproof hotels built in an era when most were of wooden construction. In 1913, he bought two Stanley steamers, among the first in the county, to transport his guests from the Delaware Water Gap railroad station to and from the inn.

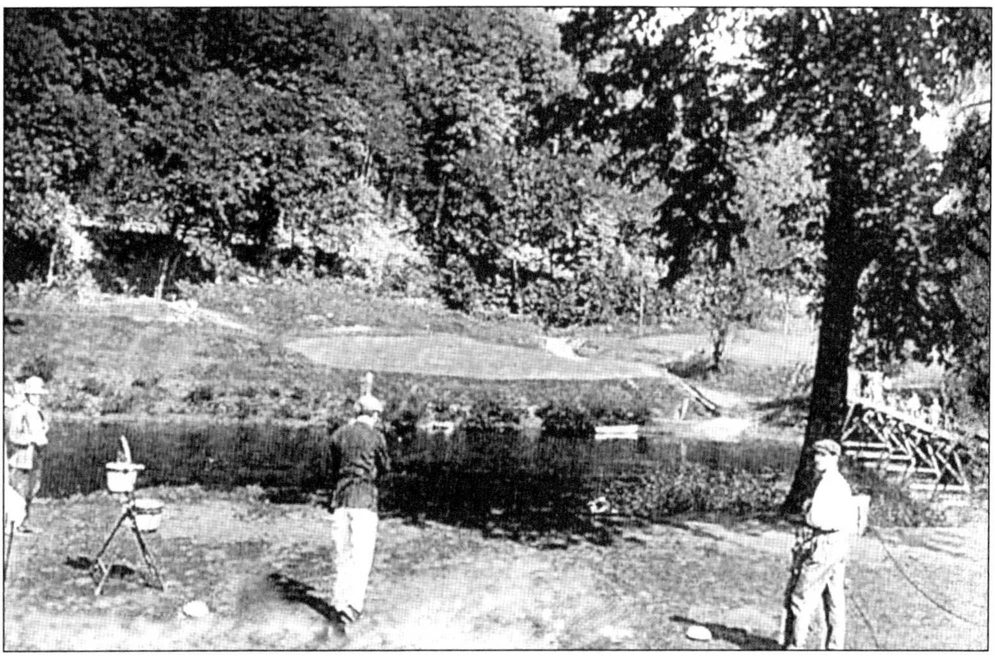

The original golf course at Shawnee, designed by the famous golf architect A. W. Tillinghast, was the first professionally designed course in the United States. In 1938, in the PGA golf championship, Paul Runyan defeated Sam Snead, who was Shawnee Inn's golf pro at the time. This was C. C. Worthington's second course, with the first being Caldeno, near the gap. The original nine-hole Shawnee course later grew to 27 holes.

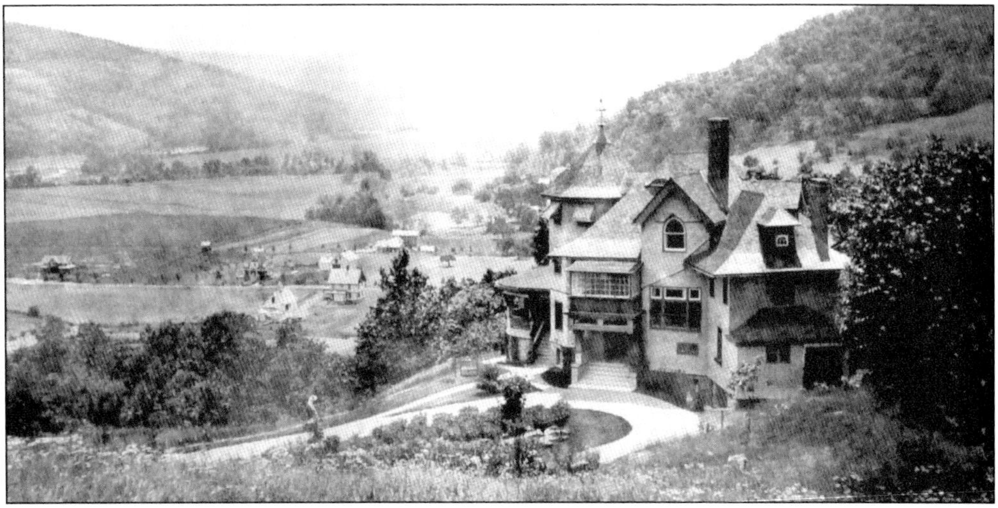

Charles C. Worthington built the mansion known as Hillbrow in the early 1900s. Its interior contained intricately carved paneling, imported crystal chandeliers, and leaded-glass windows. Musicians from Shawnee Inn who later stayed there could enjoy the spectacular view of the valley below and of the Delaware Water Gap. A May 1976 fire destroyed the house.

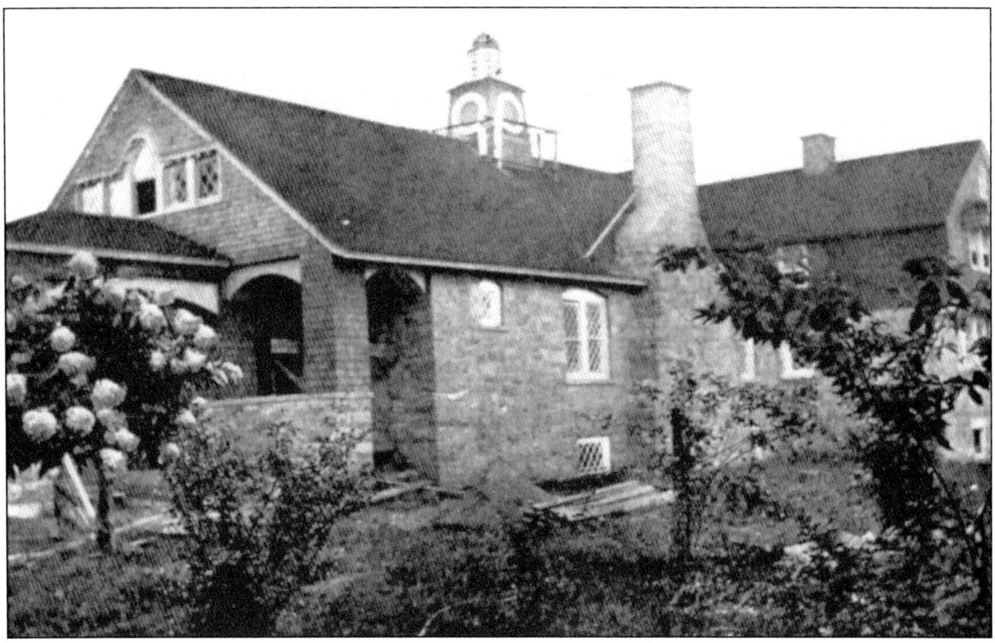

Worthington Hall, an entertainment center built in 1904, was another of Charles Worthington's creations. From 1904 until World War II, the Shawnee players performed, and beginning in 1943, Fred Waring and the Pennsylvanians broadcast radio programs there. It later housed the Shawnee Fire Company. Ironically, a June 1985 fire mainly destroyed the building. Through the efforts of the Kirkwood family, the building was restored and operates today as Shawnee Playhouse.

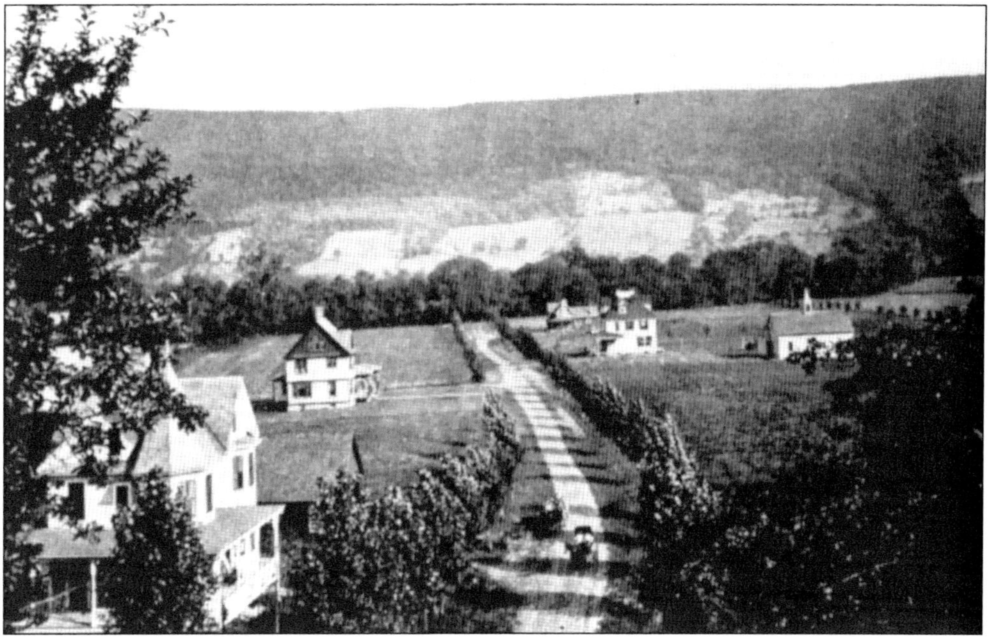

Minisink Land Company, whose president was Webster Eilenberger, developed building lots along the former Walker Ferry Lane, renaming it Minisink Avenue. The land company built its first house in 1903. This is a 1905 view of the homes.

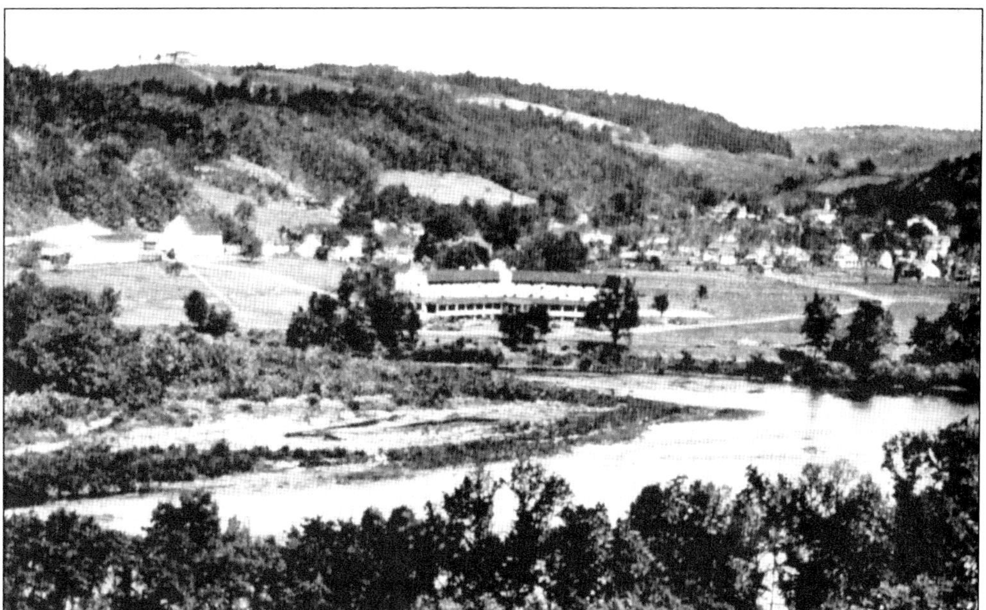

This is an early-1900s aerial view of Buckwood Inn, called Worthington's "Gem of the East." The open field to the left of the main building is now the site of the golf course. Mosier's Knob and Mount Nebo are in the background.

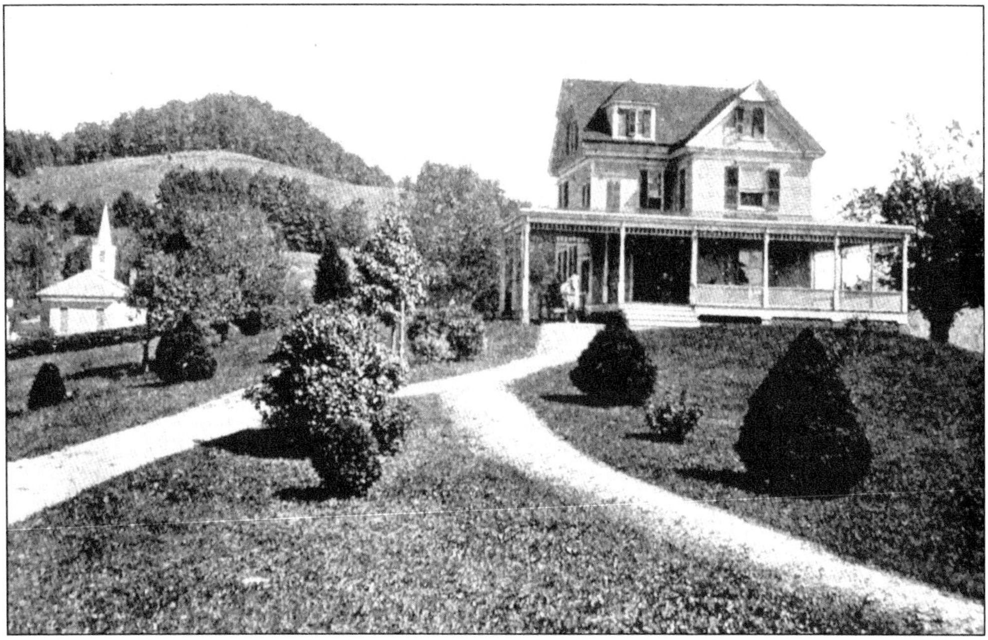

Frank LaBar, general agent for Provident Life Insurance Company in Philadelphia, first occupied this home, called Antock House. Built in 1896, the large three-story house contained a number of rooms for servants' quarters on the first floor. A horse stable, servants' quarters, icehouse, and a carriage house stood outside the home. E. B. Edwards later bought Antock, converting it to a summer boardinghouse.

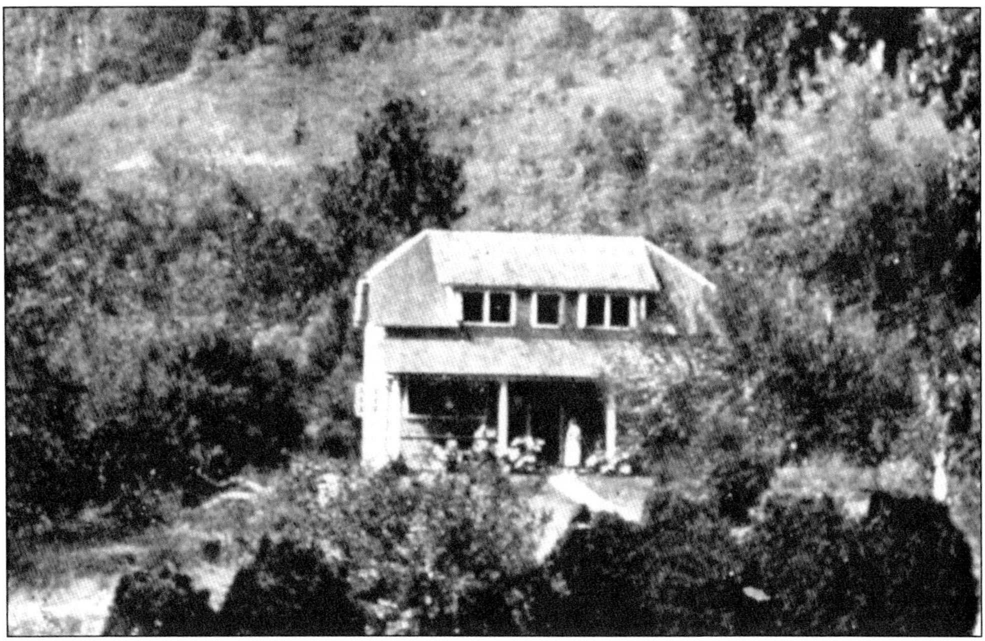

In 1920, the Antock House was torn down, and a newer one took its place. Building materials salvaged from the Antock were used to construct this newer home on the property, the Leventritt house, which was nicknamed the Bungalow. Walter Wyckoff, of the former Wyckoff's department store in Stroudsburg, and his wife live there now.

Fred Waring, accompanied by wife Virginia Waring, accepted one of the many awards he was granted in his long musical career. Fred bought the Buckwood Inn in 1943, renaming it Shawnee Inn. Waring and his group, the Pennsylvanians, centered their musical programs at the inn, and numerous celebrities such as Arnold Palmer, Dwight Eisenhower, Lucille Ball, Jackie Gleason, Art Carney, and a throng of others assembled at the resort.

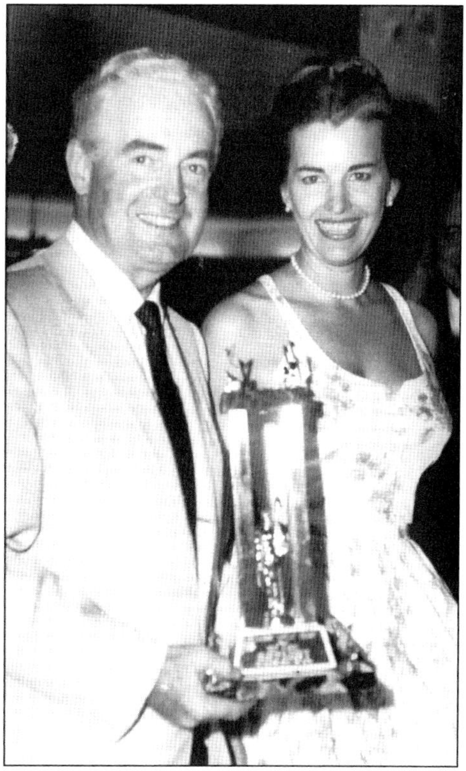

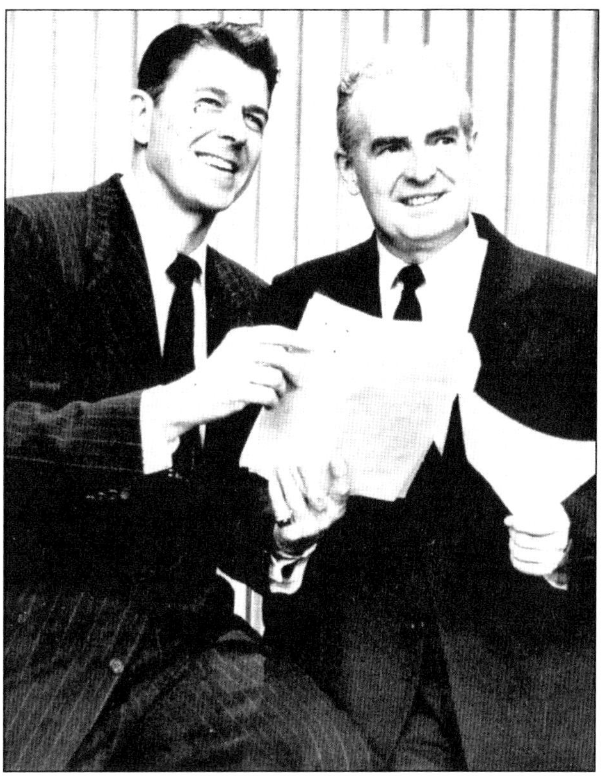

This photograph gives us a rare glimpse of two very charismatic and famous figures together. Fred Waring, friend to presidents and common folk alike, touched many lives with his talent and ability. On this occasion in 1954, Waring and his Pennsylvanians appeared on *General Electric Theater*, which Ronald Reagan hosted.

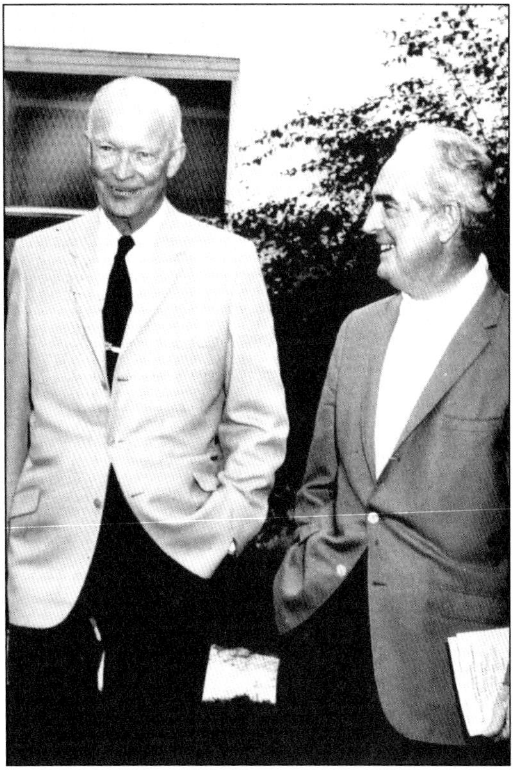

Pres. Dwight D. Eisenhower enjoyed a good game of golf and a visit with his friends at Shawnee. He is seen here with Fred Waring in 1963, when Fred presented him with the Fred Waring Sportsmanship Award. (Photograph courtesy of Waring Archives, Penn State University.)

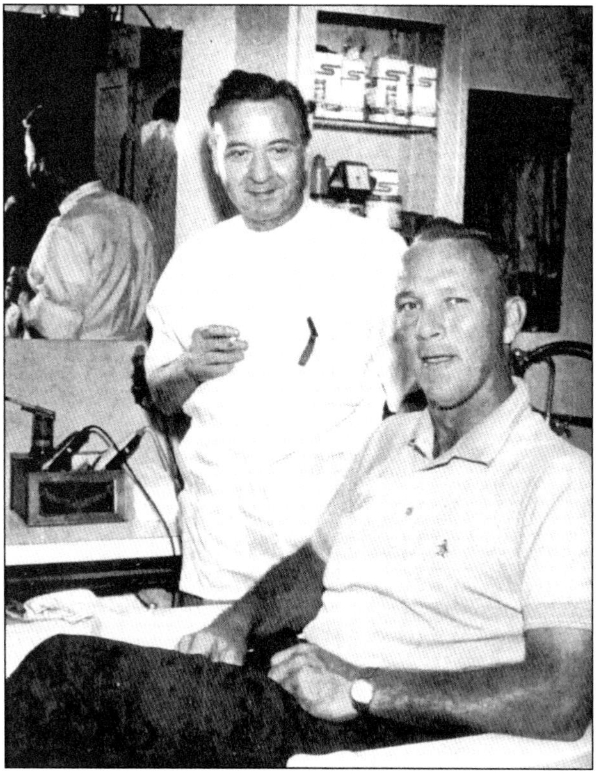

Arnold Palmer stops by the Shawnee Inn's barbershop for one of Tony Summa's haircuts. The famous golfer was a frequent guest at the inn, where he met his wife, Winnie, a Monroe County resident. (Photograph from personal collection.)

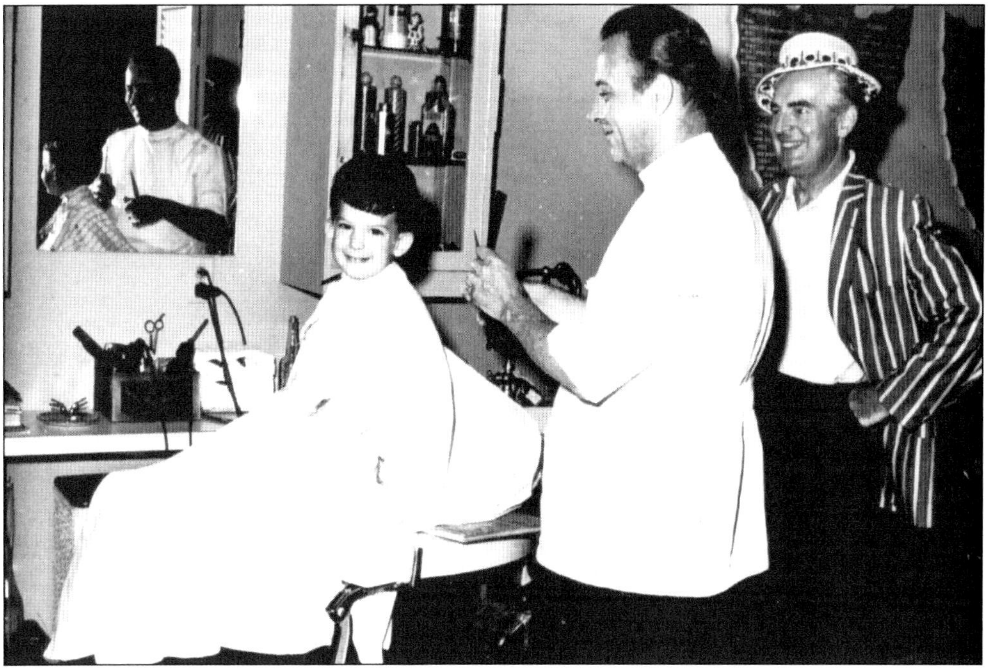

Fred Waring's son Malcolm gets his locks trimmed. Malcolm is the son of Fred and Virginia Morley Waring and the youngest of Fred's children. (Photograph from personal collection.)

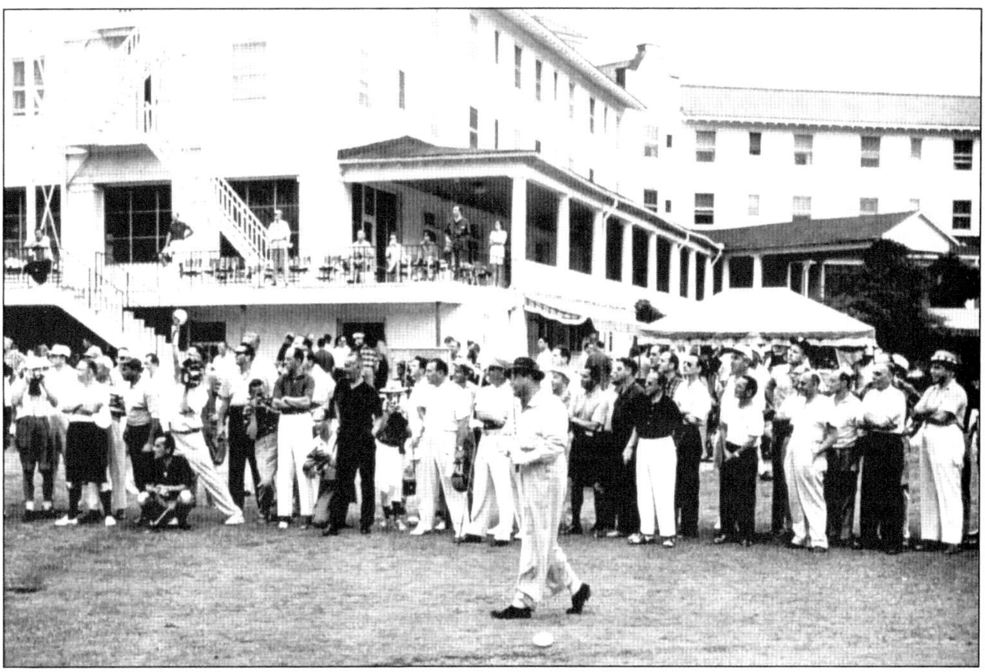

Guests at Shawnee Inn gathered around to watch Jackie Gleason at the first tee. Jackie learned to play golf at the Shawnee Inn and Country Club. He was reportedly so intent on improving his game that he once played two 27-hole rounds of golf in one day. He spent many summers at Shawnee. (Photograph courtesy of Shawnee Inn and Country Club.)

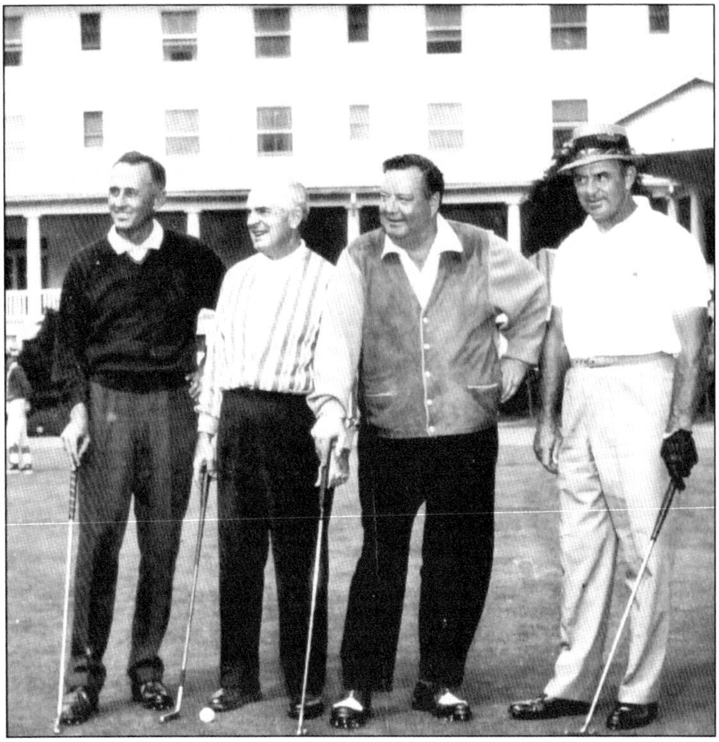

Golf greats Art Wall Jr. and Sam Snead teamed up with the Great One (Jackie Gleason) and musical genius Fred Waring for a golf foursome at Shawnee Inn. Pictured from left to right are Wall, Waring, Gleason, and Snead. Sam Snead recently had a Shawnee inn, formerly Mimi's Streamside, renamed in his honor. (Photograph courtesy of Waring Archives, Penn State University.)

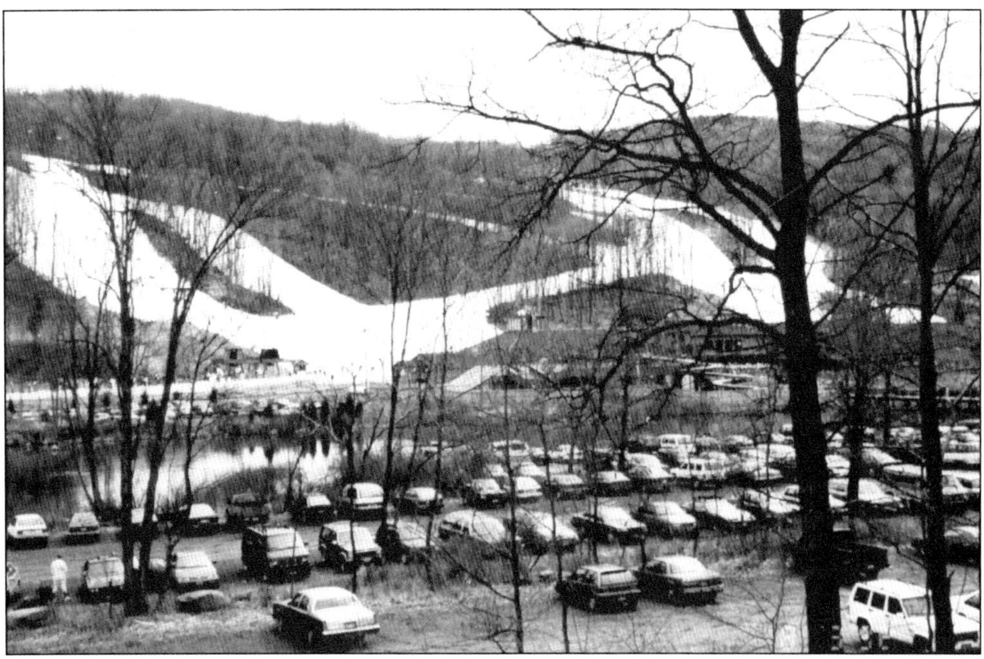

Shawnee Mountain Ski Area is now in its 30th year of operation. In 1974, Karl Hope, a Philadelphia real estate developer, bought Fred Waring's Shawnee business interests. Hope tore down several buildings in Shawnee and began a timesharing enterprise. As an adjunct to his business enterprises, Hope built Shawnee Mountain Ski Area, hiring Olympic gold medal winner Jean-Claude Killy as director of ski operations.

Jacob Mosier and wife, Mahala, operated this observation tower, which was advertised as the "highest point in Eastern Pennsylvania with an unobstructed view showing the entire range of country in three states, from the Wind Gap to the Catskill Mountains." The admission fee was 15¢. Reportedly, thousands of visitors visited the Knob. Jacob and his wife died in 1926, and the tower gradually deteriorated.

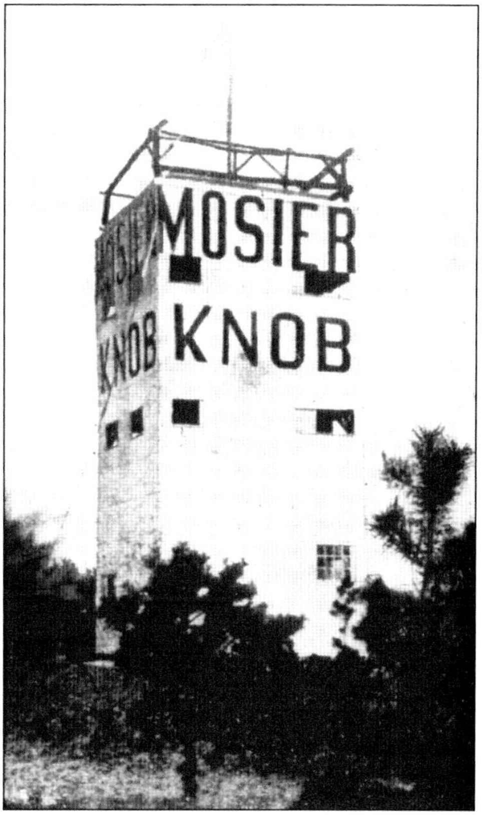

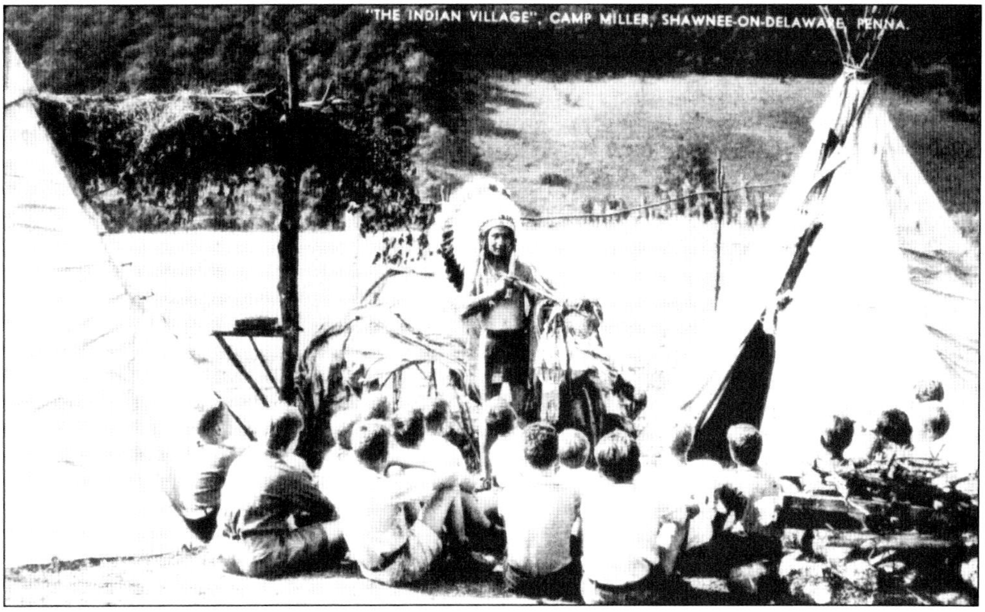

At Camp Miller, boys gather around for an educational presentation of Native American culture. Camp Miller was one of three summer camps for youths situated along River Road near Shawnee. This and the others, Camp Ministerium and Camp Hagan (a girls camp), were taken by the government for the Tocks project.

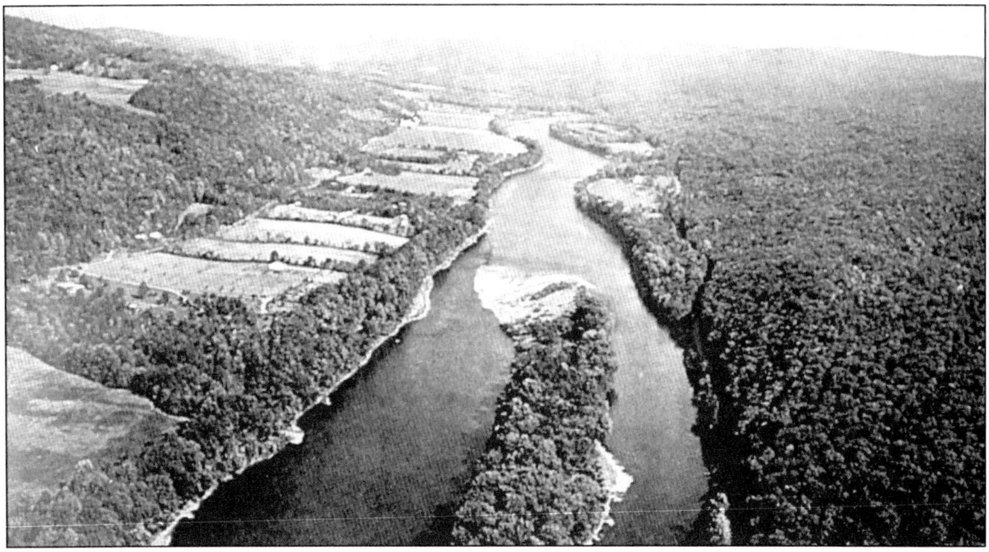

This is Tocks Island, located six miles above Delaware Water Gap on the Delaware River. In 1956, the Army Corps of Engineers planned a massive 160-foot dam at this location, the largest east of the Mississippi. The Tocks Island Dam project would have flooded 12,000 acres from here to Port Jervis, New York, a distance of 40 miles. The proposal called for 72,000 acres for the dam and recreation area. (Photograph courtesy of Al Koster.)

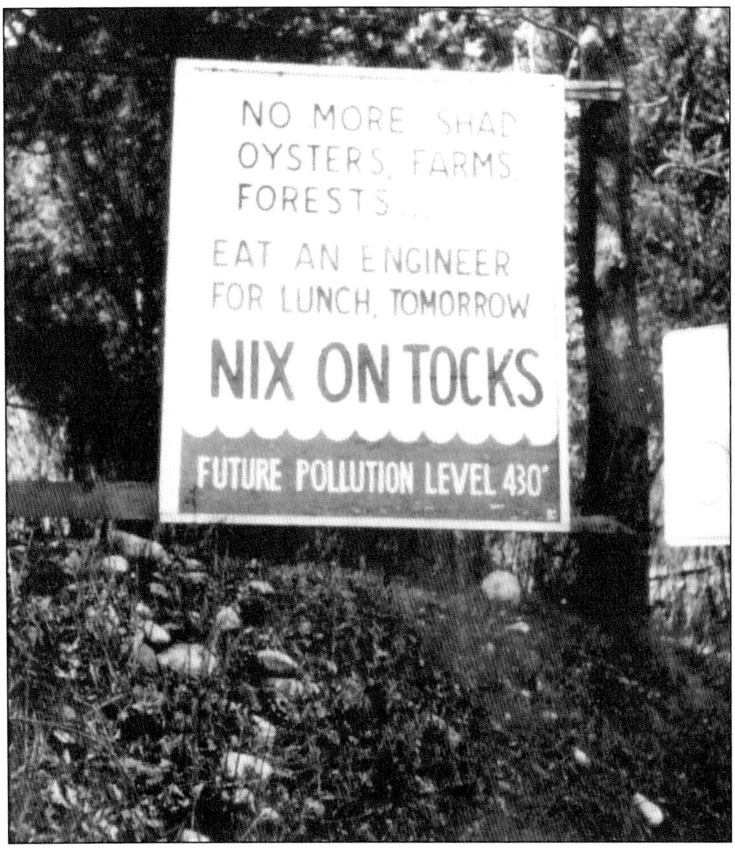

This sign is one of many expressing great local opposition to the Tocks Island Dam project. As eminent domain proceedings began, local opposition grew. Citizens banded together in a David and Goliath–like struggle between local individuals and government forces. Shawnee residents were among the most vocal, effective activists who eventually brought about the defeat of the dam project. The Delaware Water Gap Recreation Area exists today; the dam does not.

Four

MARSHALLS CREEK

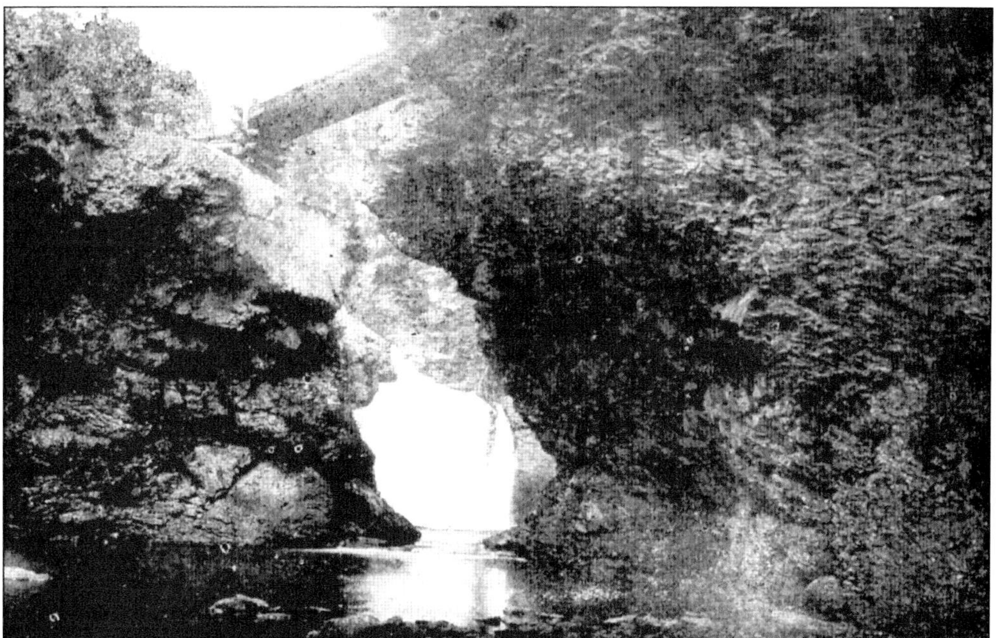

Marshalls Falls is the first of a series of falls lying along Marshalls Creek. The creek rises in the northwest part of Middle Smithfield Township and runs south through Smithfield Township, in which the village of Marshalls Creek is located. The creek, the village, the falls, and Marshalls Lake were all named for Edwin Marshall, the runner who took part in the Walking Purchase of 1737. Marshall did not live in this area, and it is doubtful he even set foot here. While the walk he was hired to perform gained the provincial government of Pennsylvania a great deal of land, its injustice also led to later bloodshed when conflicts arose during the French and Indian War.

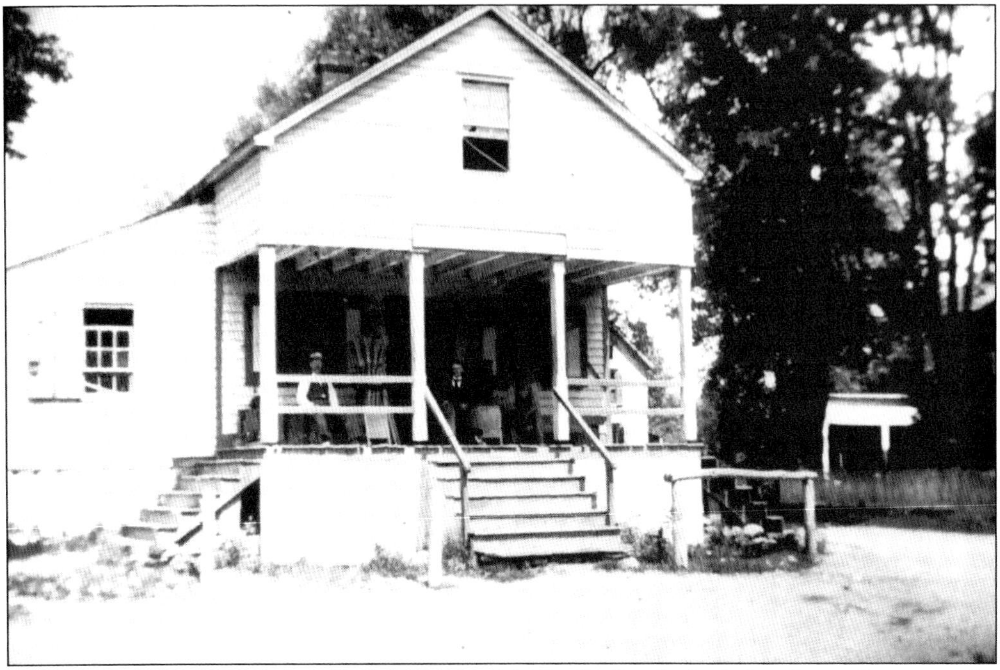

This is an early view of the general store in Marshalls Creek, built by Henry Peters in the early 1800s. William Peters succeeded him, continuing to operate the store and nearby gristmill. In 1865, Elias D. Huffman bought a half-interest in the store and mill and, a few years later, purchased Peter's share. The store has remained in the family ever since. (Photograph courtesy of David MacDonough.)

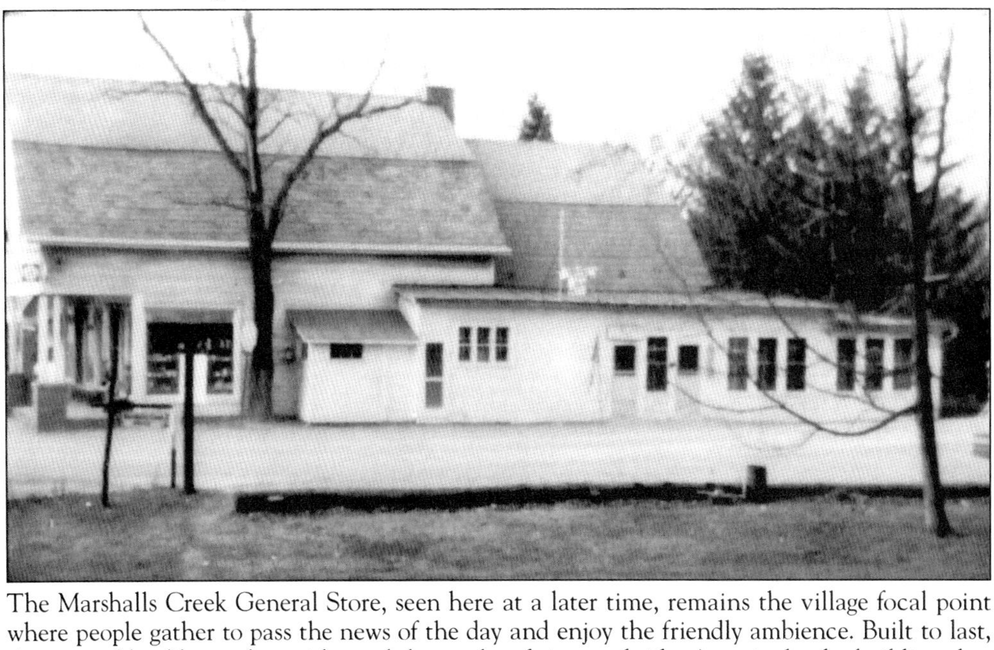

The Marshalls Creek General Store, seen here at a later time, remains the village focal point where people gather to pass the news of the day and enjoy the friendly ambience. Built to last, the venerable old store has withstood the marks of time and tide. Amazingly, the building that stands within yards of Pond Creek has remained unscathed through various floods the area has endured. (Photograph courtesy of David MacDonough.)

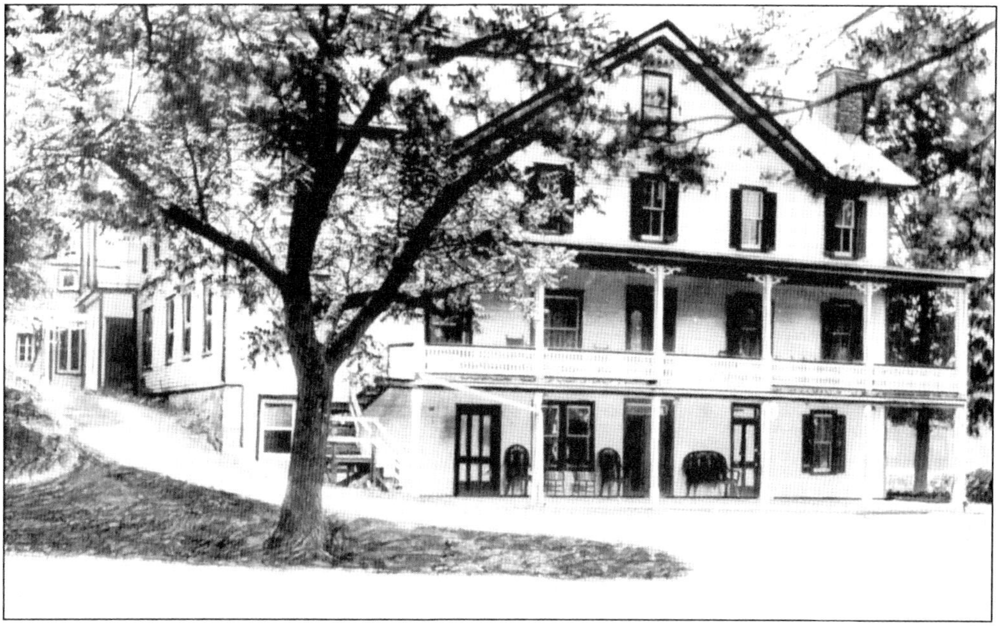

The Marshalls Falls House was built in 1887 by E. D. Huffman. It stood across the street from the general store, roughly where Mr. Z's supermarket now stands. Originally a stagecoach stop, the building was expanded into a large hotel by Elias Huffman in the 1870s. Officials of the Fernwood resort bought the property and razed it on February 28, 1980, to build the mini-mall across the street.

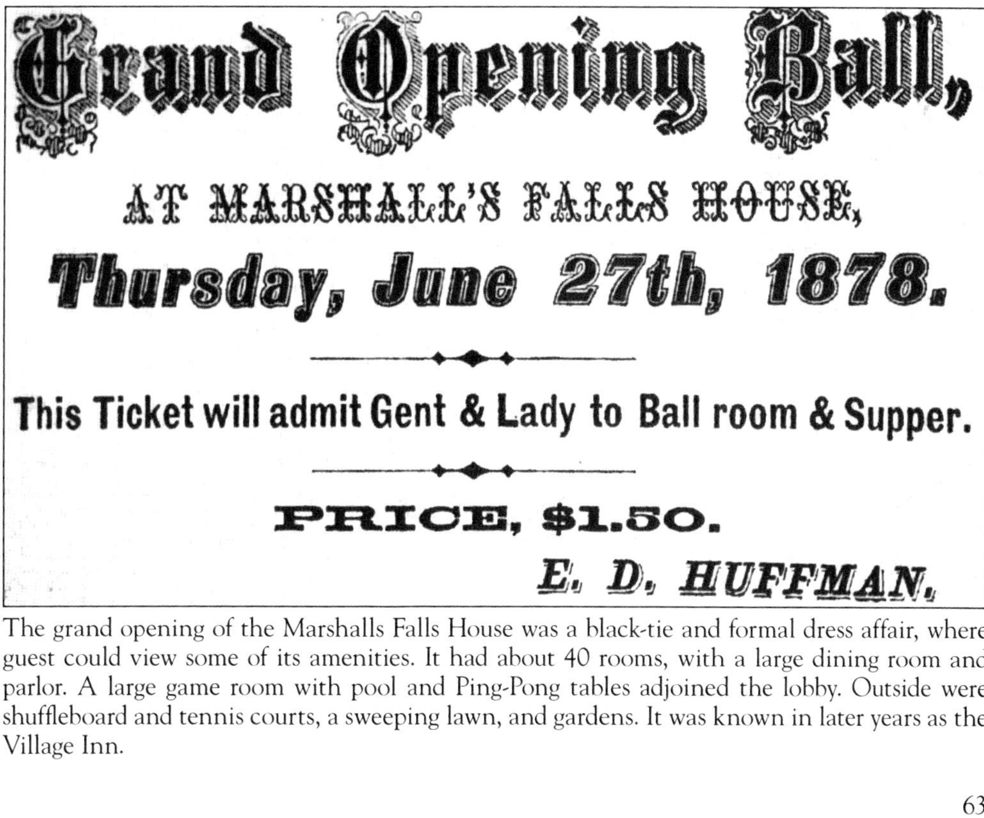

Grand Opening Ball,

AT MARSHALL'S FALLS HOUSE,

Thursday, June 27th, 1878.

This Ticket will admit Gent & Lady to Ball room & Supper.

PRICE, $1.50.

E. D. HUFFMAN.

The grand opening of the Marshalls Falls House was a black-tie and formal dress affair, where guest could view some of its amenities. It had about 40 rooms, with a large dining room and parlor. A large game room with pool and Ping-Pong tables adjoined the lobby. Outside were shuffleboard and tennis courts, a sweeping lawn, and gardens. It was known in later years as the Village Inn.

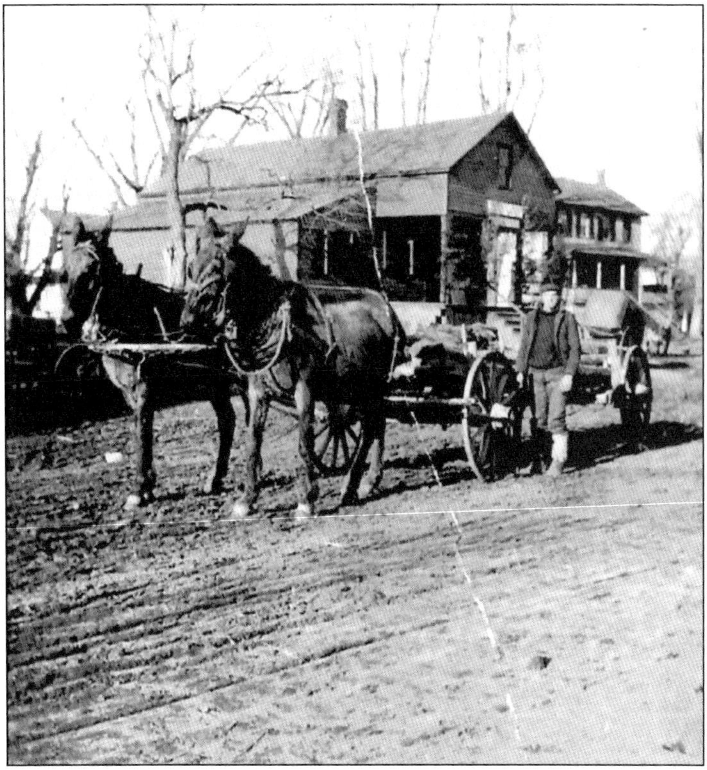

This picture shows E. D. Huffman walking beside his wagon along what is now Route 209 in Marshalls Creek. Among his many enterprises, Huffman owned a sawmill across the street, where he cut mine ties. The ties were shipped by railroad to the coal regions of northeastern Pennsylvania. The Delaware Valley Railroad that ran behind the Huffman property was convenient to Huffman's business. (Photograph courtesy of David MacDonough.)

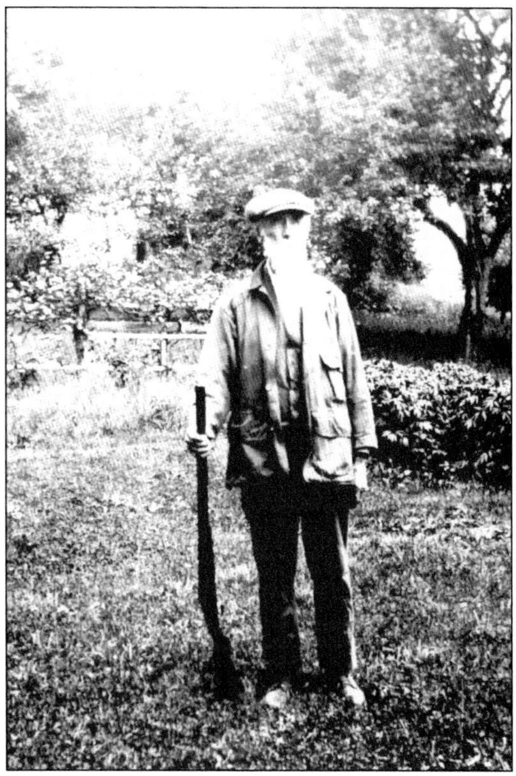

Elias D. Huffman is shown sporting his long beard, of which he was quite proud. Huffman was born in August 1841, the grandson of John and Mary Huffman, early pioneers of Middle Smithfield Township. He became postmaster of Marshalls Creek in 1867, when he took over the general store. Huffman was the ancestor of many area families. (Photograph courtesy of David MacDonough.)

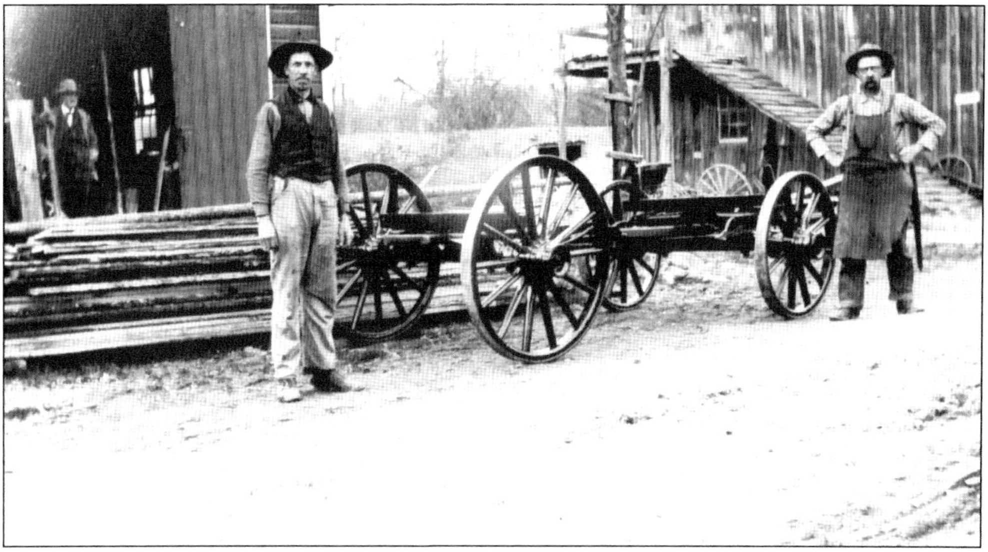

Before the advent of the automobile and even afterward, blacksmiths played a vital role in lives of citizens. The blacksmith shop in Marshalls Creek lay beyond the general store. In the photograph, smithy Amzi Miller stands at the far right. (Photograph courtesy of David MacDonough.)

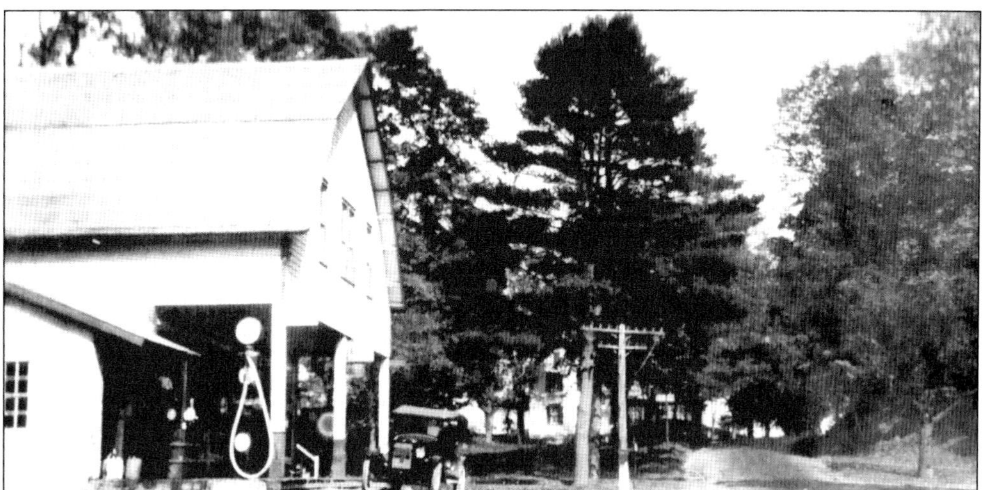

The old blacksmith shop gradually gave way to the gas station, one of the first in the county. It was run by Norman Huffman, Elias D. Huffman's son. The station burned about 1942. (Photograph courtesy of David MacDonough.)

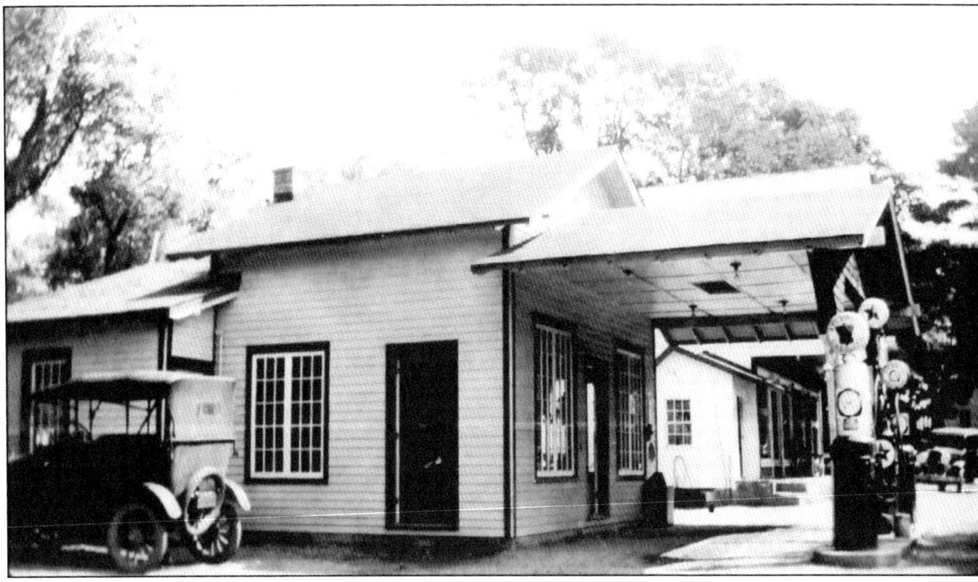

This newer gas station replaced it at this vital intersection, as things are apt to happen in strategic locations in life. The building still stands, appearing much different today but remaining in ownership of the Huffman family. (Photograph courtesy of David MacDonough.)

The TITANIA HOUSE,

MARSHALL'S CREEK, PA.

A Quiet, Refined Summer Home Among the Mountains.

House and Fountain Supplied with the Coldest and Purest Spring Water.

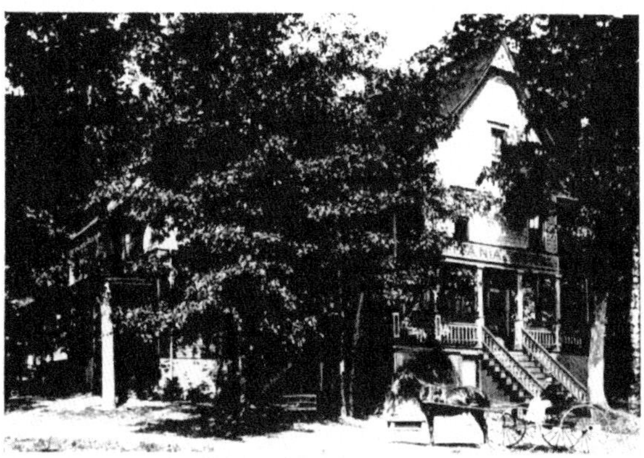

The Only Hotel at the Falls.

Delightful Scenery. Invigorating Air.

Perfect Drainage. Dry Gravel Walks and Drives.

JAMES T. WOLFE, Proprietor.

MARSHALL'S CREEK, PA.

The Titania House was built in 1888 and is pictured here a decade later. Its proximity to Marshalls Falls and its refined, stylish quarters made it a big attraction for guests. At the time of this photograph, J. T. Wolfe owned it. By 1911, C. H. Congdon was its proprietor. The building stands today as a private residence.

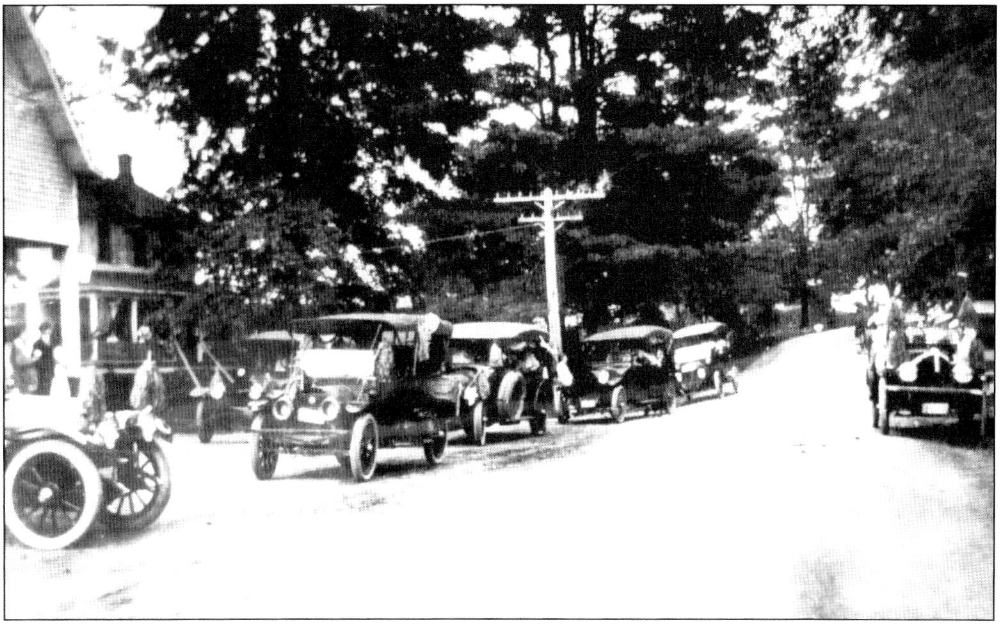

Pennsylvania governor Gifford Pinchot stopped by the general store in Marshalls Creek, along with his entourage. The village rarely ever saw such a display of automobiles then, and it must have created quite a stir. Pinchot, a noted forester and conservationist, began serving his second term of office in 1930. He worked toward highway improvement, and this stretch of highway was among one of his pet projects.

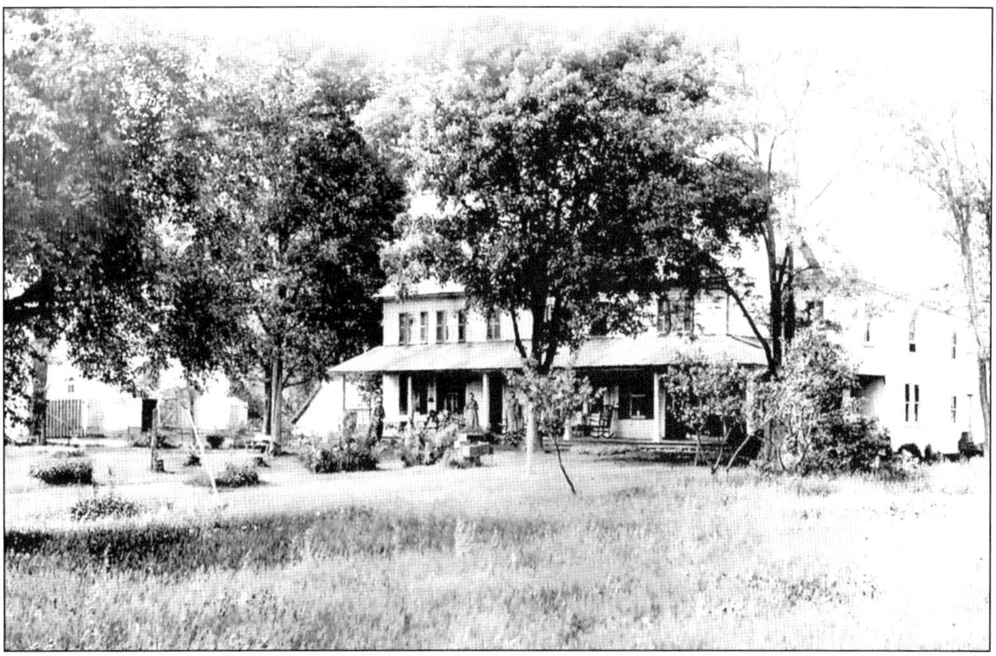

Mountain Manor was built around a log cabin originally constructed in the 1700s. Although it is not known who built the cabin, the first recorded property owner was Dr. Philip Bush, who was the son of the Philip Bush who donated land to the Lutheran church in Craig's Meadows. Bush built an addition to the two-story log cabin, which is now the lobby of the main house.

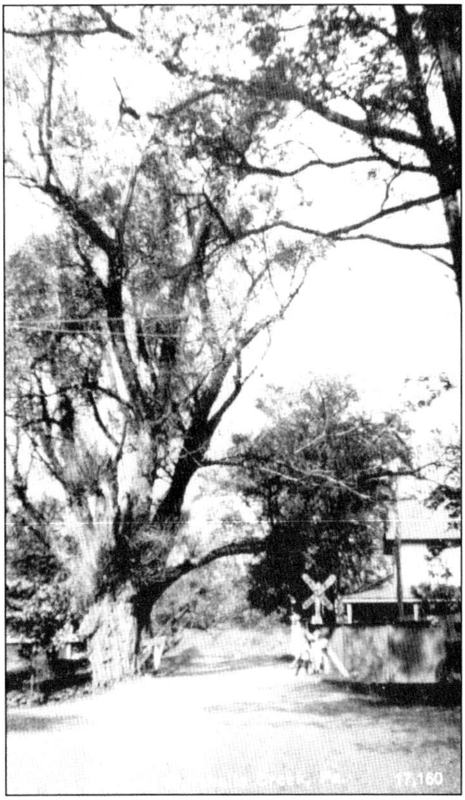

This is an early view of the lane that later became Route 402, looking down toward where today Marshalls Creek Fire House stands. The railroad sign along the willow-lined road has long since disappeared, as have the trees.

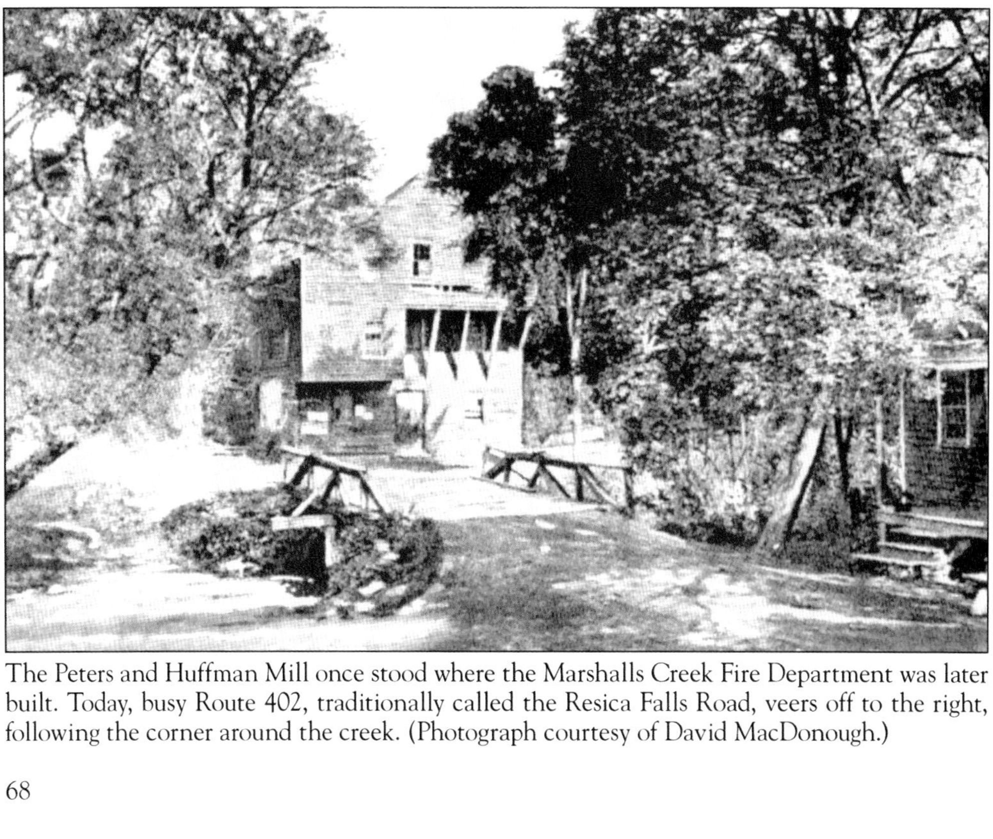

The Peters and Huffman Mill once stood where the Marshalls Creek Fire Department was later built. Today, busy Route 402, traditionally called the Resica Falls Road, veers off to the right, following the corner around the creek. (Photograph courtesy of David MacDonough.)

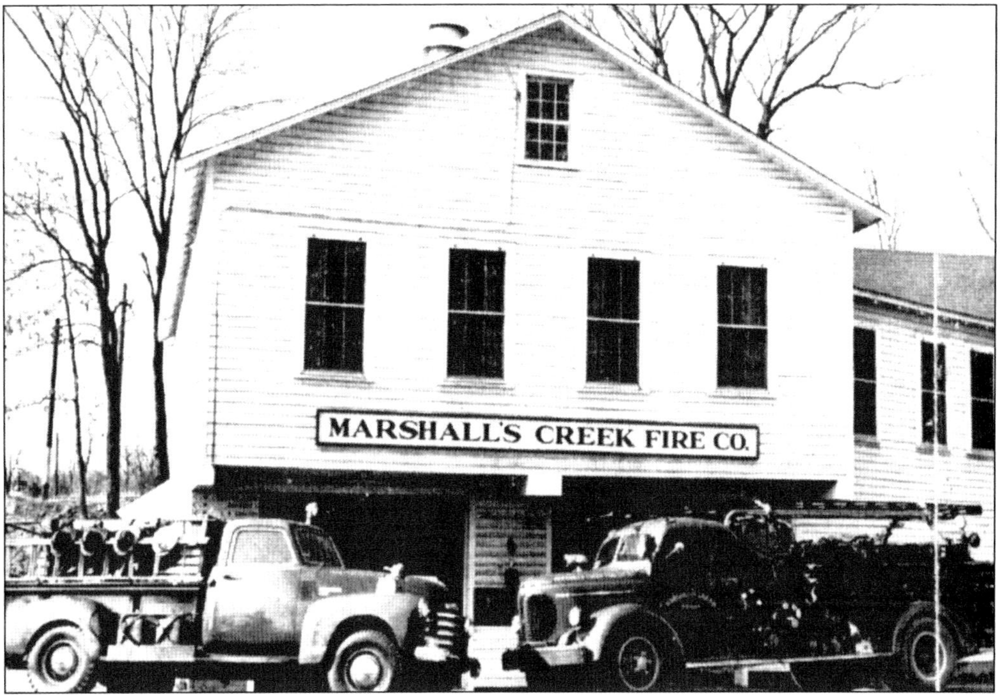

The Marshalls Creek Company, organized in 1945, built its first firehouse on the location of the old mill site. Three of the company's firemen lost their lives in 1963 when a tractor trailer carrying a load of explosives blew up near the Pocono Reptile Farm in Middle Smithfield Township. (Photograph courtesy of Roger Hartmann.)

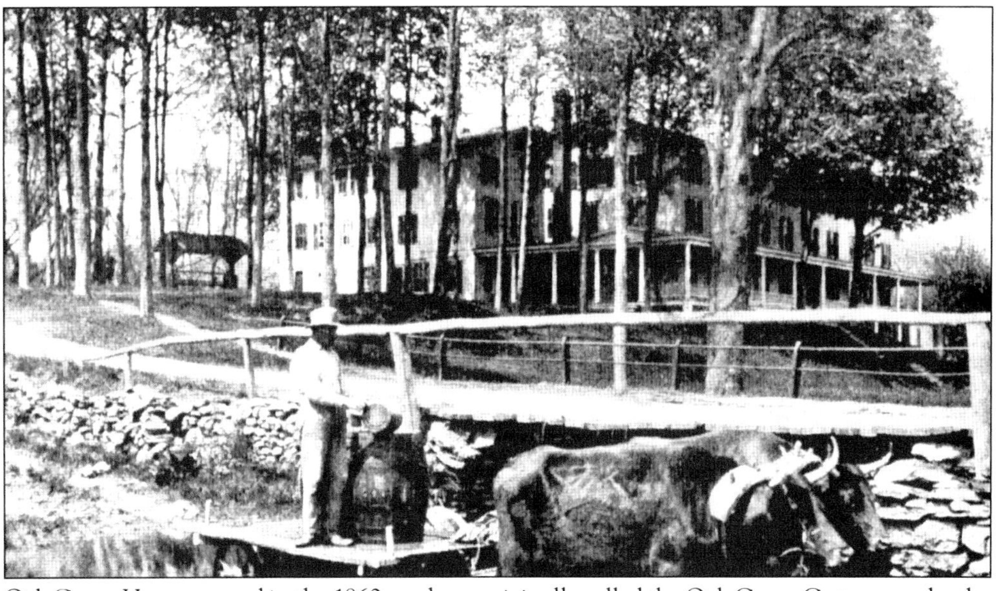

Oak Grove House opened in the 1860s and was originally called the Oak Grove Cottage, under the ownership of Case V. Smith. The cottage grew to resort size after undergoing several remodelings. It had its own railroad station on the Delaware Valley Railroad from 1904 to 1938. It took its name from the grove of oaks that sheltered it, keeping it cool on even summer's hottest days.

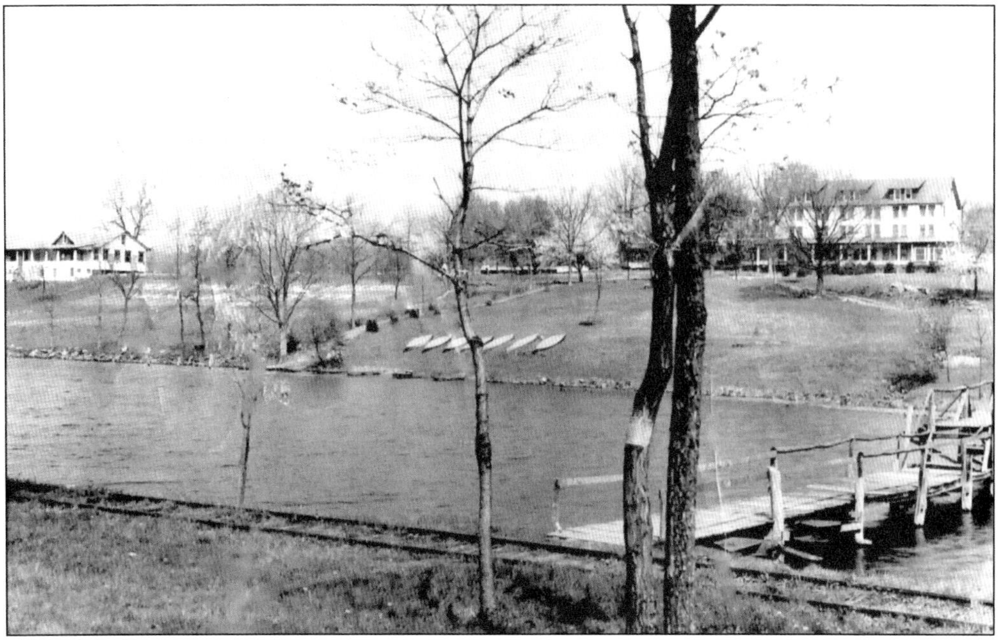

Mountain Lake House, earlier known as the Lake Marshall House, was owned and operated by Jay and Edith Huffman. Four generations of the Huffman family kept up the tradition. Lake Marshall stands in front of the resort complex. The resort recently closed.

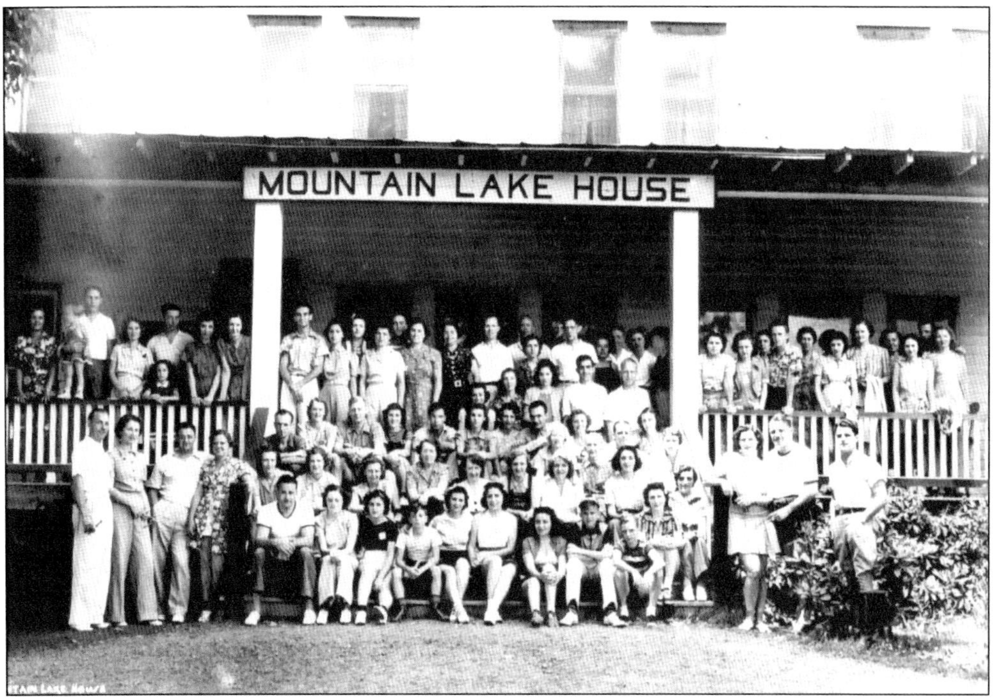

The Mountain Lake House catered to group dinners for class reunions, local service club dinners, weddings, and similar events. The people pictured in front of the main building appear to be enjoying themselves. Ken Fritz, social director, is seen in the first row on the far right. (Photograph courtesy of Robert Huffman.)

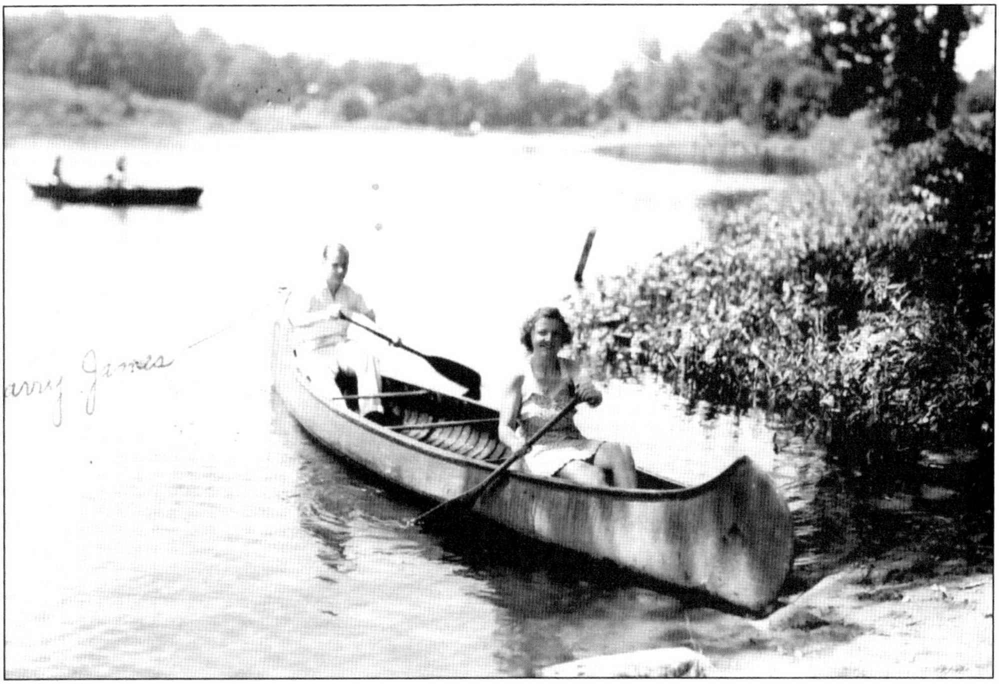

Famed bandleader Harry James enjoys a canoe ride on Lake Marshall. He was among a number of celebrities who visited the Mountain Lake House. (Photograph courtesy of Robert Huffman.)

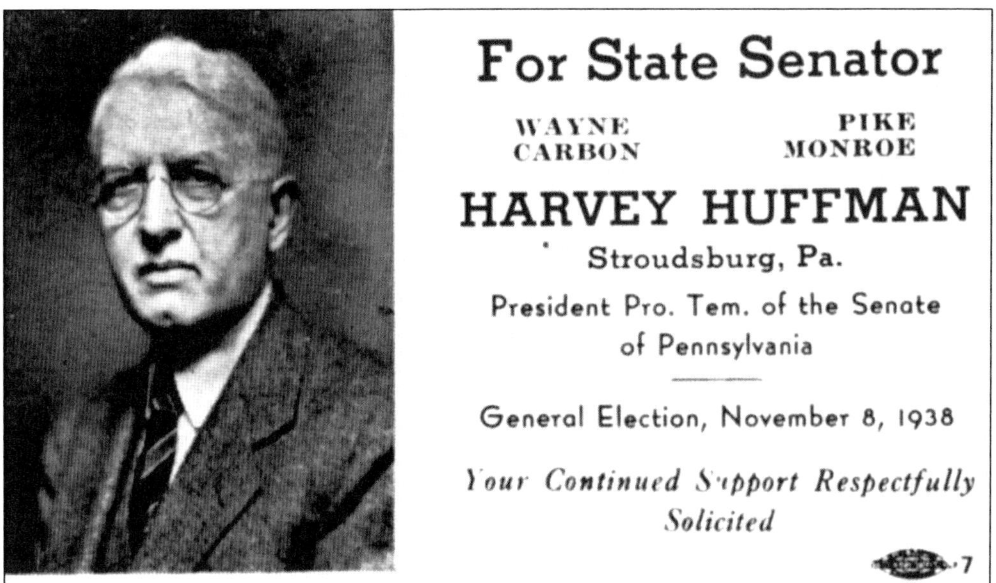

Marshalls Creek native Harvey Huffman served as a member of the state senate for the 14th District (1911–1914, 1923–1930, and 1935–1938). He died in office on November 30, 1938. Huffman also maintained a law office in Stroudsburg.

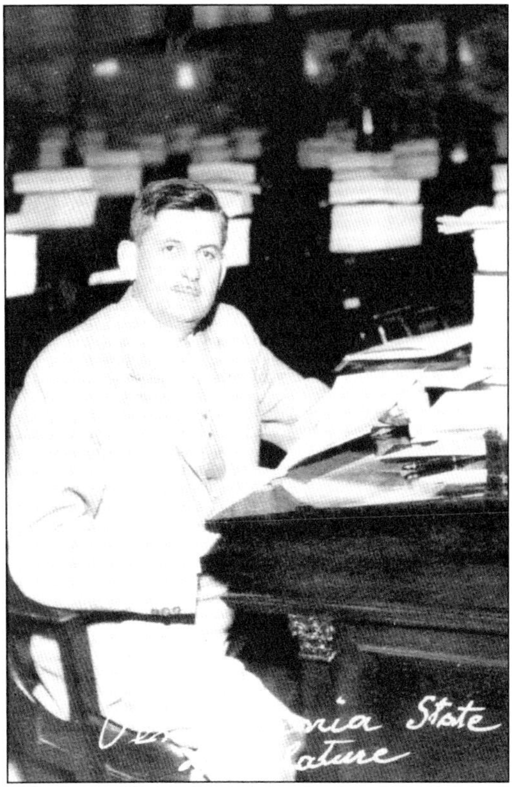

Van D. Yetter Jr. symbolized the work ethic of "pull yourself up by your bootstraps" rural America in his rise from farm boy to legislator. He served in the Pennsylvania House of Representatives for 10 years with two-year terms in the years of 1954, 1958, 1960, 1962, and 1964. As a businessman, he sold farm equipment and small trailers and mobile homes. (Photograph courtesy of Katherine Yetter.)

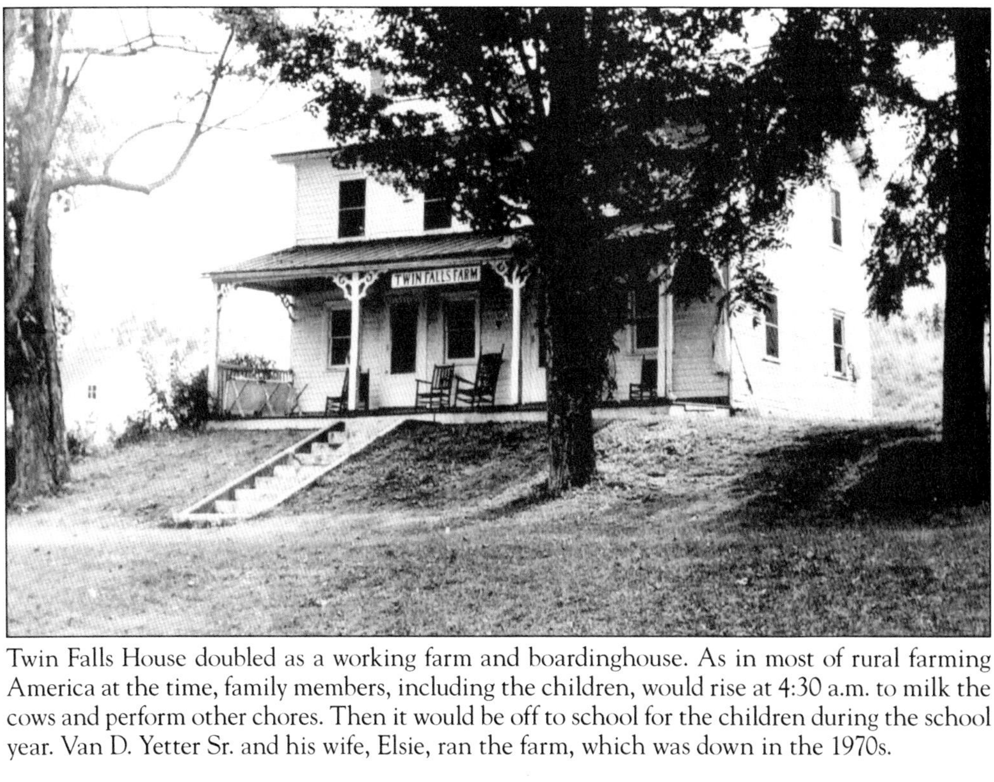

Twin Falls House doubled as a working farm and boardinghouse. As in most of rural farming America at the time, family members, including the children, would rise at 4:30 a.m. to milk the cows and perform other chores. Then it would be off to school for the children during the school year. Van D. Yetter Sr. and his wife, Elsie, ran the farm, which was down in the 1970s.

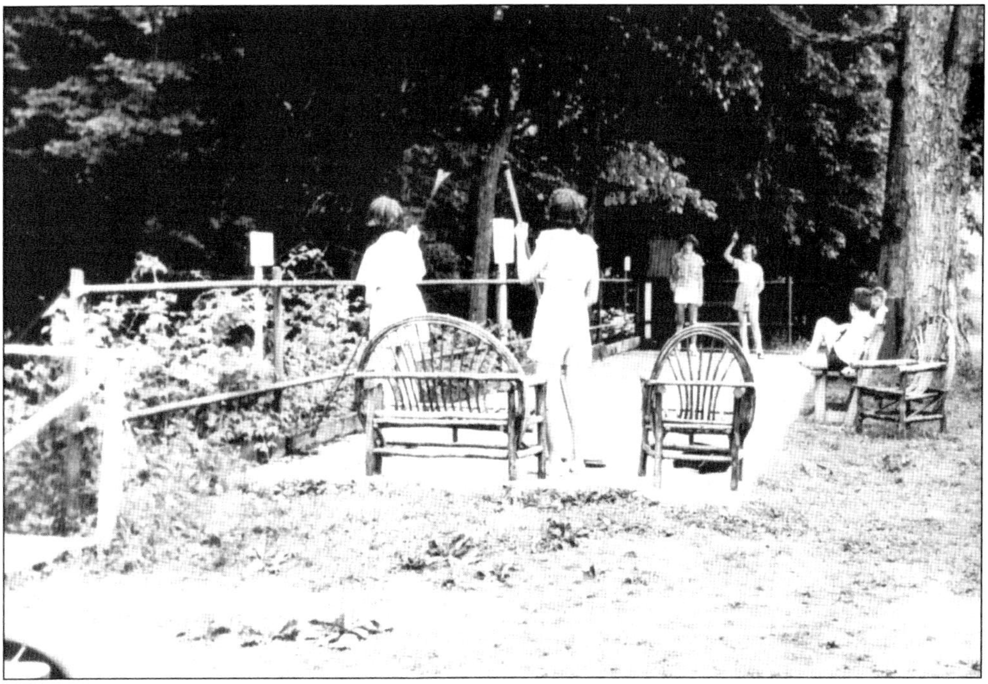

Shuffleboard contests between the various boardinghouses and resorts were common in the early part of the 20th century. This is a picture of the court at Twin Falls House, where these ladies no doubt were practicing for a fierce competition with a rival lodge. (Photograph courtesy of Katherine Yetter.)

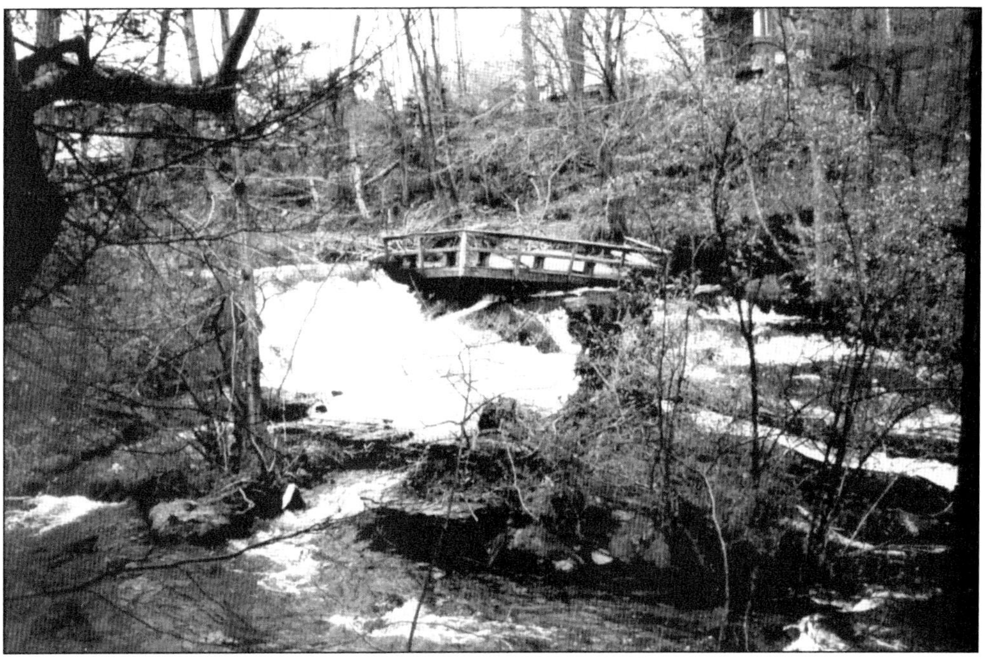

The bridge over Twin Falls was close to Seven Bridges Road. This area is now part of Waterfront Park, a public recreation area owned by Smithfield Township.

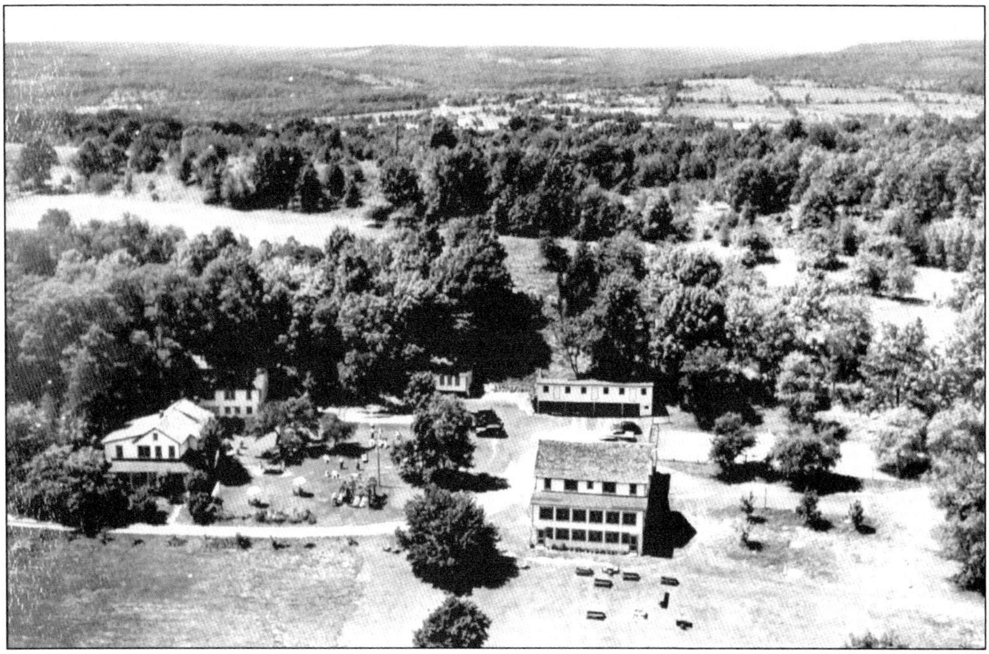

Mr. and Mrs. Eschenback purchased Sunset Hill Farm from John Mahl, initially turning it into a boardinghouse and then a small resort. The lodge, seen in the foreground, contained guest rooms, a dining room, kitchen, and recreation hall. On the left is the homestead, with 13 additional rooms for rent. The inn, located on Mount Nebo Road between Shawnee and Marshalls Creek, closed in 1989. (Photograph courtesy of Hilda Bachelder.)

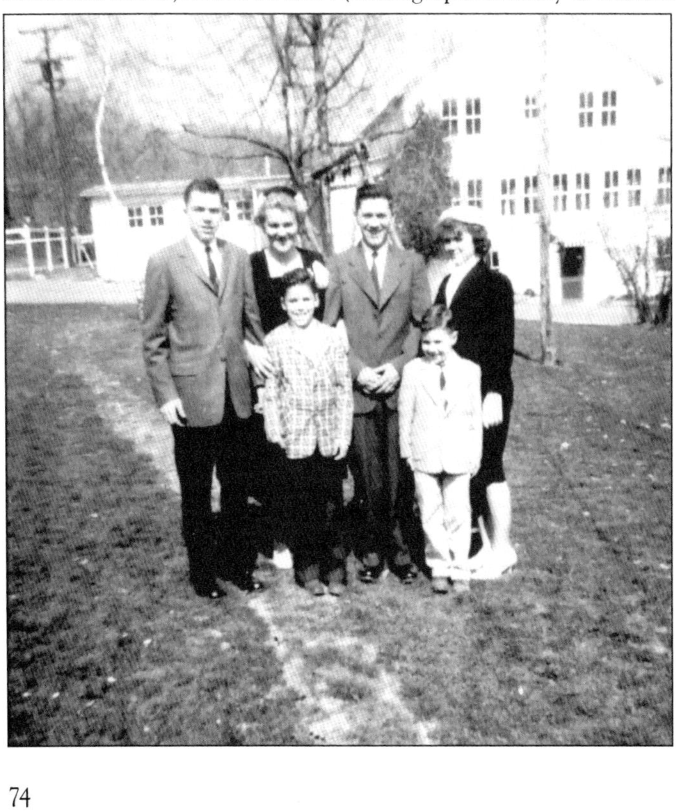

The Butz family enjoyed an Easter Sunday outing at Sunset Hill Inn. Pictured from left to right are Bruce, Margaret, Lawrence, Joyce, Brian, and Boyd Butz. The original farm became a boardinghouse in 1920. A short walk up the hill offers a splendid view of Mosier's Knob and Shawnee. Margaret Butz's sister, Hilda Bachelder, and her husband own the property. (Photograph courtesy of Margaret Butz.)

Five

Through Middle Smithfield

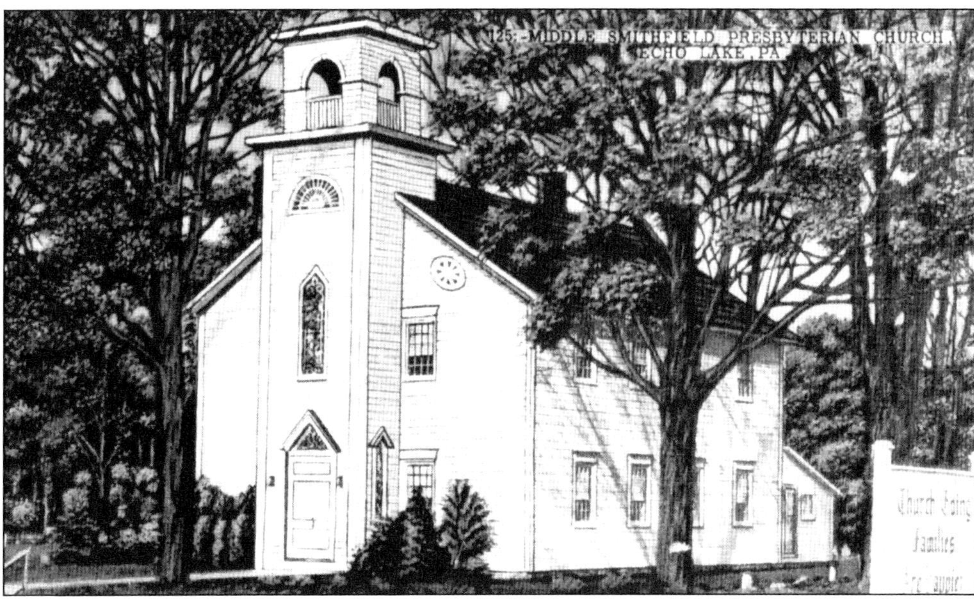

The Middle Smithfield Presbyterian Church was built in 1833. John Coolbaugh donated the land and timber for construction of the church. The congregation had been meeting since 1814 at Mr. Coolbaugh's house. Rev. Jacob Field, also Stroudsburg's pastor, held services there while also tending to his Stroudsburg congregation. Coolbaugh lent his name to a postal address involving the surrounding area. The advent of the Delaware Valley Railroad made this area ripe for tourism, with stops along the railroad line creating more post addresses. Middle Smithfield Township alone had the majority of these stops and railroad stations with Oak Grove, Frutchey's, Coolbaugh, Delaware Valley House (later known as Regina's), Coolbaugh (later known as Echo Lake), Turn Villa (later Echo Lake House), and Shoemakers Station.

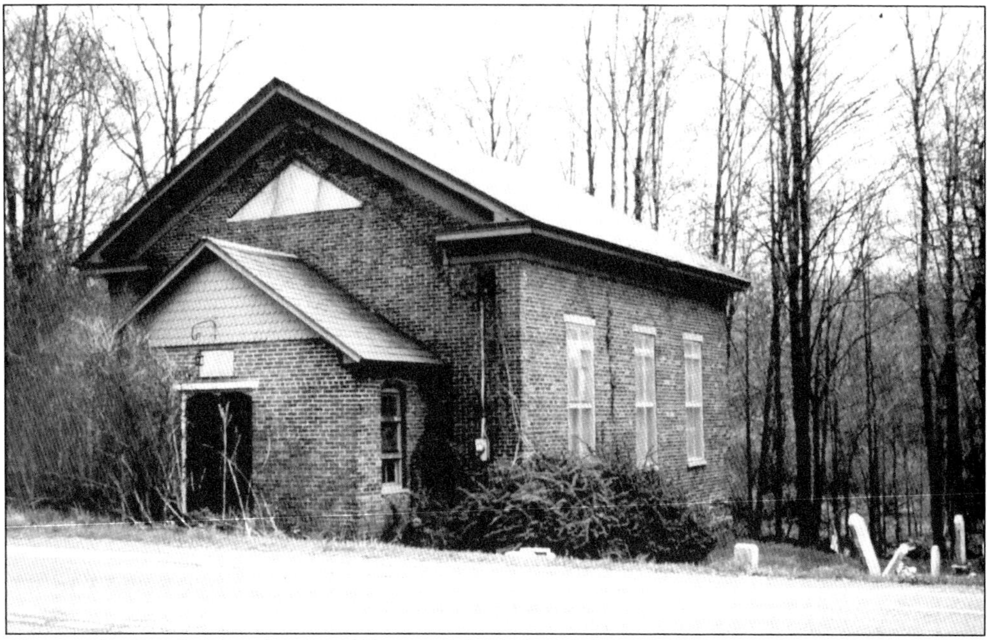

The Wesley Brick Church of Middle Smithfield closed down in 1952. It was of the Methodist denomination and was affiliated with the East Stroudsburg Methodist Church and served by its ministers. The cemetery is interfaith; one side is a Jewish cemetery, and the other is Methodist. The building later operated as an antique shop for several years.

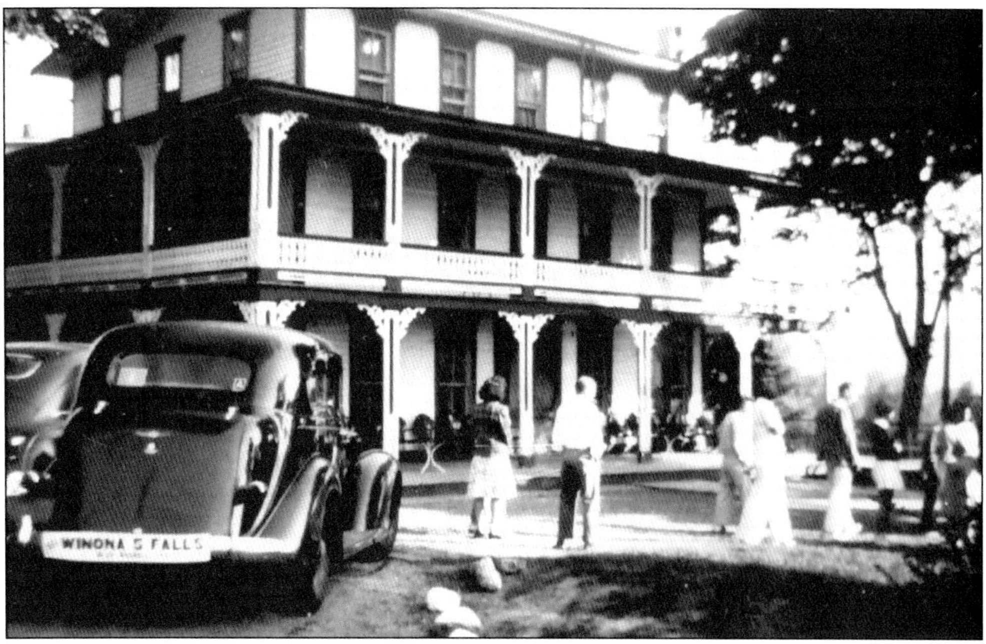

Turn Villa, seen in this 1942 picture, was owned at the time by Al and Elsie Rosenberger, who renamed it from its former designation as Echo Lake Farms. Joseph Kulick, late principal of Middle Smithfield School, served as recreation director at the resort and took guests on trips to area attractions. The bumper stickers on the cars indicate guests had visited Winona Five Falls. (Photograph courtesy of Helen Sirola.)

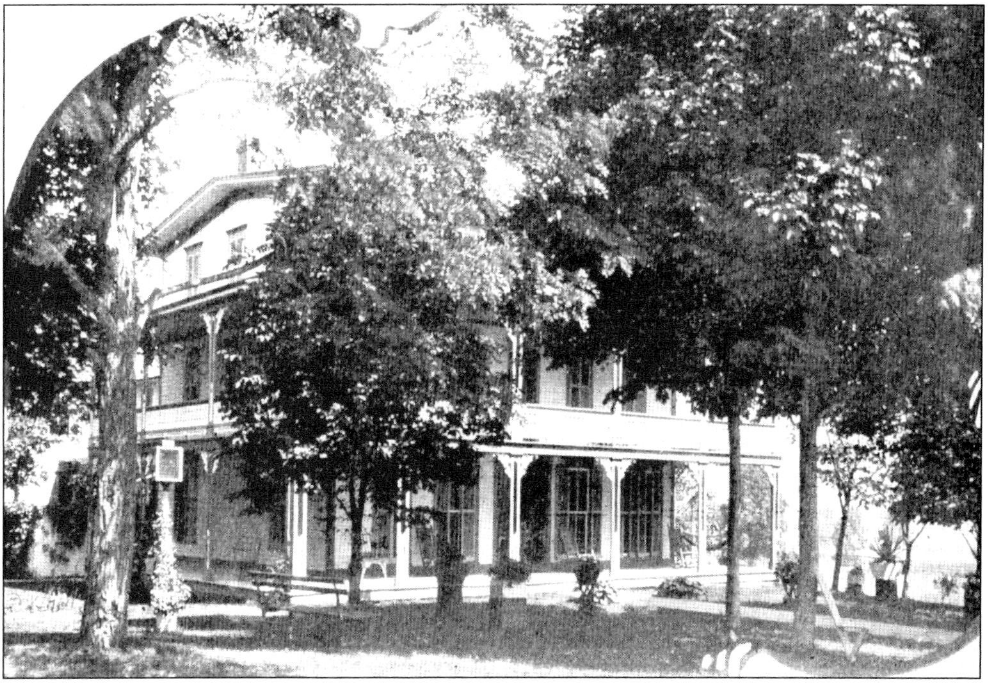

The Ridge View House was owned and operated as a boardinghouse by Melchoir D. Turn when this 1896 photograph was taken. It was located three miles from Bushkill in the village then known as Coolbaugh.

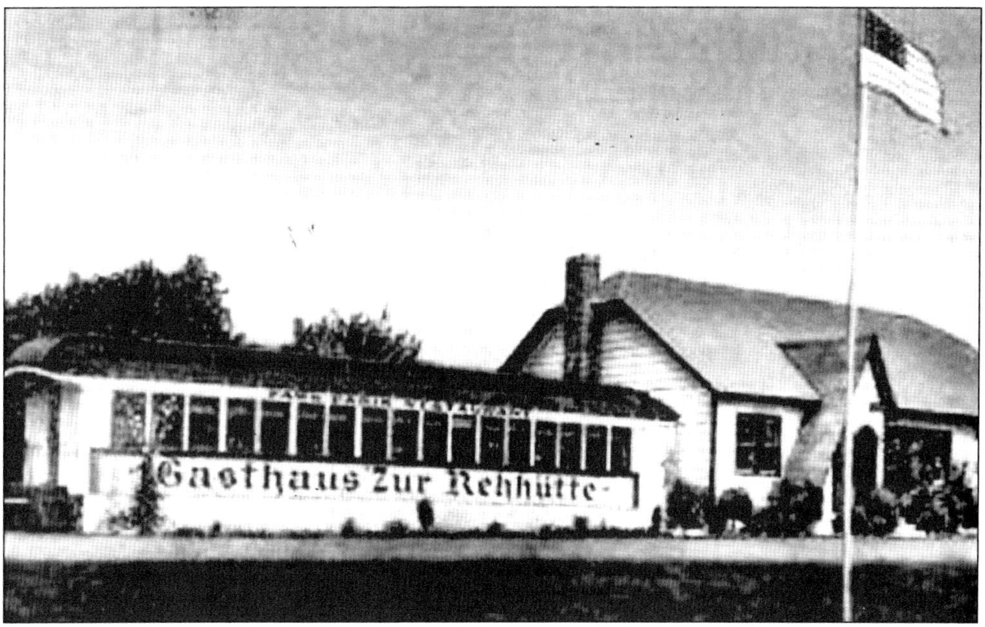

In the late 1920s, Al Rosenberger built Fawn Cabin with materials from a barn behind his house. It had hand-hewn beams and a slate roof. When the Delaware Valley Railroad disbanded, he bought the line's one railroad coach car and attached it to the diner. The Sirola family owned Fawn Cabin from 1953 to 1962. It was later known as Heddy's Restaurant and is currently the Steak and Rib.

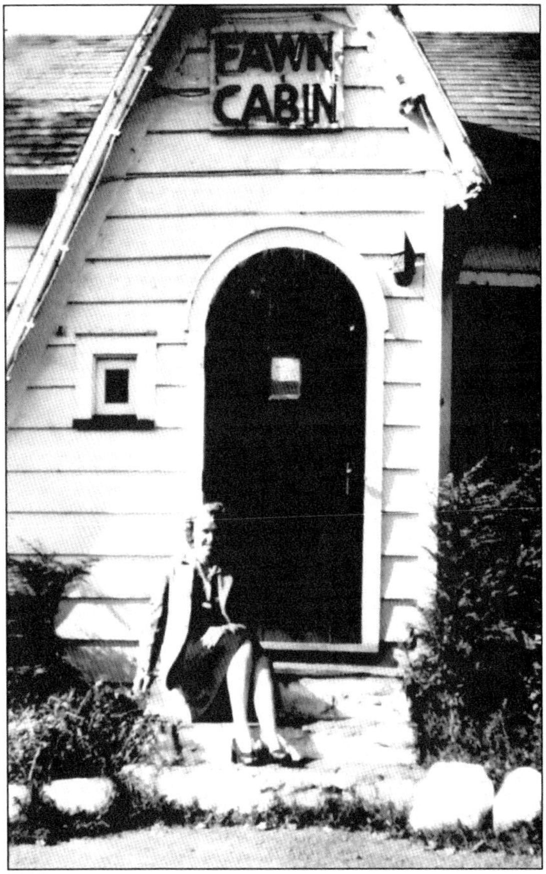

Helen Sirola is seen sitting on the steps of Fawn Cabin in the 1940s. She had recently been discharged from the service, having served her country in World War II. The distinctive doorway still remains as part of the building's architecture. (Photograph courtesy of Helen Sirola.)

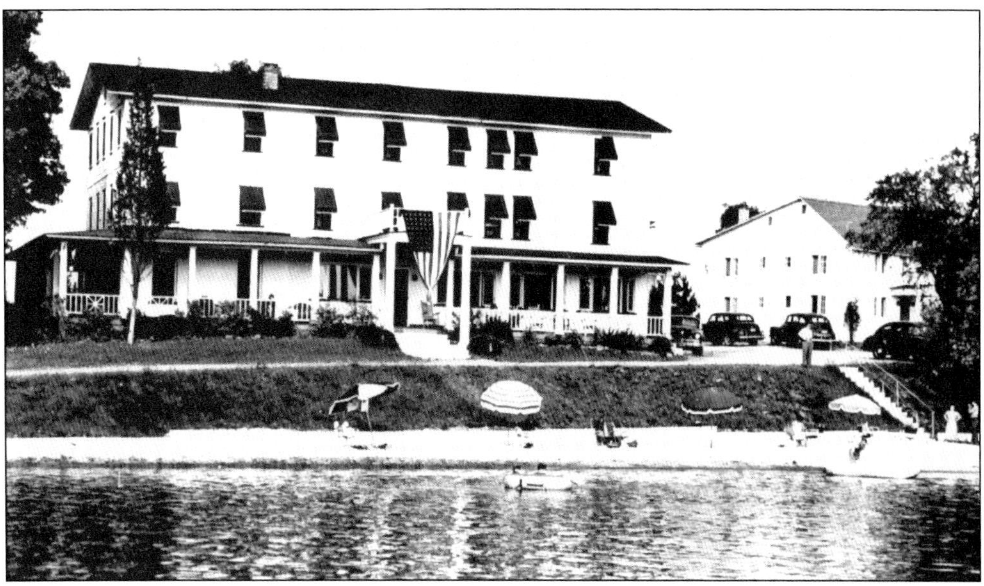

Blue Ridge began as a campground owned by Morris and Joseph Kutay. Frank Kristoff operated the Blue Ridge Inn and Resort from 1968 to 1977. The restaurant was destroyed by fire and later rebuilt, with various owners operating it.

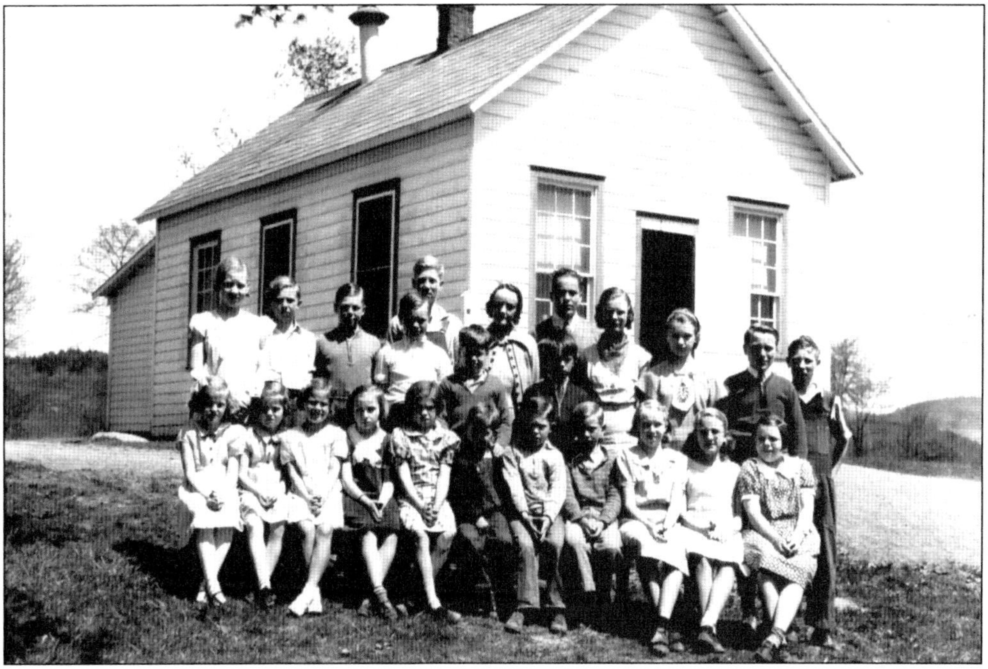

Frutchey's School was another one-room schoolhouse that stood along Route 209. Pictured from left to right are (seated) Freida Lesoine, Doris Lesoine, unidentified, Elfreda Winkel, Arlene Freeman, unidentified, ? Freeman, unidentified, Helen Overfield, Lillian Warner, and Minnie Balmoos; (standing) Beulah Ludwig, Durling Ace, Leonard Mosier, Richard Ace, Claude Ludwig, Charles Booth, Dorothy Miller, Dick Primrose, Charles Primrose, Evelyn Ace, Mary Lou Warner, Gene Mosier, and Albert Ludwig. (Photograph courtesy of Helen Sirola.)

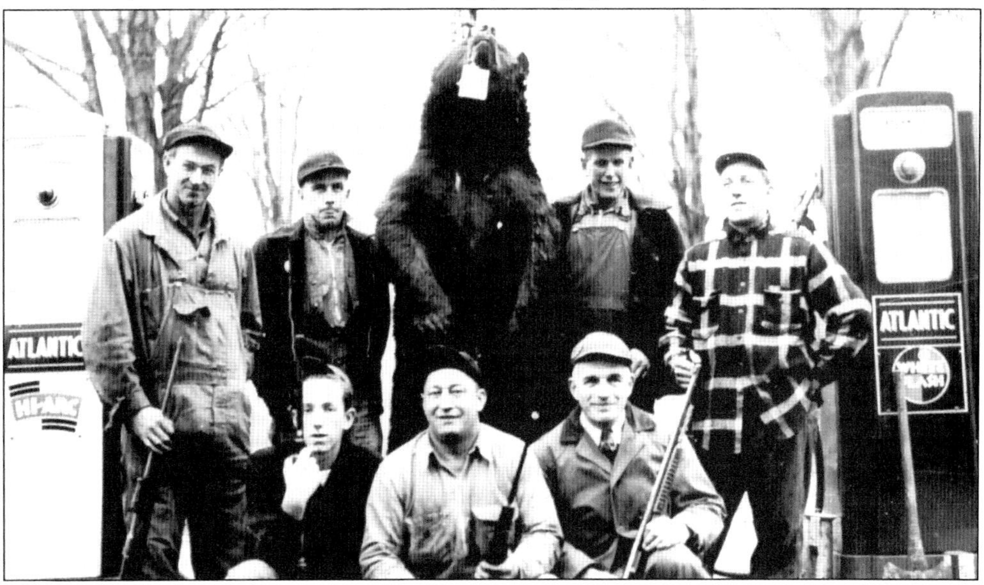

A member of this hunting party bagged this prize bear, which the group is seen showing off in front of Ernie Booth's gas station. From left to right are (first row) George Dewitt, Ernest Booth, and Sterling Schoonover; (second row) Roy Squires, Irvin Smith, George Overfield, and Alvin Dewitt Jr.

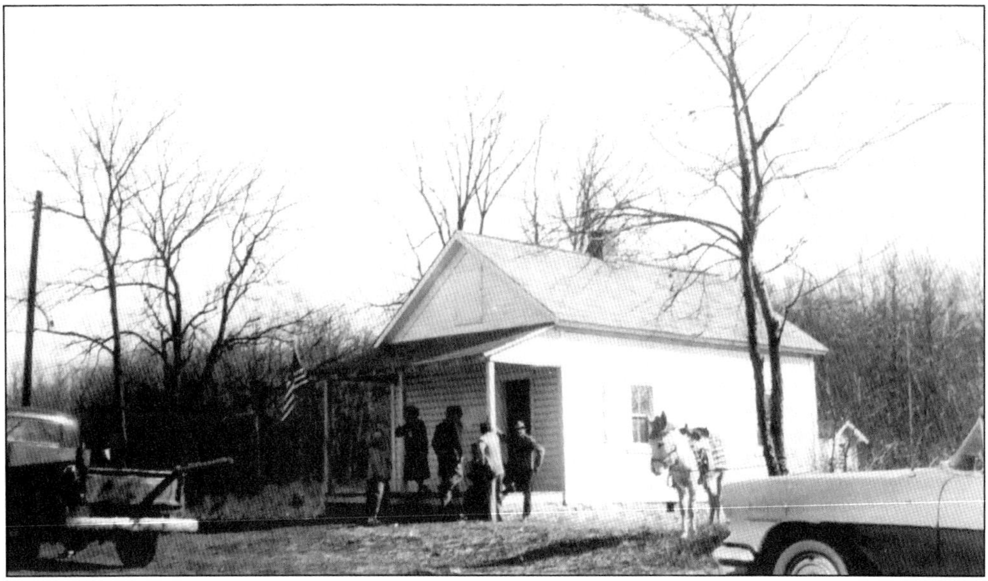

From the 19th century on, election houses such as this one in Middle Smithfield were built to provide polling places for those living in rural areas. This building stood on Route 209 near the entrance to Mount Nebo Road. Members of the Democratic Club posted their mascot and symbol of their party nearby. (Photograph courtesy of April Duganieri.)

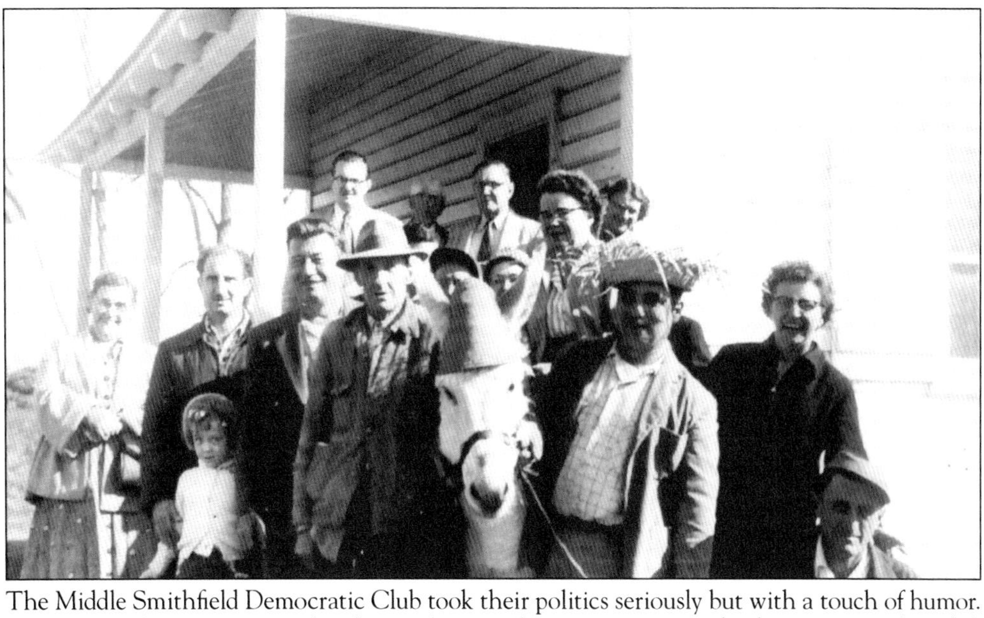

The Middle Smithfield Democratic Club took their politics seriously but with a touch of humor. Here we see their group near the election house. The campaigners in the front row are, from left to right, Mrs. Pascarella, Pascarella's daughter, Mr. Pascarella, Ernie Booth, Ed Howey (owner of the donkey), Ernie George (with straw hat), Verna Riedmiller, and Frank Smith (kneeling). The others are unidentified. (Photograph courtesy of April Duganieri.)

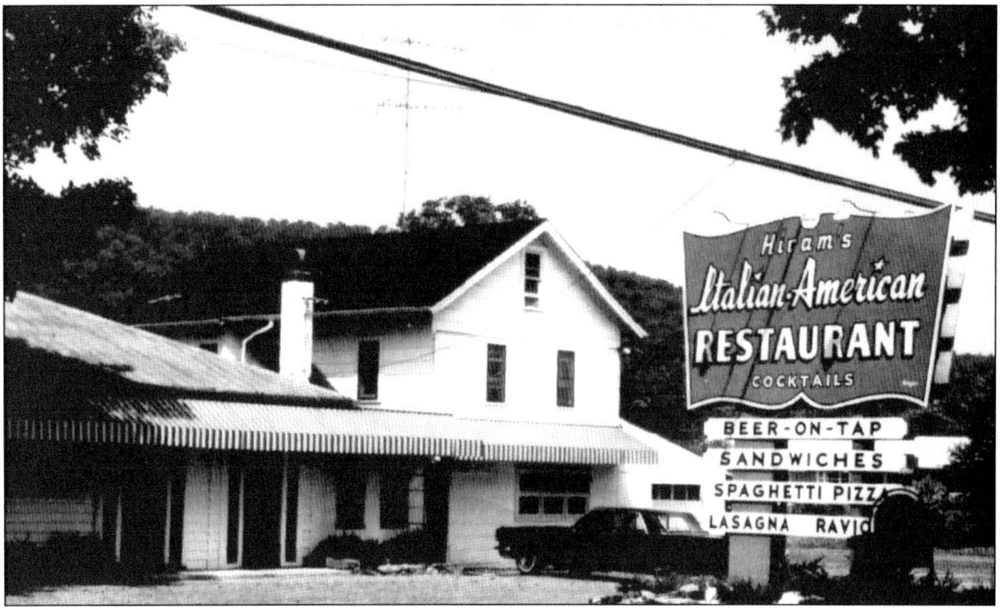

In 1946, Mike and Pauline Sirola purchased 10 acres of land next to the ball field near Bushkill. They began their business by operating a hamburger stand and serving baseball players and tourists. Soon after, they expanded the business to a restaurant and continued it as Hiram's Rest. In 1962, their son-in-law and daughter, John and Mary Petrizzo, took ownership, renaming it Petrizzo's Restaurant. A third generation now operates the restaurant.

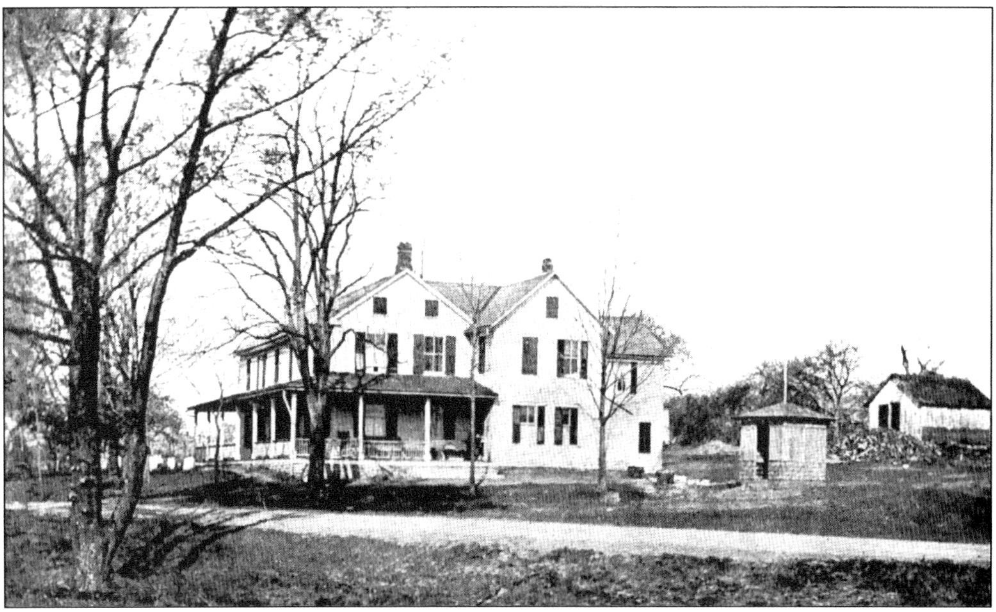

In 1914, Edward and Anna Regina bought the hotel originally known as the Delaware Valley Hotel and renamed it the Regina and, later, Regina's Hotel. It stood on Route 209 where it intersects with Hollow Road. Their son Ted and his wife, Ellen, later owned the hotel and acquired a liquor license. The Delaware Valley Railroad stopped here on its way from Stroudsburg to Bushkill.

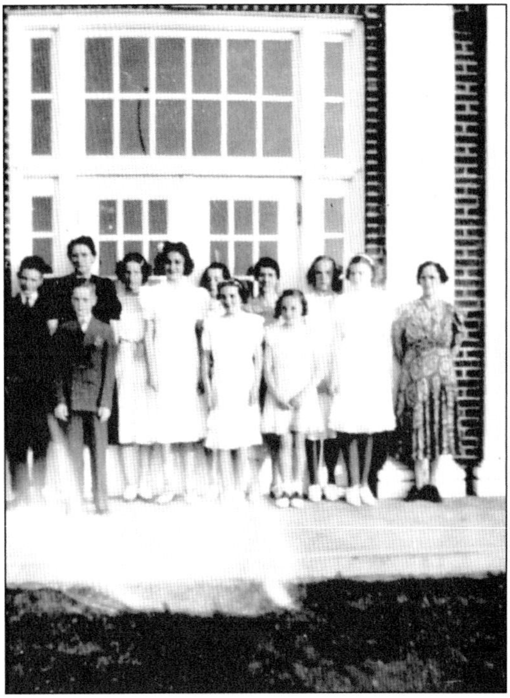

Eighth-grade students pose on the occasion of their June 1937 graduation at the Middle Smithfield School. From left to right are (first row) Art Hines, Harold Sebring, Lewis Scheller, Rita Schoonover, Josephine McCole, Elfreda Winkle, Marjorie Lanterman, and Edith Courtright (teacher); (second row) Magdaline Peters, Doris DeWitt, Anges Oliver, Cora Strunk (teacher), and Helen Overfield. (Photograph courtesy of Rita Laubner.)

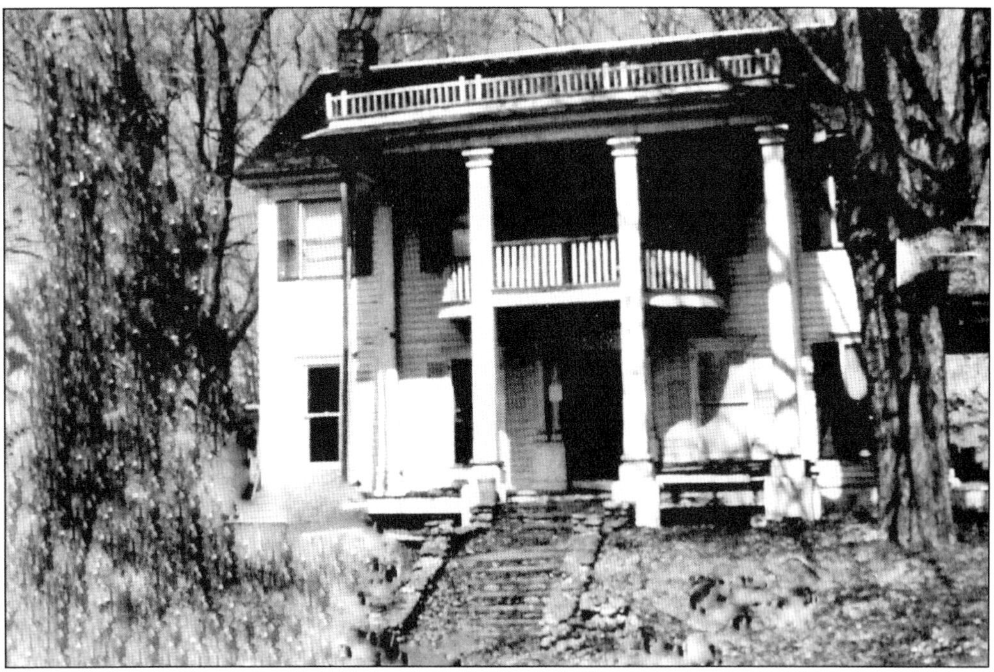

Built around 1840, the John Van Campen–Coolbaugh house has a fascinating history. It was reputedly used as part of the Underground Railroad during the Civil War. Charles Peters, the entrepreneur who developed Bushkill Falls, lived with his grandmother at the house after his mother died. Known as Joan of Arc during Prohibition, the building was a notorious speakeasy, with gangsters such as Legs Diamond and Dutch Schultz as visitors. (Photograph courtesy of Marge Law.)

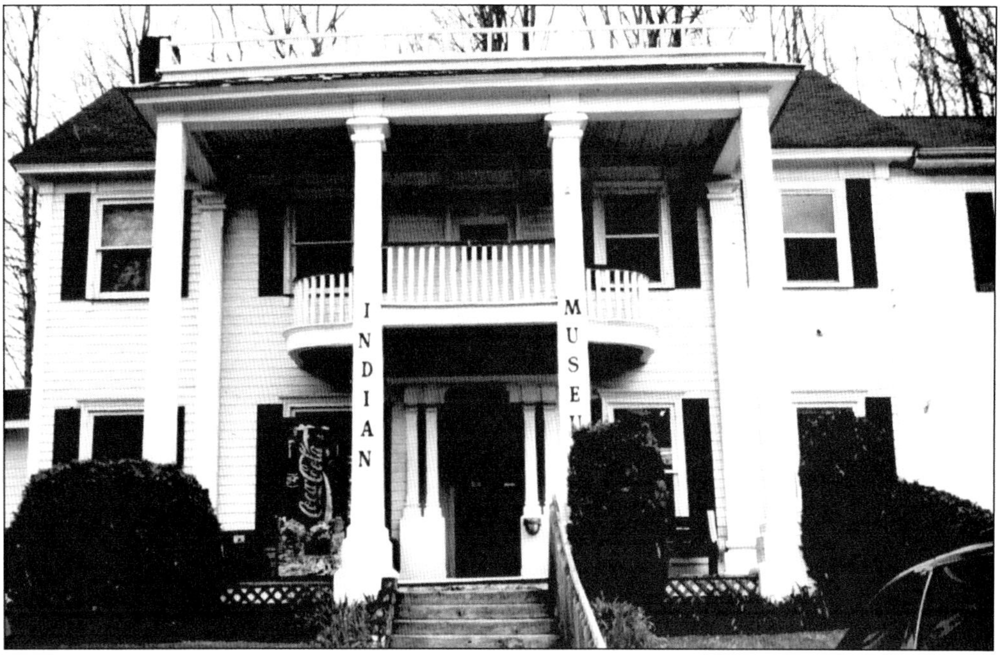

Malcolm and Marge Law purchased the Van Campen and Coolbaugh house and retrieved it from decadence. They turned it into the Pocono Indian Museum, a showcase featuring Native American culture, particularly the Lenni-Lenapes who inhabited the region. The museum conducts educational tours of exhibits and offers a gift shop dedicated to Native American souvenirs.

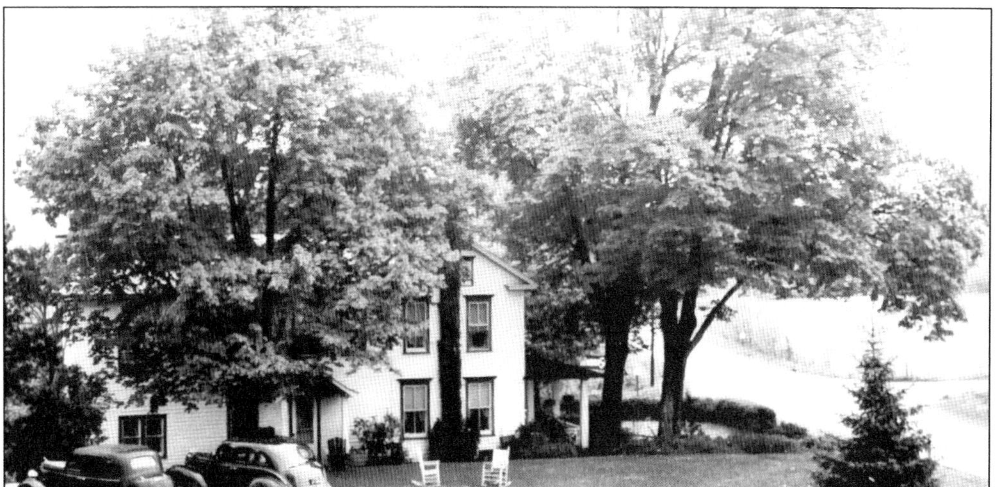

DeWitt's Inn, one and a half miles south of Bushkill, was built on land purchased by Samuel Dewitt in the 1870s. Four generations of the Dewitt family operated the inn. The surrounding village, known as Shoemakers, had its own post office. Alvin DeWitt Sr. later took over the inn from his father. The inn was later renamed Winona Falls Lodge. It was sold in 1977 and later demolished by the Rank Corporation.

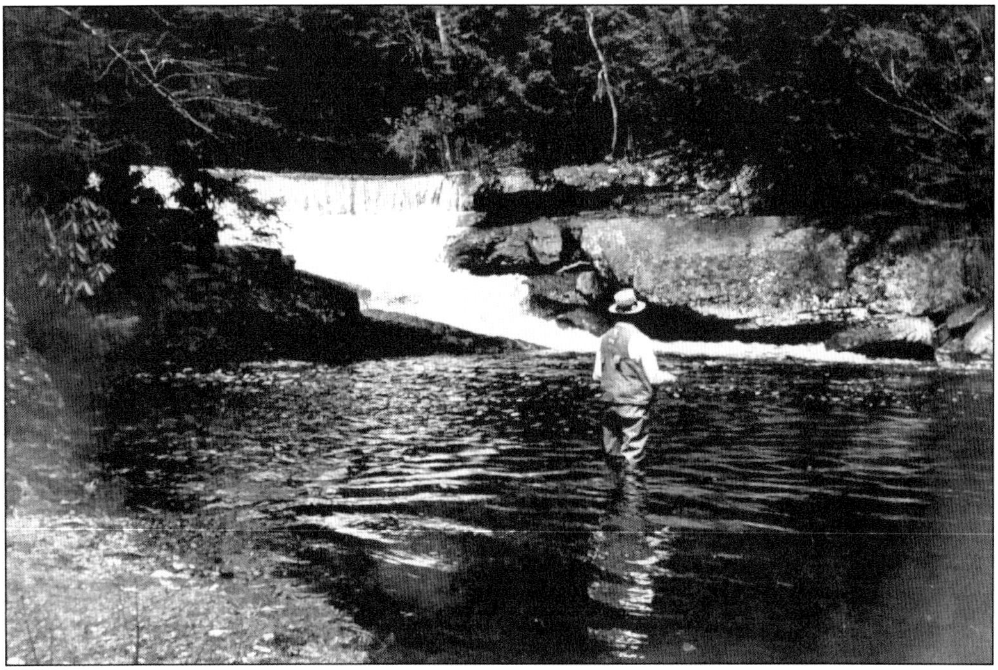

Bill Schoonover enjoys angling in the serene waters below Winona Five Falls. An avid fisherman, he had a keen awareness of the best fishing spots. Bill owned the Bushkill Restaurant for many years. The falls is one of a series located on Saw Creek. (Photograph courtesy of Rita Laubner.)

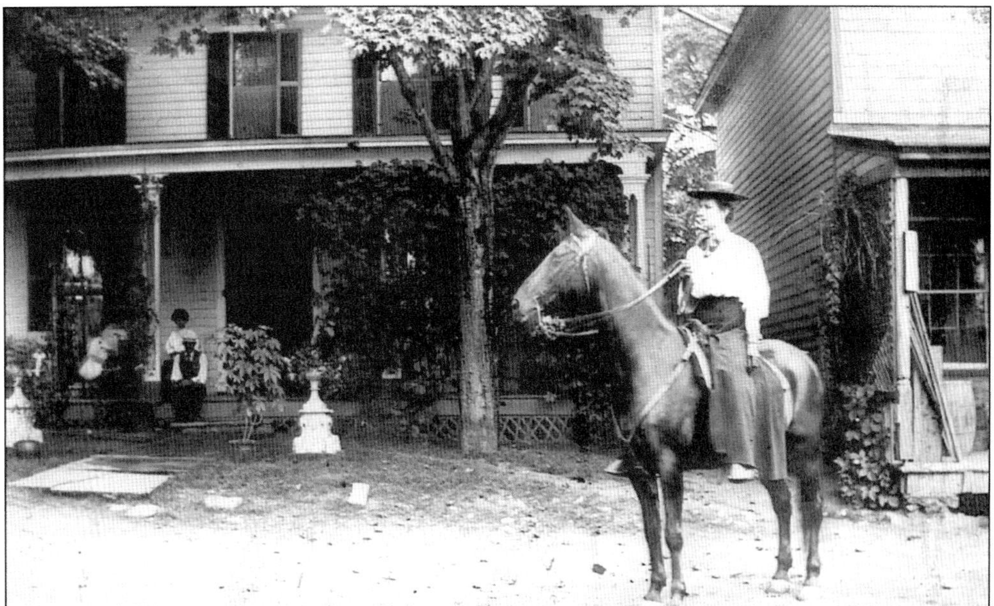

This equestrienne in front of DeWitts Inn apparently disdained the practice of riding sidesaddle. The year was 1905, and she was a thoroughly modern woman. Pictured on the left is the boardinghouse, and on the right is the Shoemakers post office, both of which have been demolished. (Photograph courtesy of George DeWitt.)

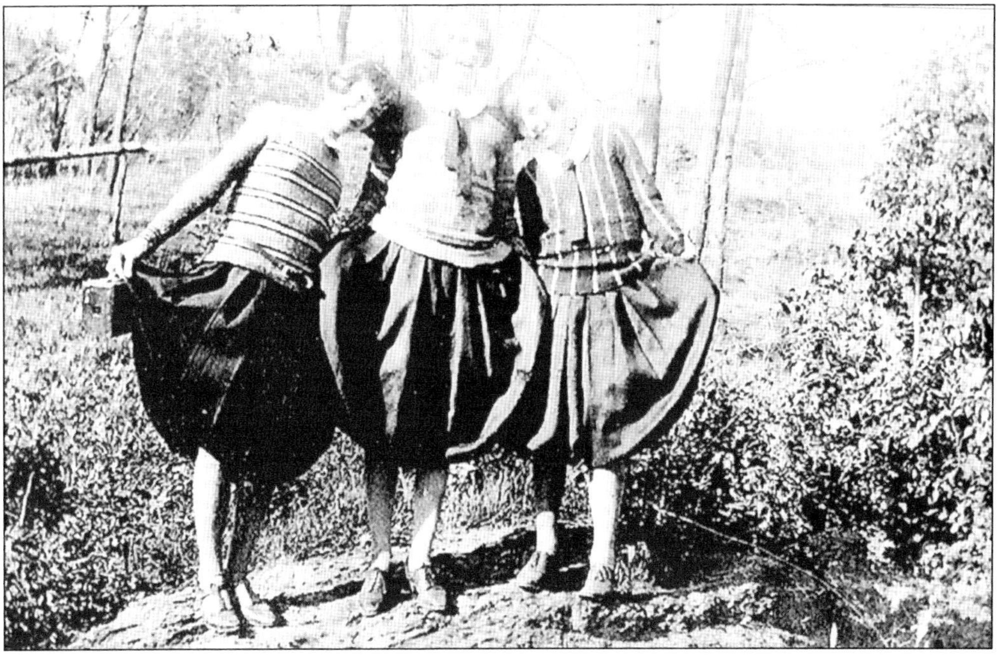

The so-called Bloomer Dancers are, from left to right, Marguerite Litts, Mildred Smith, and Ruth Smith, posing for the camera at Winona Five Falls. Amelia Bloomer had earlier popularized the balloon-type garment that manufacturers named after her, and women had recently won the vote. In this 1920s picture, the ladies are no doubt celebrating their liberation. (Photograph courtesy of Katie Angle.)

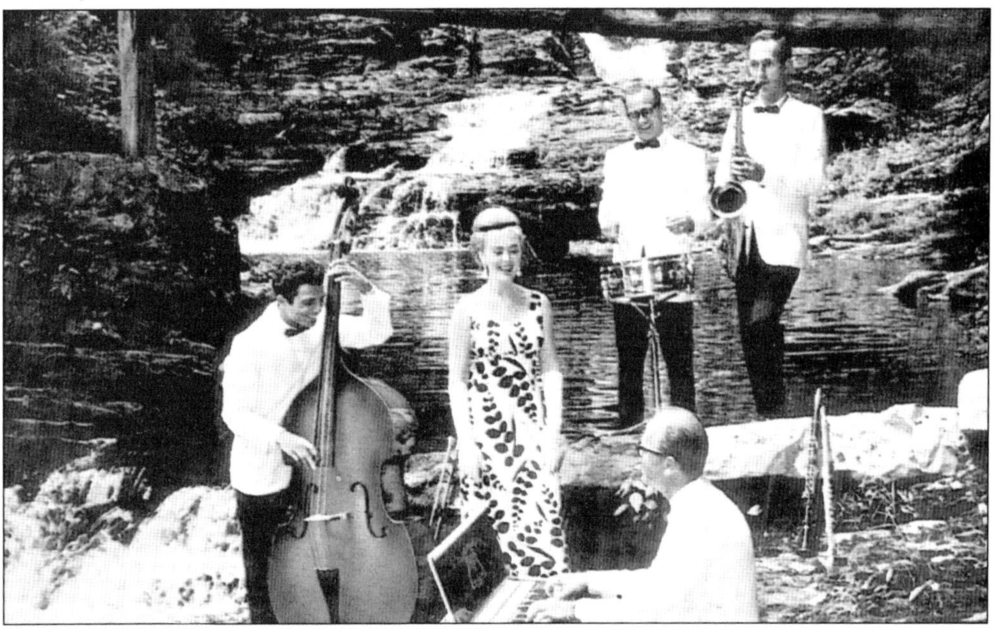

Bill Barth's Quartet Plus One appeared nightly at Fernwood from the mid-1950s to the mid-1970s. The group is pictured here in front of Winona Five Falls. From left to right are Tony Ardito (bass fiddle), Beverly Barth (lead singer), Bill Barth (keyboard), Tony Colondo (drums), and Jimmy Kiess (saxophone).

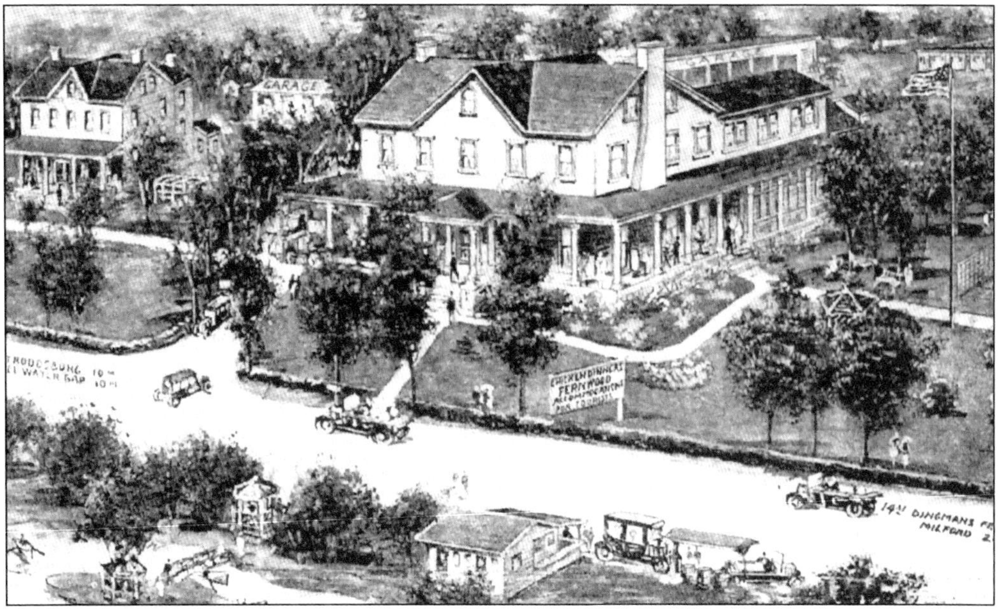

As with many small and large resorts in the Poconos, Fernwood first operated as a tourist house. Henry and Helen Ahnert started a chicken farm and opened their doors to the public in 1921, specializing in chicken dinners. During World War II, the Ahnert brothers operated a machine shop there and later made Champion sparkplugs as a subcontractor for the company.

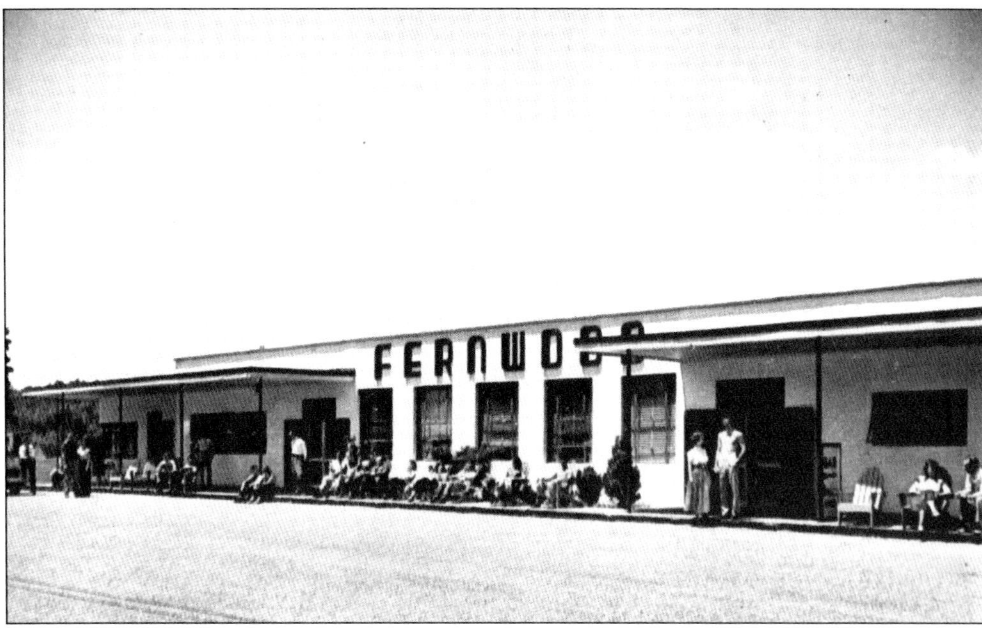

This is a 1950s view of Fernwood. The building was later destroyed by fire, as was a dormitory in a separate fire. Fernwood Resort opened in 1949. Ahnert Enterprises opened the Villas at Fernwood in 1979 and Outdoor World in 1981. The Rank organization acquired Ahnert Enterprises in 1988, and the company became known as Rank-Ahnert. In 1993, the company name changed to Resorts USA, a company within the Rank organization.

Six

Bushkill, the Village That Disappeared

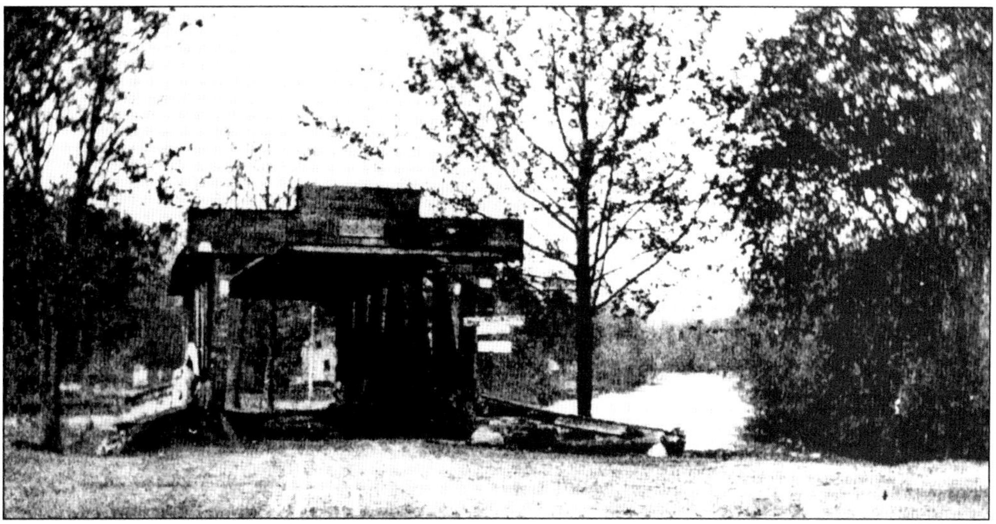

This covered bridge, called the County Line Bridge, was constructed in 1837, the year Monroe County was formed. It was built by William Brodhead and was replaced in 1897 by an iron one. When Monroe was partitioned off from Pike County, the Big Bushkill Creek became the boundary line. This structure marked the line of separation. The northern side of the bridge became part of Pike County and the southern section, called Maple Grove, became a part of Monroe County. The creek it spanned and the village it divided, both called Bushkill, came from the Dutch "little stream" or "little river." Bushkill, the village, was among the hardest hit of all the areas that lay in the path of the proposed and now defunct Tocks Island Dam project. Little remains of the once prosperous village. People new to the area are little aware that a thriving village once existed here. Former residents paying a return visit view this as a ghost town, and most lament its passing.

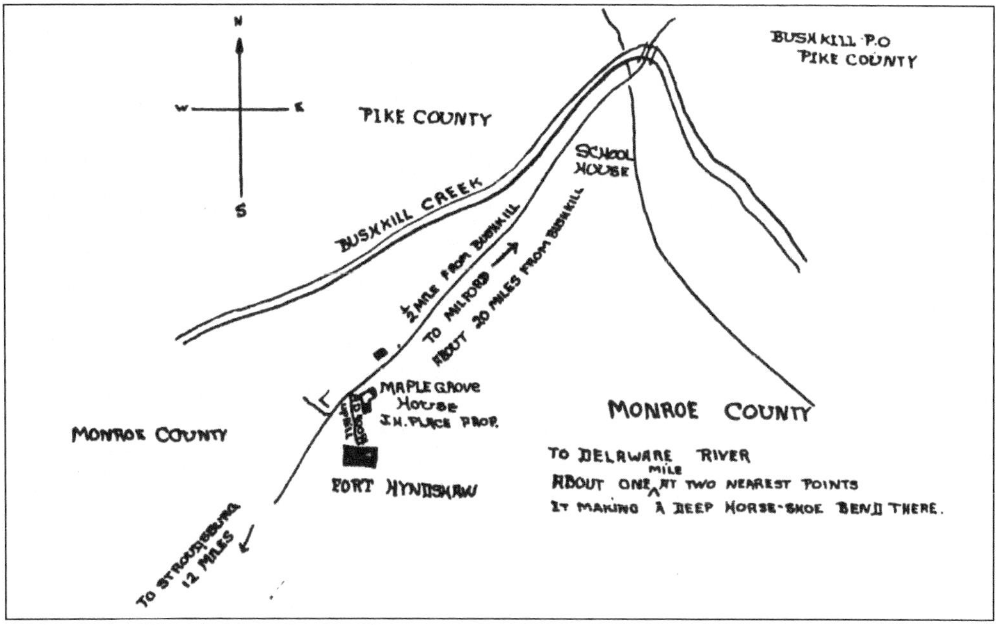

In the Bushkill area, as in others, Indian attacks were rampant during the French and Indian War. In response, Benjamin Franklin ordered a series of forts to be built along the Blue Mountains. Fort Hyndshaw on the Maple Grove side of Bushkill, was built in 1756. The log fort was described in colonial reports as a square about 70 feet each way, very lightly "staccaded" (*sic*), and clear all around for 300 yards. (Sketch courtesy of Pennsylvania Archives.)

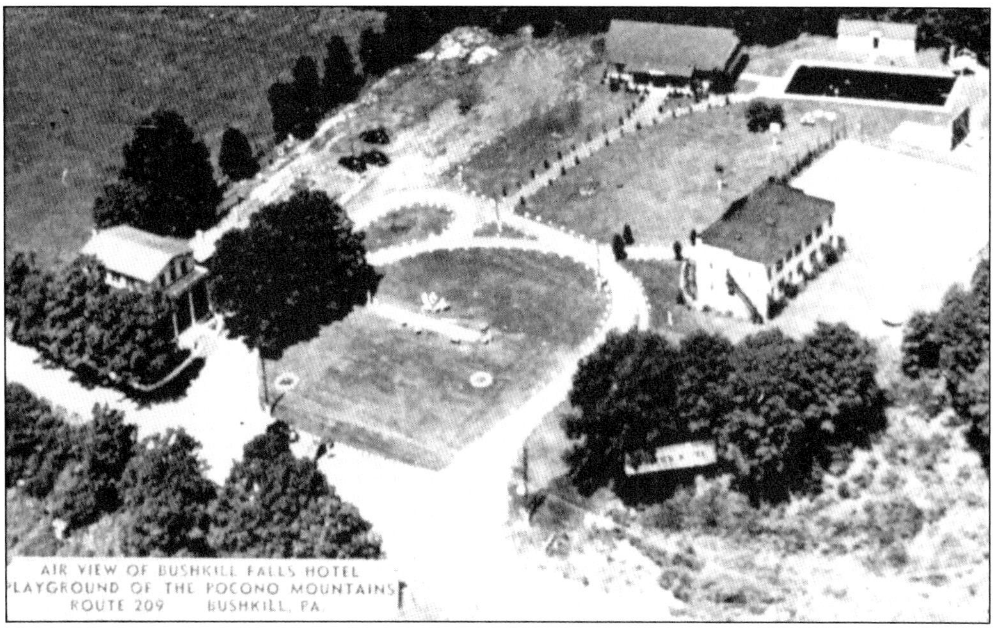

Jacob Place ran the Mountain View House, and his widow operated it after he died in 1902. Various owners followed. At the time of the photograph, Frank and Elsie Pipher owned and operated it under the name of Bushkill Falls House. The aerial view of the resort indicates the expansion of an original small boardinghouse into a large resort area. This property became a casualty of the Tocks project.

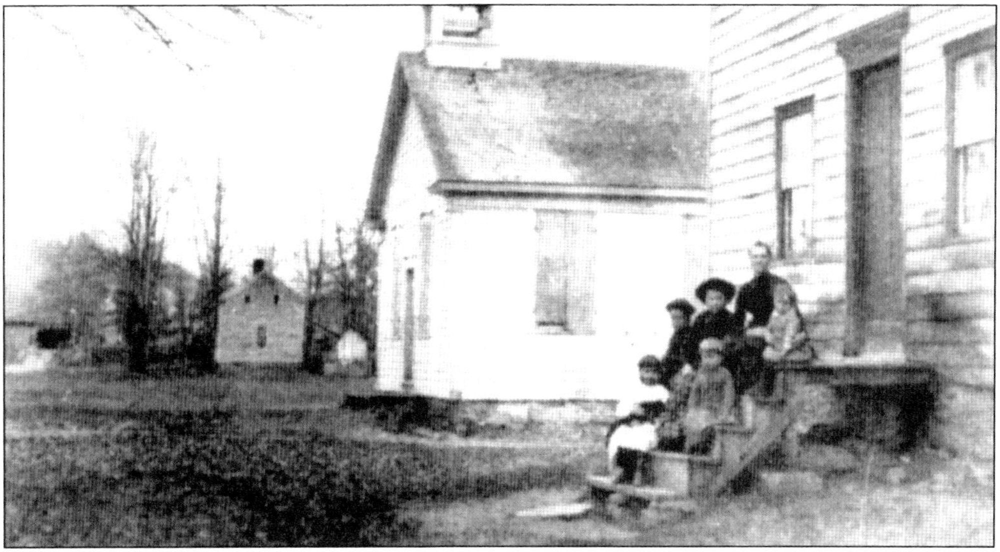

The Maple Grove School was located on the Monroe County side of Bushkill. In the early 1920s, Father Butler felt the parish needed a Catholic church in this area, so he arranged to purchase the schoolhouse and converted it into a church. On June 23, 1923, he read the first mass here. In the early years, parishioners and visitors could attend services every Sunday from May to October.

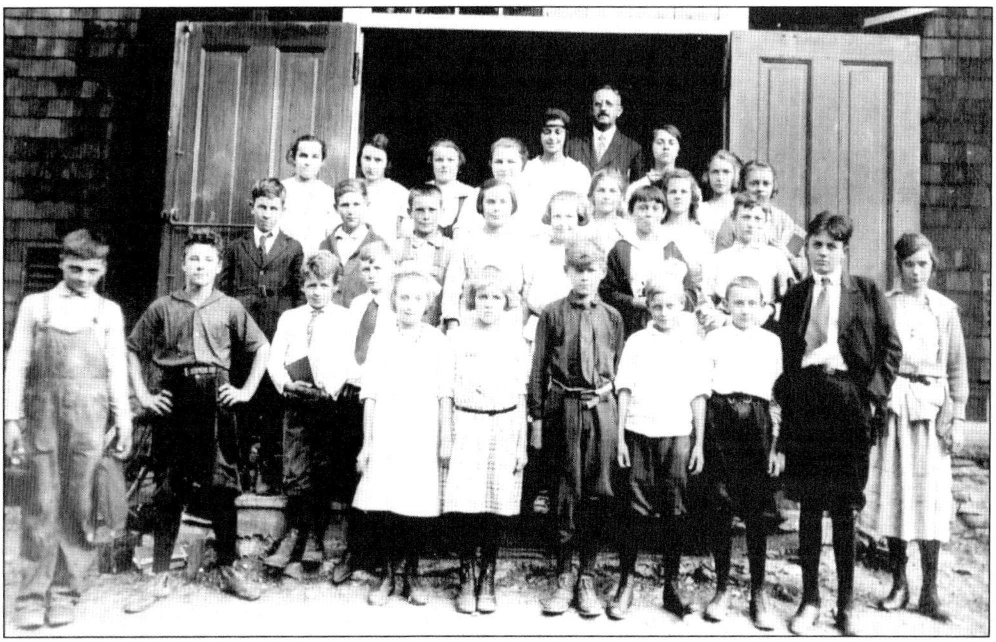

Students pose in front of the Maple Grove one-room schoolhouse. From left to right are (first row) unidentified, ? Van Why, unidentified, unidentified, Jennie Garris, Mildred Garris, unidentified, Gershom Litts, Jacob Schouppe, Richard Van Why, and Adelaide Schouppe; (second row) Lawrence (Lonny) Van Why, Allen Garris, Mildred Smith, Ruth Smith, Marguerite Litts, Nancy Van Why, Olive Schoonover, Eileen Eshback, and Albert Howey; (third row) unidentified, unidentified, unidentified, unidentified, Leola Lee, unidentified teacher, Gertrude Eshback, unidentified, and Frances Schoonover. (Photograph from private collection.)

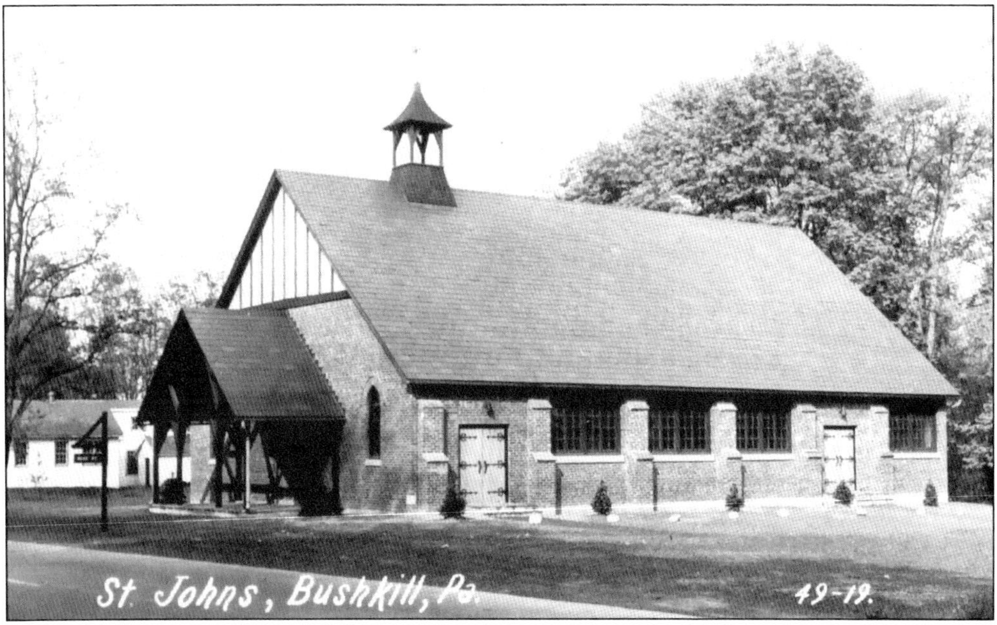

St. John's Church was built and dedicated in the late 1940s. The land it occupied was taken by the government for the Tocks Island Dam project, and the diocese leased the church from the National Park Service until 1990, when the diocese built the newer church farther south on Route 209. The building is now maintained by the park service and serves as a meeting hall.

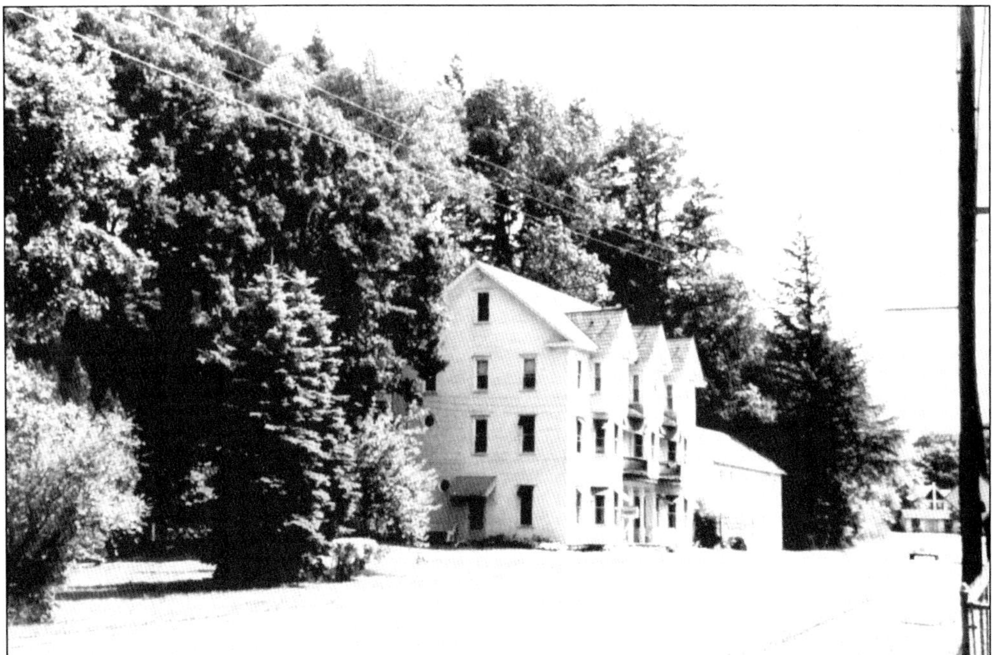

William Hemingway built the Bushkill Roost, situated north of and across the street from the blacksmith shop. The four-story building served as a boardinghouse. Percy Depue owned it, and his wife, Amy, operated it after his death. Later, the proprietor rented space for stores on its lower level.

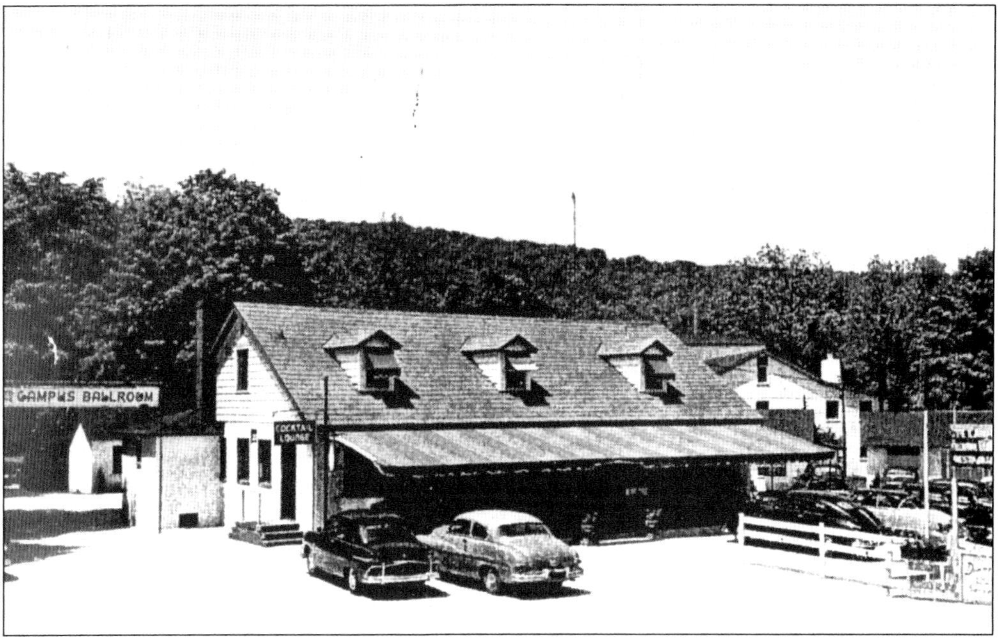

This is a view of the Campus, owned by Harold Auten, a man Bushkill folks addressed as "Captain" Auten. Very few Bushkillites know they had a war hero in their midst. Auten emigrated from England, where he had won the Victoria Cross for valorous service in the English Channel. In 1918, Lieutenant Auten commanded HMS *Stock Force* when it was torpedoed by a U-boat and very badly damaged. He was later promoted to commander.

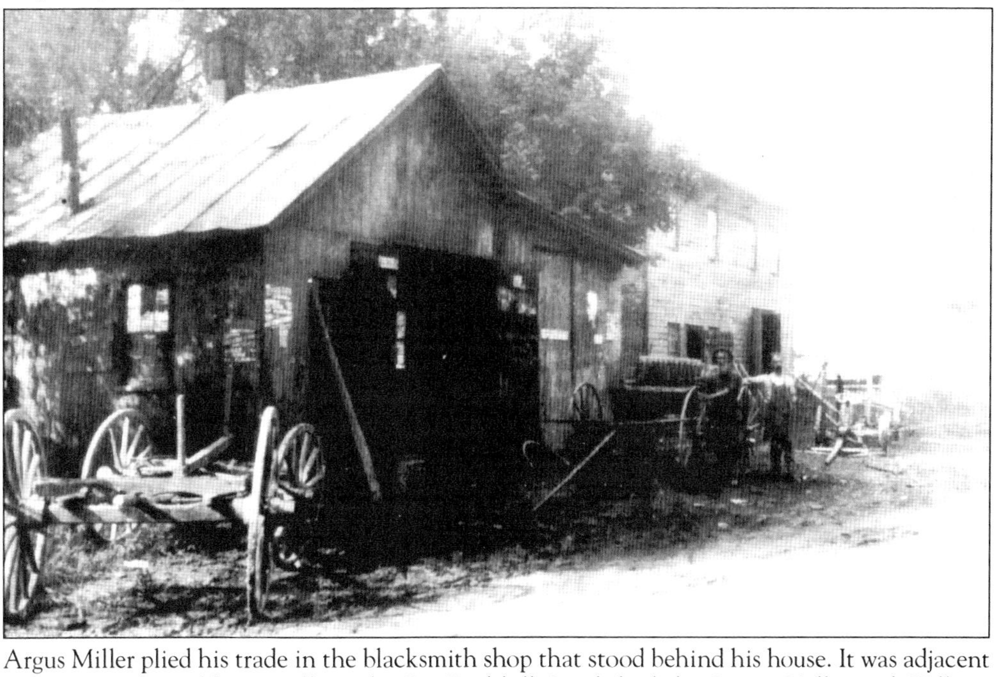

Argus Miller plied his trade in the blacksmith shop that stood behind his house. It was adjacent to the site of an old gristmill on the Big Bushkill Creek built by Simon Heller and William Clark. Preceding Argus Miller at this location was an earlier blacksmith, Jim Carson, followed by "Pappy" Dunbar in the 1880s.

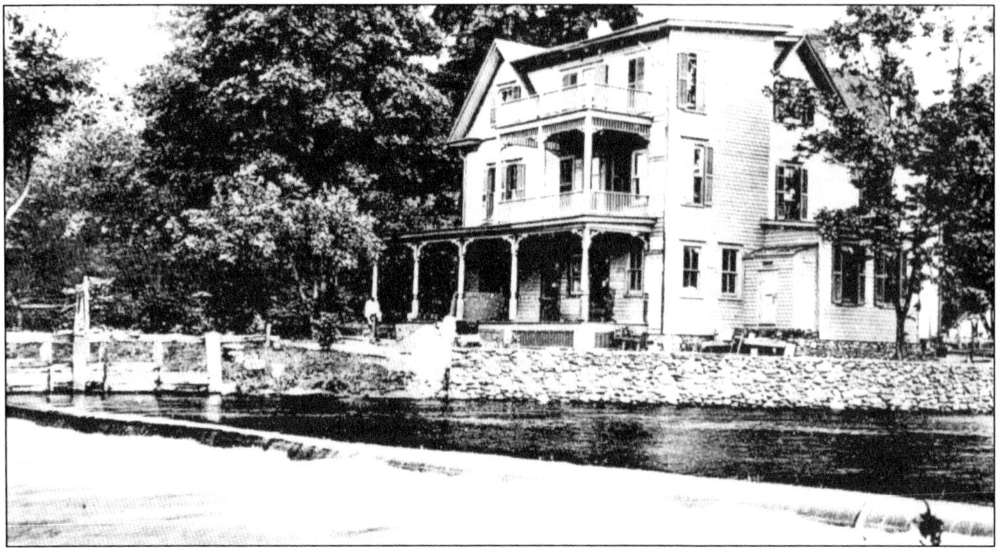

Germonds opened under the ownership of Monsieur A. Camile Germond, who advertised his marvelous French cuisine. This is an early-1900s view of the restaurant. The unpaved road in front later became Route 209. Behind it stood Swartzwood's Dam, which originally supplied power for Jacob Klaer's spoke factory. Ernest Fleischman and the Burns family later owned the hotel. It became a casualty of the Tocks Island Dam project.

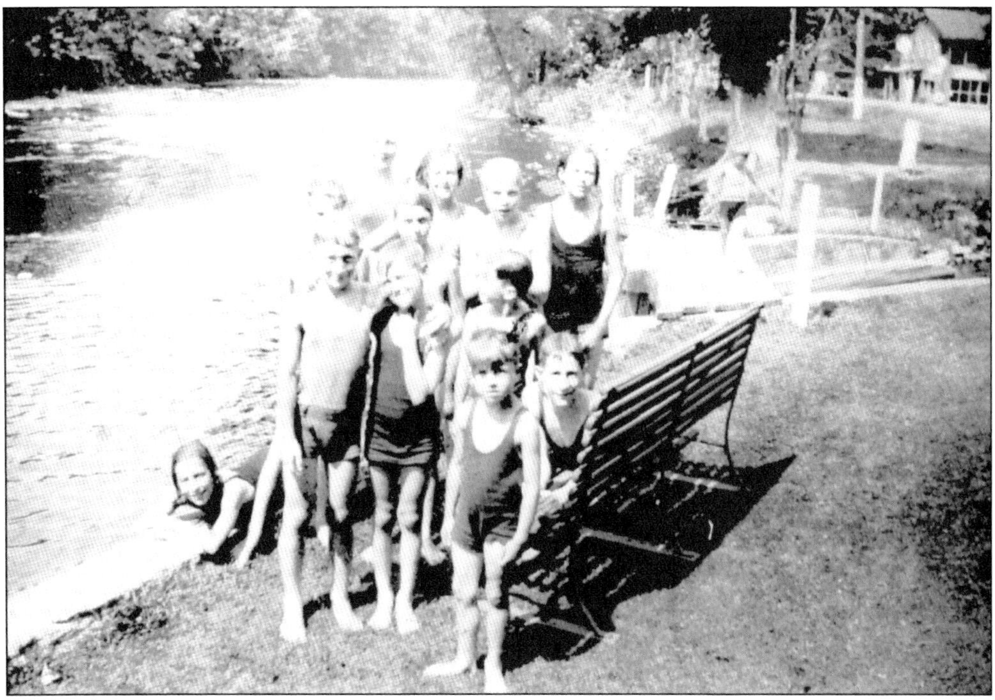

Local children enjoy swimming behind Germonds. They are identified as Charles Turn, Grace Carpenter (lying on wall), Margaret Garris, John Turn, Russell Scheller, Hilda Carpenter, Marjorie Carpenter (partially hidden), Marjorie Butz, Helen Turn, Evelyn Scheller, Esther Carpenter, and Shelia Crowley.

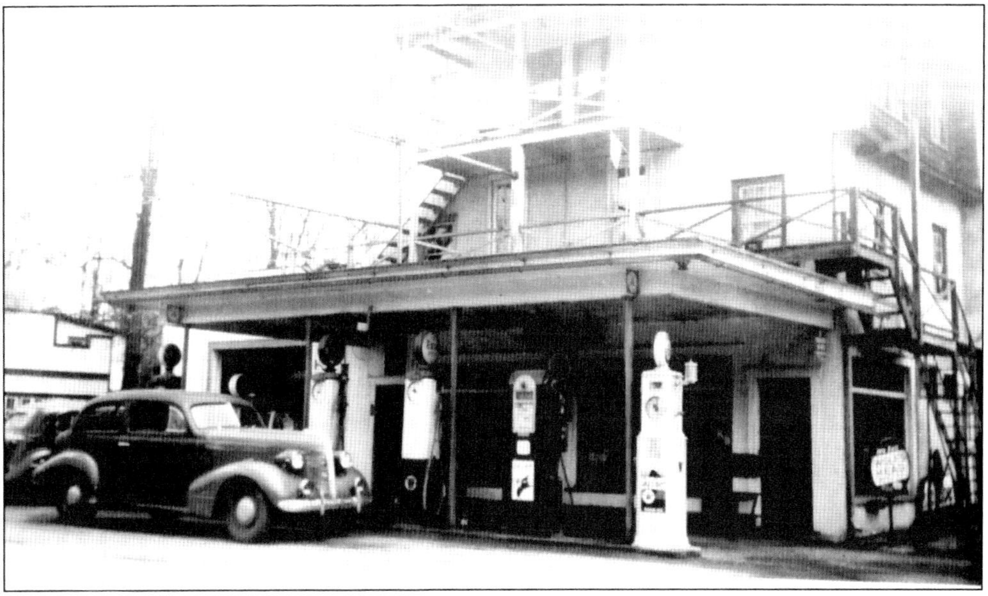

This photograph of Butz's Garage shows a vintage car in front of the building. The garage opened around 1920 under the ownership of Russell Scheller. Frank Butz worked at the garage for a while and then went into business with Argus Miller at the blacksmith shop. He later purchased the garage and gasoline station. Butz sold the garage to Walter Peeney, and it burned in the early 1950s. Another garage replaced it. (Photograph courtesy of Lawrence Butz.)

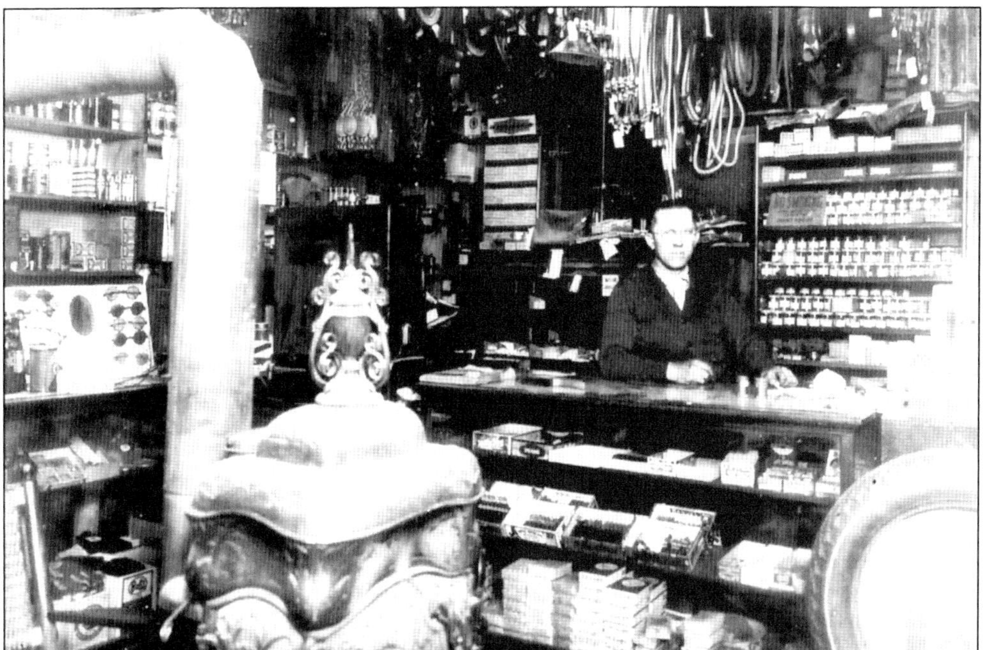

Frank Butz stands behind the counter at Butz's Garage. The picture was taken around 1932. Tidy rows of parts and supplies are arranged on the counters. The garage was often frequented by villagers who found themselves cheered by the friendly warmth of Frank Butz even more than the ornate potbellied stove. (Photograph courtesy of Kemmie Garris.)

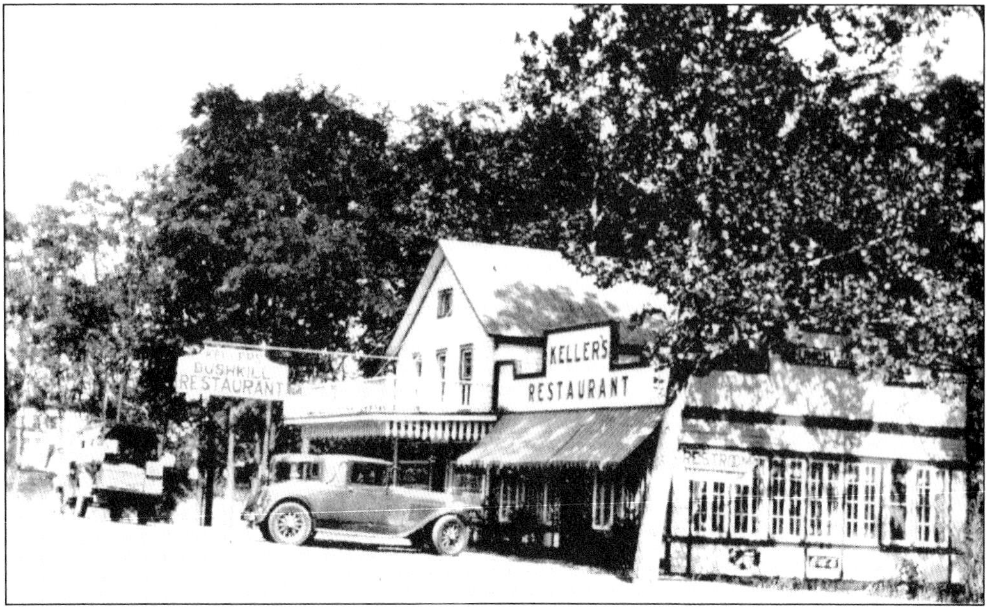

Russell Scheller opened the Bushkill Restaurant, followed by his son-in-law Luther Keller. The last owner of record was William Schoonover. The building stood alongside Butz's Garage until the garage was destroyed by fire. The restaurant building was taken for the proposed Tocks Island Dam project and was later demolished.

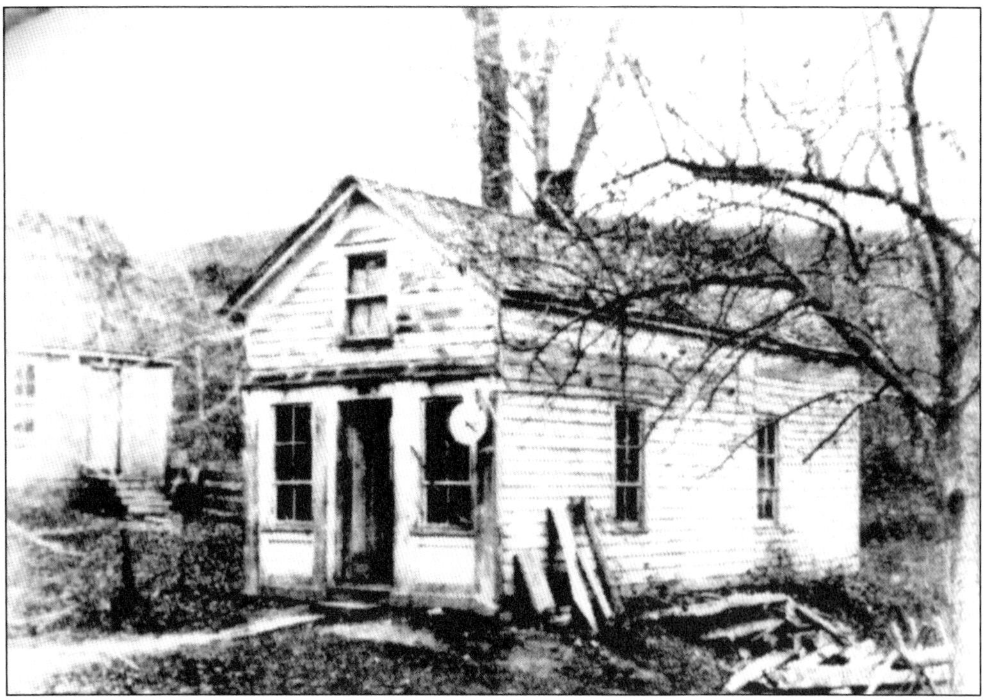

It was rare to find a watchmaker's shop in a small village such as Bushkill, but one reportedly existed after, and perhaps before, the Civil War. Gabriel Layton noted in his diary in the 1860s that he "went to Bushkill and left my watch with C. Custard to be repaired." Many years later, Moses Abel repaired watches in this watchmaker's shop on the Maple Grove side of Bushkill.

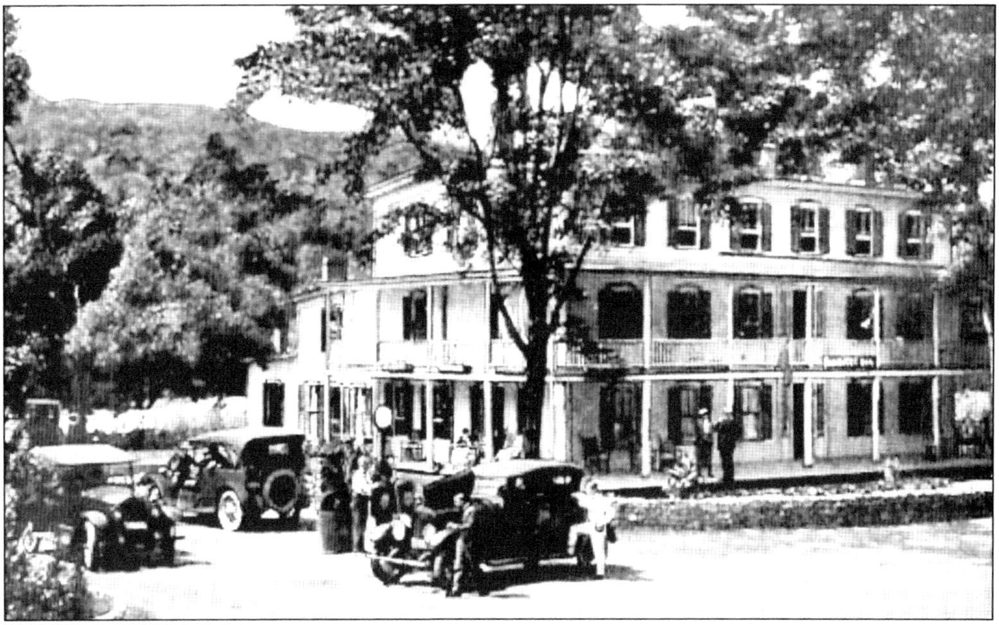

The Maple Grove, owned by J. H. Place, stood on the Big Bushkill Creek. He also owned the gristmill behind it. A swing bridge crossed the creek, with one end attached to the mill and the other to a buttonwood tree along the creek road. In 1912, Joseph C. Kennedy took ownership of the hotel and renamed it the Bushkill Inn. He advertised the inn as being convenient for auto parties.

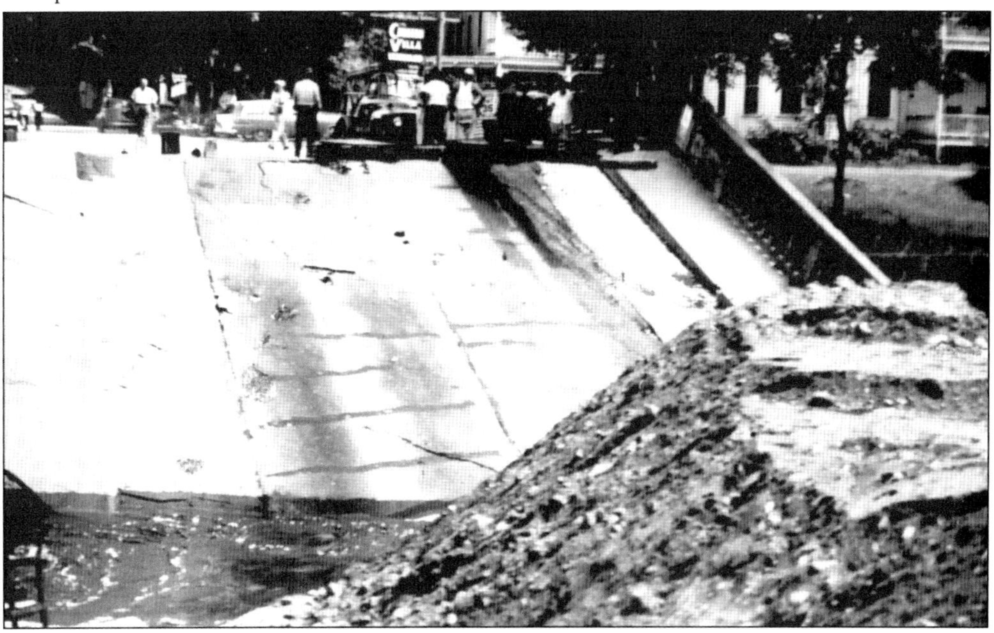

The flood of 1955 created havoc along the Big Bushkill Creek, backing water up to some buildings, buckling the roadway along Route 209, and destroying the bridge. However, the damage was minimal, considering the destruction and loss of life in nearby areas. Note that beyond the bridge, the Peters House had been renamed Country Villa, then operated by the Friedman brothers.

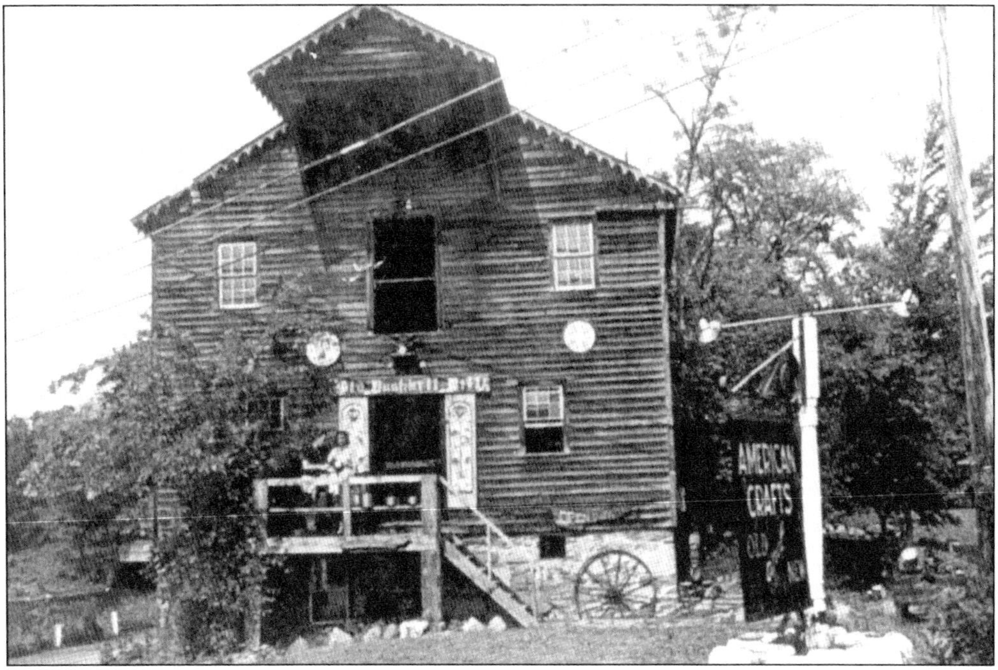

The old gristmill stood close to where Route 209 intersects with Creek Road. Colonial records and old maps point to this as the site where Manuel Gonzalez first built a mill. Henry Peters later erected a gristmill on the site. In more recent years, the mill served as a recreation center and craft shop. Following the Tocks Island Dam proposal, it was destroyed by a fire.

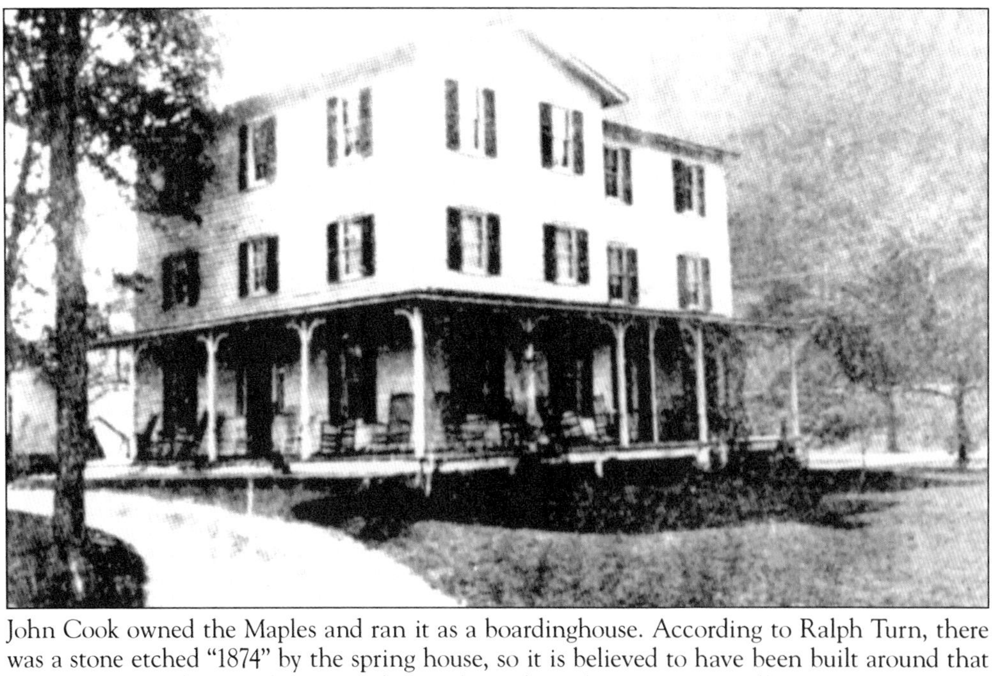

John Cook owned the Maples and ran it as a boardinghouse. According to Ralph Turn, there was a stone etched "1874" by the spring house, so it is believed to have been built around that time. Cook also bought the Riverside Hotel at a later date. His son William was a partner of Cook and Turn's General Store.

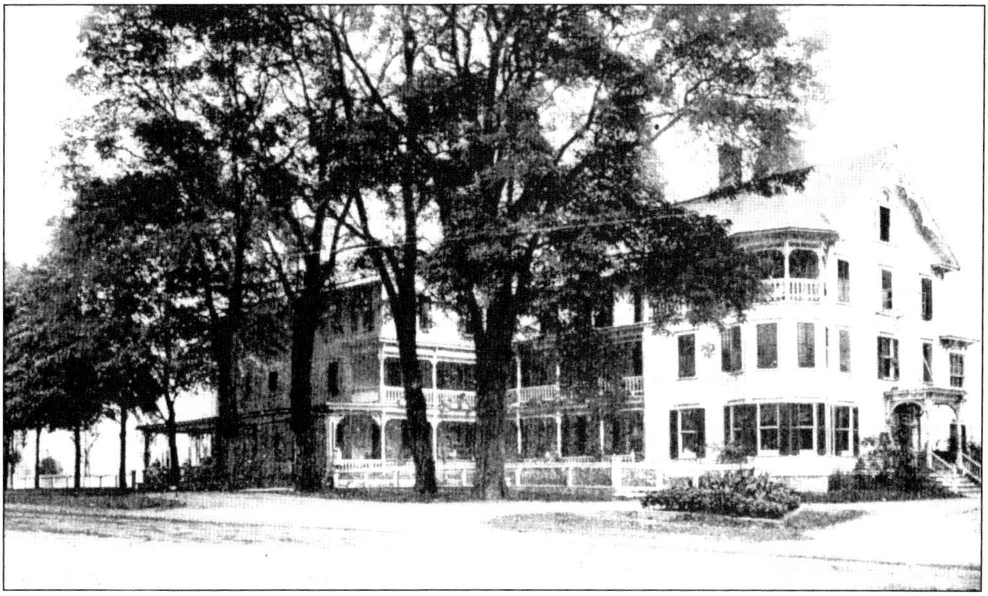

The Peters House was built on the site of one of the earliest known residences of Bushkill. Manuel Gonzalez lived in a log house, where he operated a public house as early as 1750. Israel Bensley stayed there a while, and John Heller later suspended a sign with a brown jug advertising his tavern. In 1860, Charles R. Peters built a new hotel on the site.

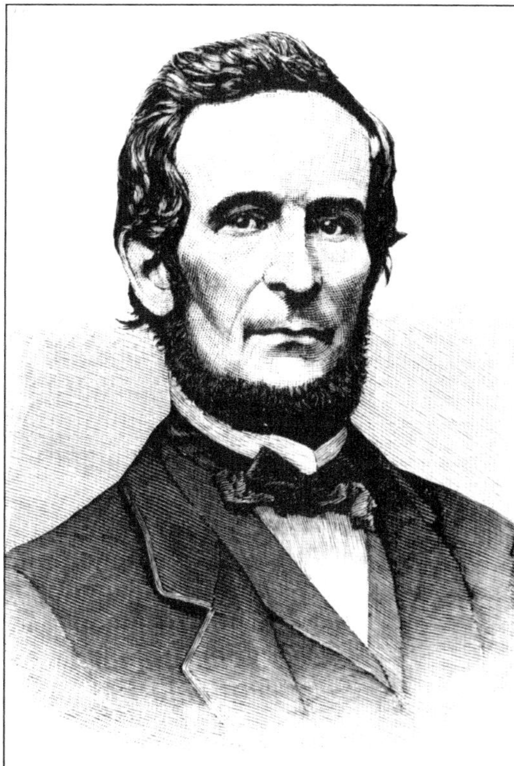

CHARLES R. PETERS.

Charles R. Peters (1822–1867) married Elizabeth Coolbaugh, whose father owned much of the land in Bushkill. He was the son of Henry Peters (1787–1857) and Sarah Gonzalez (or Gunsaules, as it was sometimes spelled) Peters, granddaughter of the original pioneer. As witnessed by the dates, Charles lived only seven more years after he built the Peters House. His widow operated it until descendants took over.

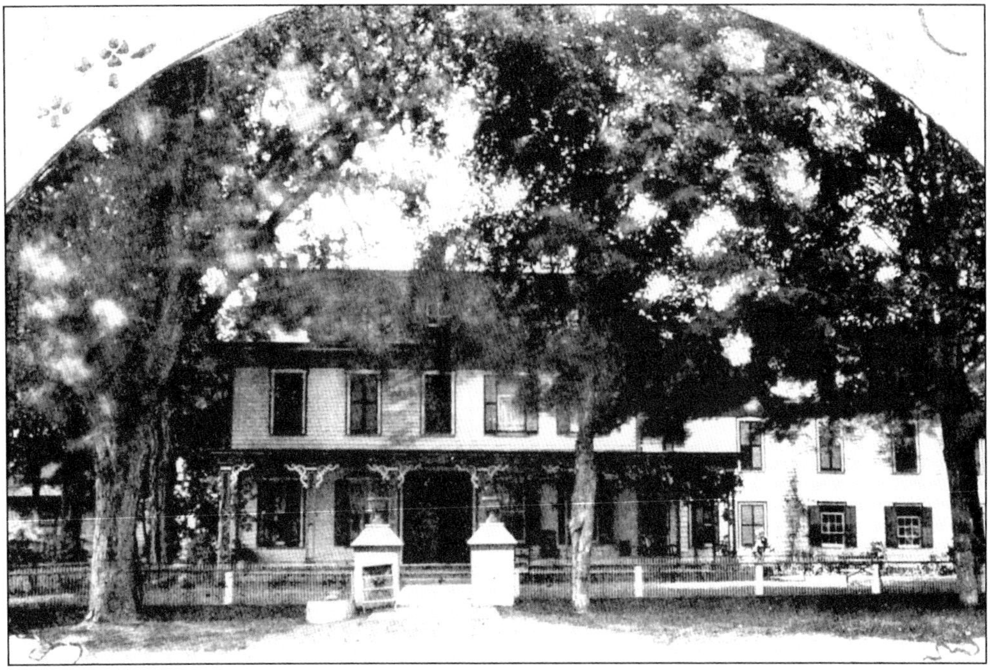

The Gonzalez House, built in 1874, stood directly across from the Peters House. Samuel G. Peters, brother of Charles, who built the Peters House, was its proprietor. In 1857, Samuel became postmaster, succeeding his father, who had served as Bushkill's first postmaster.

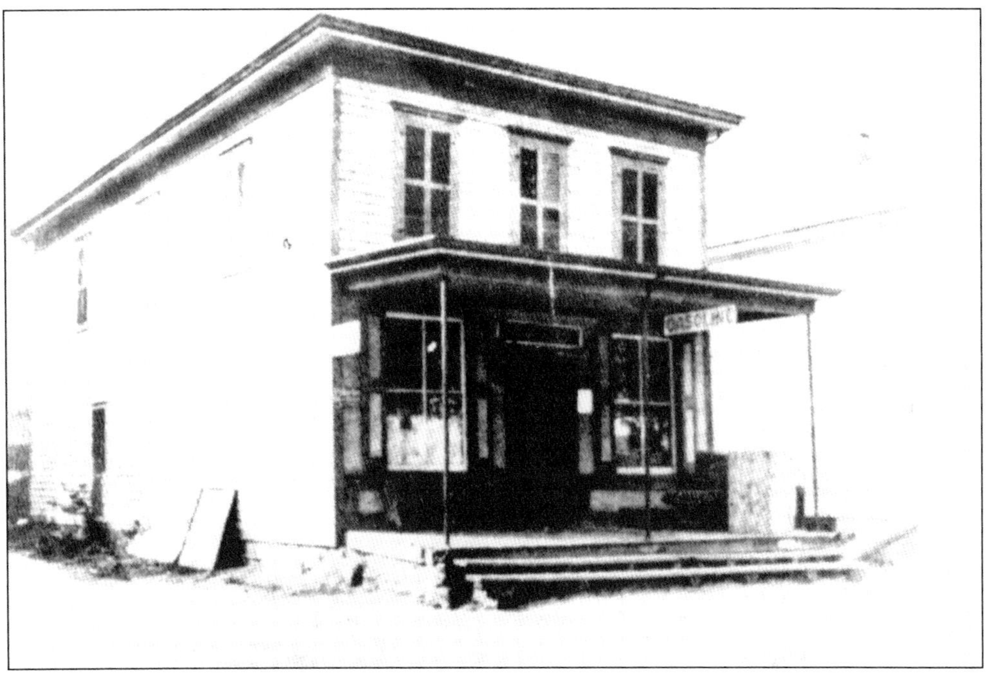

The first store where Turn's store later stood was built in 1831. It was owned by Nyce and Westbrook and operated as a trading post. The building was moved to the rear by horses and a chain-drive Mack truck when Cook and Turn took over the store.

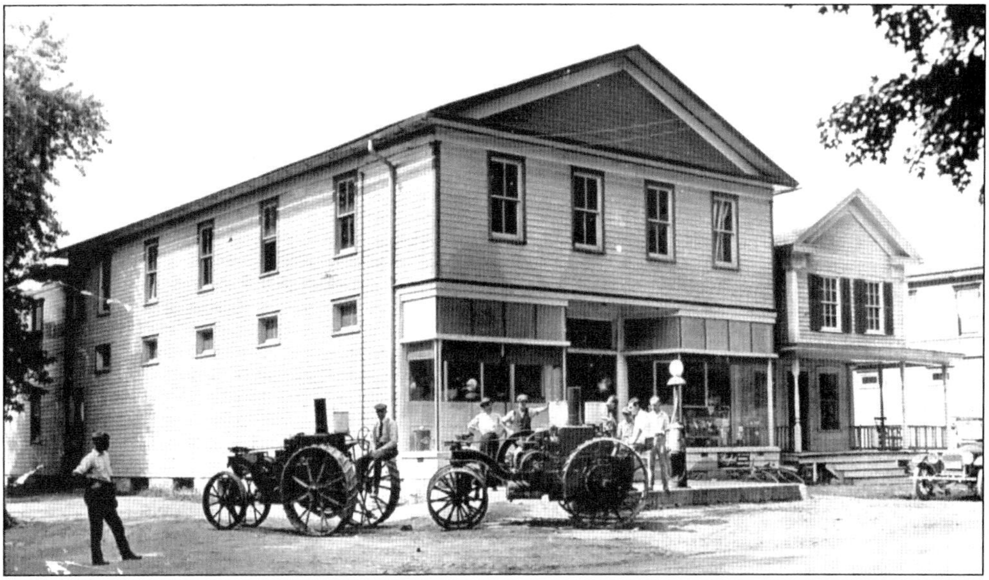

William Cook and Ralph Turn Sr. created a partnership and developed Cook and Turn's General Store, built in 1916 by Carl Werry. Seen here are the first tractors in Bushkill. Joe Nyce sits on the tractor closest to the bridge, and Ralph Turn Sr. is on the one closest to the tinsmith shop to the right of the store. Ralph Turn Jr. sold the store in 1990. (Photograph courtesy of Katherine Angle.)

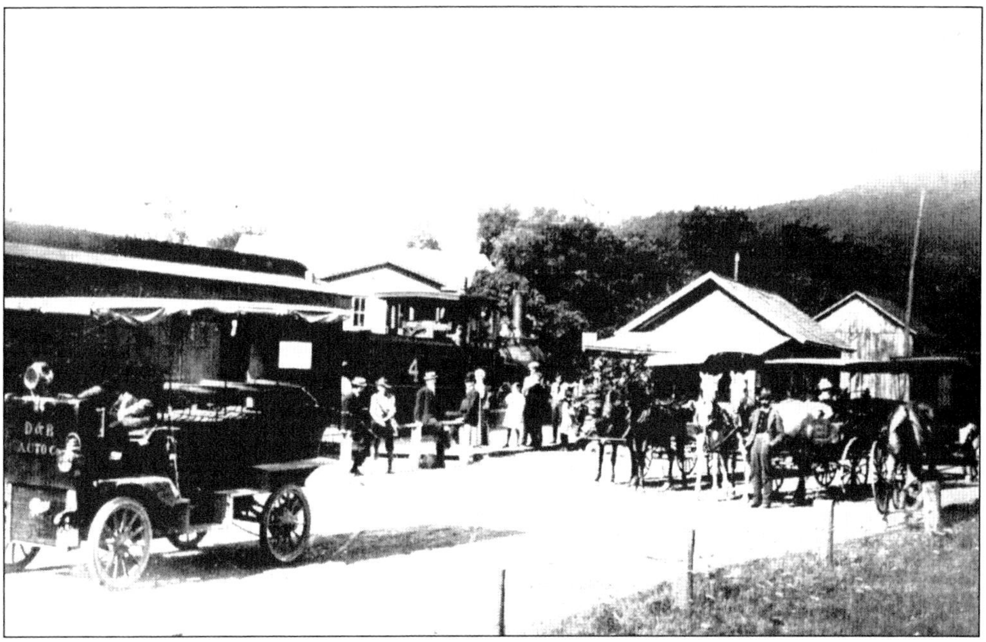

Tourists and locals alike awaited the train at the Delaware Valley Railroad Depot in Bushkill. Developed by Milton Yetter, East Stroudsburg industrialist, the railroad transported passengers and cargo. Since the East Stroudsburg station had no turntable, the train had to back up all the way to Bushkill. It carried passengers from 1901 to 1929. The railroad discontinued ice freight service in 1938, completely closing.

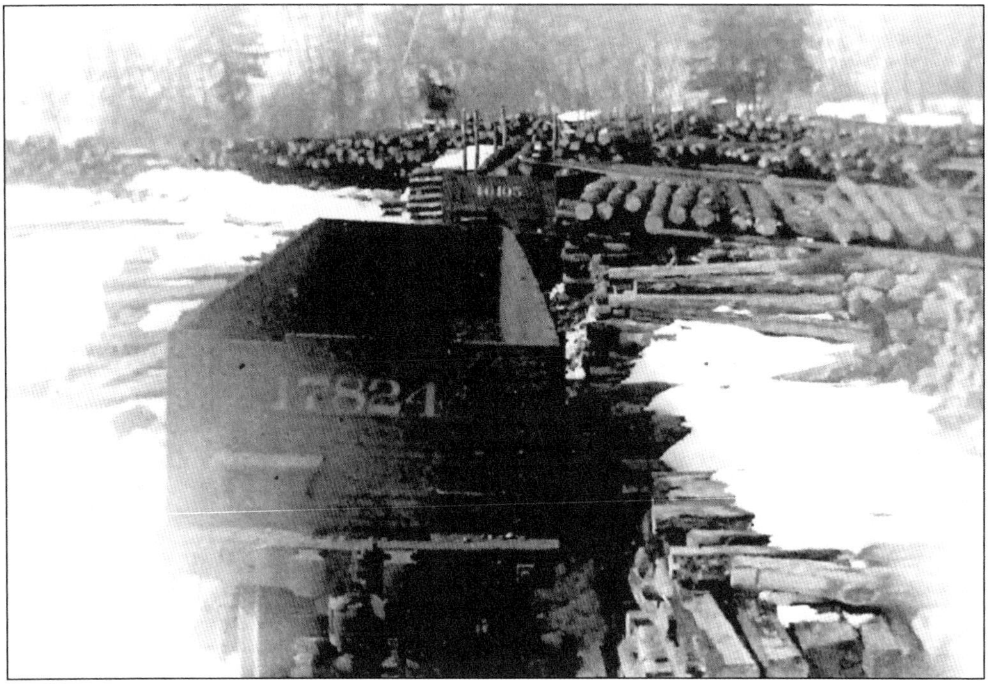

Behind Cook and Turn's General Store, log rafts stand ready for shipment. In the height of logging days, four or five loading docks stood ready. The timber collected from the forests was called "Pike County currency," for the barter system was common then. Cook and Turn's offered goods in exchange for the logs that would be converted into railroad ties or mine props. (Photograph courtesy of Katie Angle.)

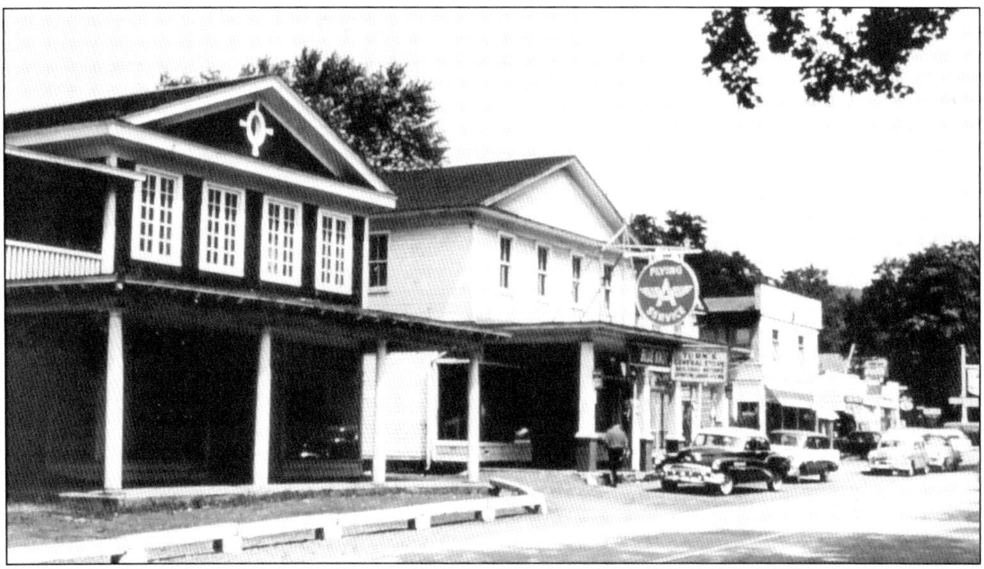

In this view looking north on Route 209, the dark building on the left is the Annex, which once held an A&P and other stores following that. The second floor served as a recreation hall. Next to that building is the Cook and Turn store, a smaller building that was once a tinsmith's shop, Rick DePue's Bar, Kessler's Soda Fountain, and a gas station on the corner. Today, only the general store and the tinsmith shop remain.

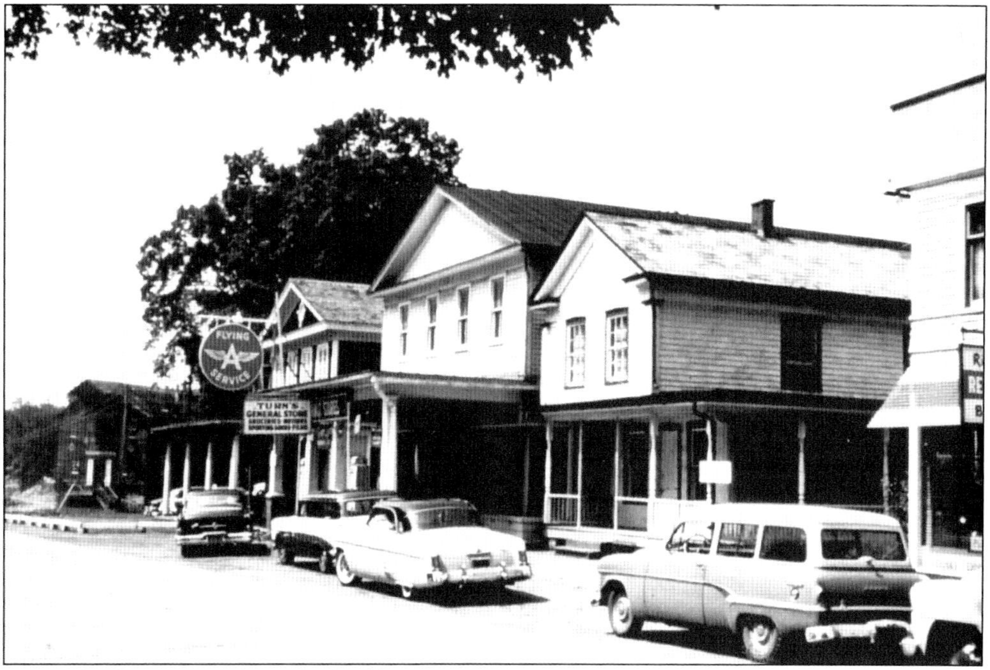

A view looking south shows the buildings in greater detail. On the far right, there is a glimpse of Depue's Bar and Restaurant, followed by the tinsmith shop, Turn's, the Annex, and the old mill. Most of these buildings were bulldozed in the 1970s for the Tocks Island Dam project, except for the historic old mill, which was destroyed by fire.

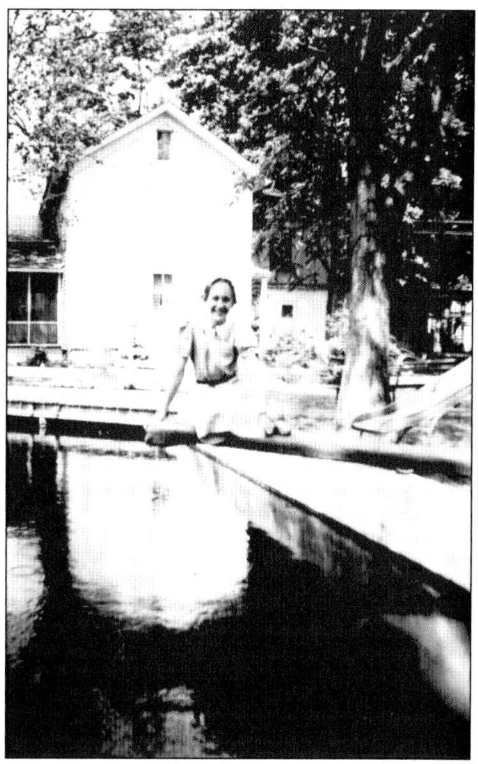

Rita Schoonover enjoyed swimming in the old millpond behind Turn's, as did many others. It provided year-round recreation. In winter, groups of people would have ice-skating parties on the frozen pool, often building a nearby bonfire and toasting hot dogs and marshmallows. The A&P store can be seen in the right background. (Photograph courtesy of Rita Laubner.)

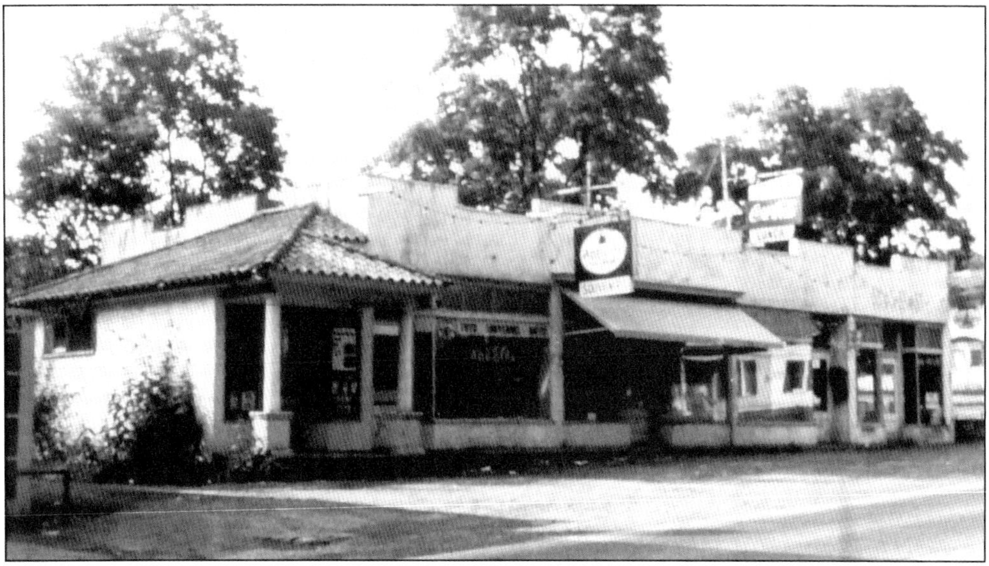

Stephen "Lefty" Barr operated Kessler's Soda Fountain and Gift Shop, a popular tourist attraction. With its fountain, jukebox, and pinball machines, it also became a favorite teenage hangout in the 1950s. Lefty was a son-in-law of Julius and Alice Kessler, who also owned an adjacent bar, which they sold to Rick DePue. It is shown here in its declining years after being taken by eminent domain for the Tocks project.

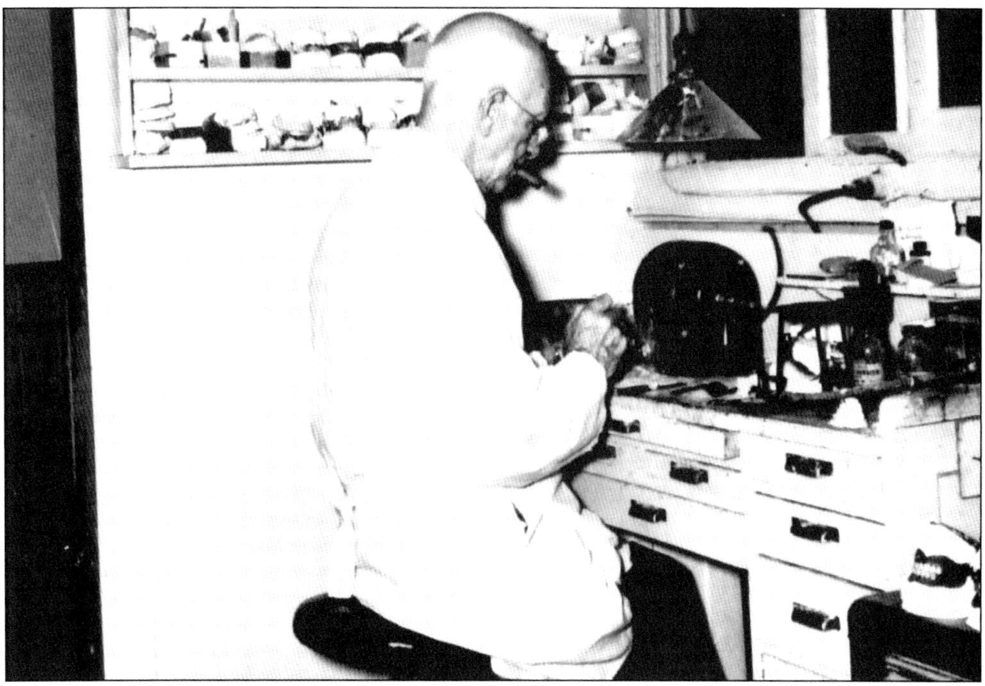

Robert B. Irwin, Bushkill's resident dentist, is shown enjoying a cigar in his dentist's office in Bushkill. Irwin graduated from the Baltimore School of Dentistry in 1902. After serving as postmaster of Nichols, New York, from 1912 to 1916, he traveled by horseback to the Stroudsburg area and opened up a dentist's office. He practiced dentistry in Pennsylvania for 50 years, with 30 of those years being in Bushkill. (Photograph courtesy of Russell Irwin.)

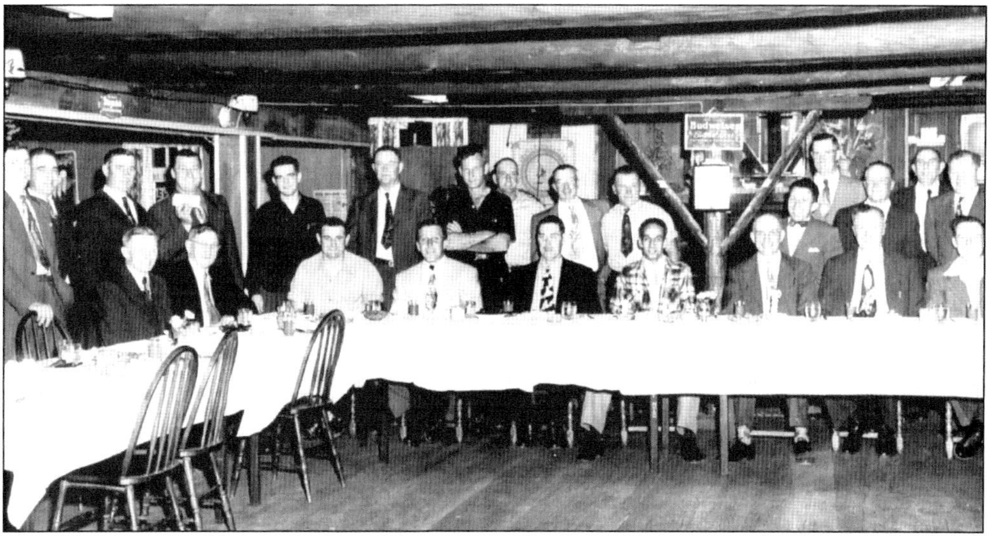

Pictured are members of Bushkill's Bowling League at Shafer's Inn, on Route 209. From left to right are (seated) Frank Butz, Ralph Turn Sr., Ralph Stettler, Alvin DeWitt Jr., Paul Depue, Louis Lee, Sterling Schoonover, Tilghman Courtright, and unidentified; (standing) Irvin Smith, Philip Angle, Albert Howey, Ernest Booth, Lester Litts, William Schoonover, Amos Booth, John Myers, Harold Riedmiller, Thomas Walters, Joe Kulick, Bob Reidmiller, Franklin Riedmiller, Chet Strunk, and Paul Courtright. (Photograph courtesy of Helen Sirola.)

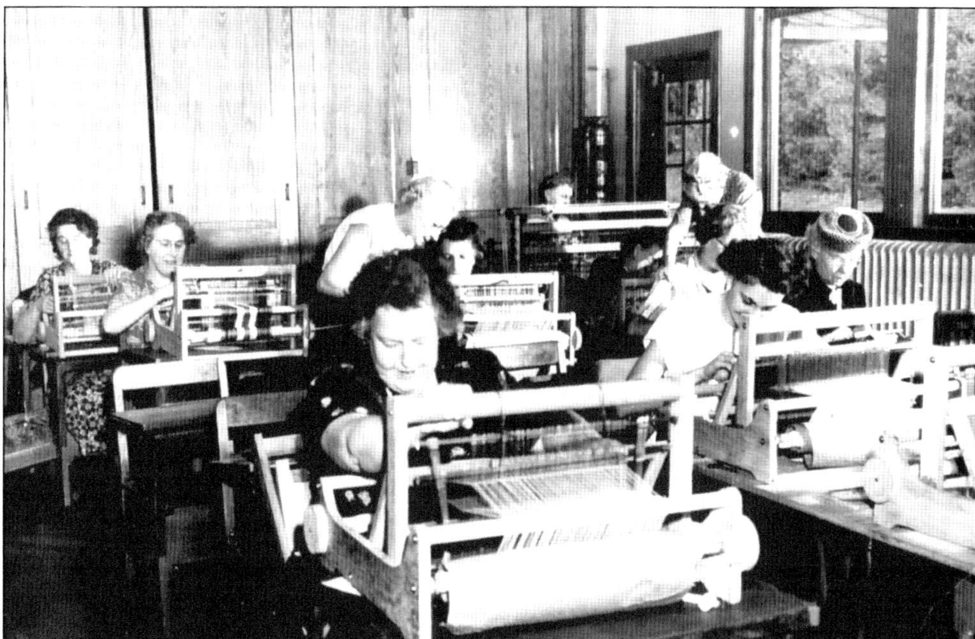

The Bushkill ladies kept alive the art of weaving by passing on their knowledge to younger generations. Harold Riedmiller built the looms for their classes. Pictured at the Bushkill School are, from left to right, the following: (first row) Marguerite Riedmiller, Rita Schoonover, and Mary Frances Riedmiller; (second row) Bess Miller, Margaret Kerr, Frances Irwin (bending over Mary Kutay), Mary Turn (in right corner), Eleanor Bartram (bending over Bertha Gierend, partially hidden), and Delores Depue (partially hidden). (Photograph courtesy of Katie Angle.)

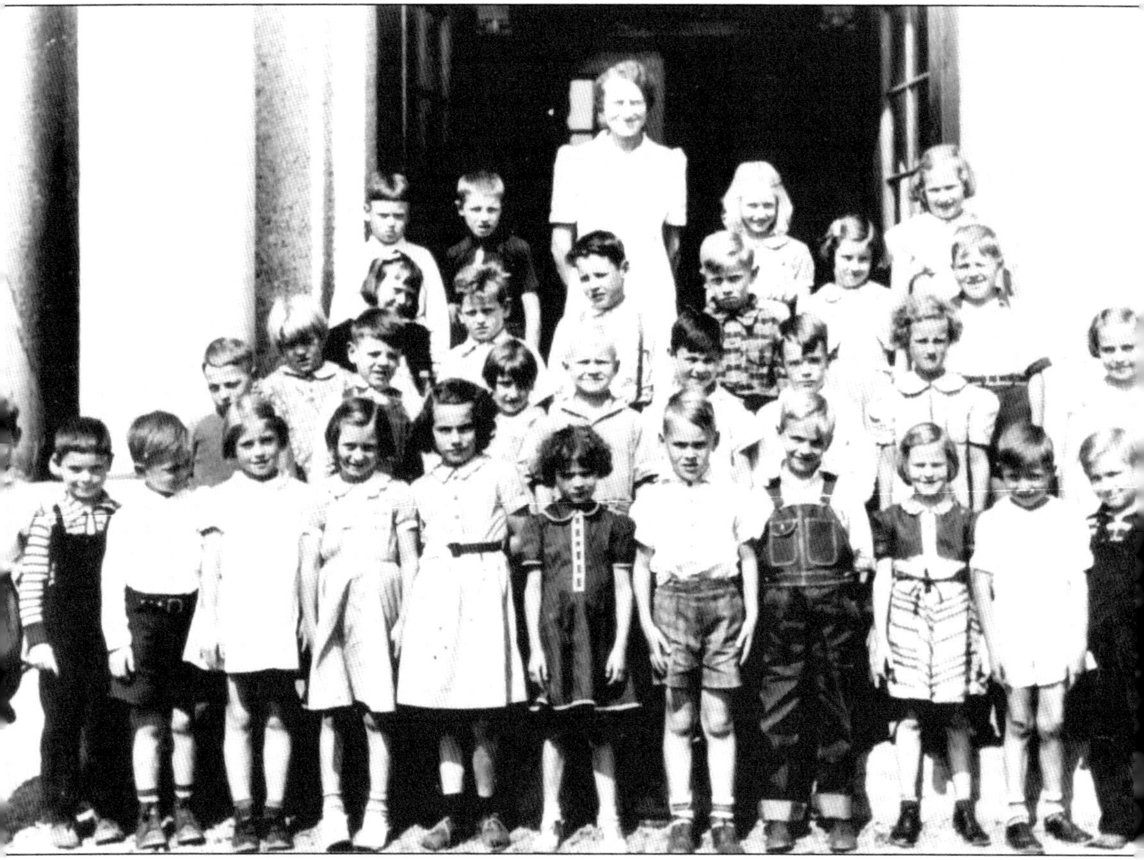

Students at the Bushkill School pose around 1940. Included in the photograph are William Bogart, Albert (Buster) Howey, Arthur Garris, Julia Garris, Freda Howey, Mildred Whittaker, Florence Schoonover, James Seese, Kenneth Dickison, Kathryn Riedmiller, Jack Whittaker, Sherman Schoonover, Richard Dickison, Shirley Fish, Irvin Hineline, Jean Myers, "Buzz" Vanermay, Raymond Steele, Thomas Dowling, Janet Schoonover, Josie Arnst, Margaret Vallershamp, John Riedmiller, Howard Dippre, Lester Bensley, Doris Dippre, Richard Butz, Delores Rouzer, and Mary Arnst. The teacher is Miss Haffling.

Seven

UP THE FOREST PARK ROAD

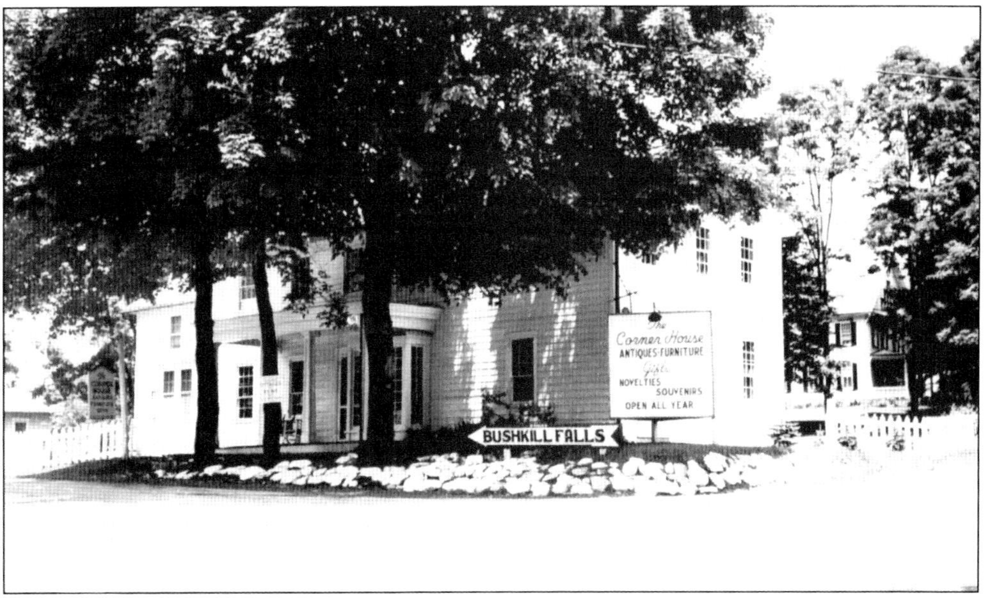

The Corner House offered many uses over the years, operating as Hollyhock Tea House and the Corner Gift Shop, as examples. The building's original section is believed to have been built in 1746. The two-story building has a fieldstone foundation. It stands as one of the few structures remaining in Bushkill in the years following the now defunct Tocks Island Dam proposal. The building lies on the north side of the road originally called the Forest Park Road and later renamed the Bushkill Falls Road. From this point close to river level, the road begins its winding course. At the point where the Sugar Mountain Road meets it, the main road follows a sinuous trail up the hill along the Little Bushkill Creek and rapidly ascends to about 1,200 feet in the Pine Ridge and Tamiment area.

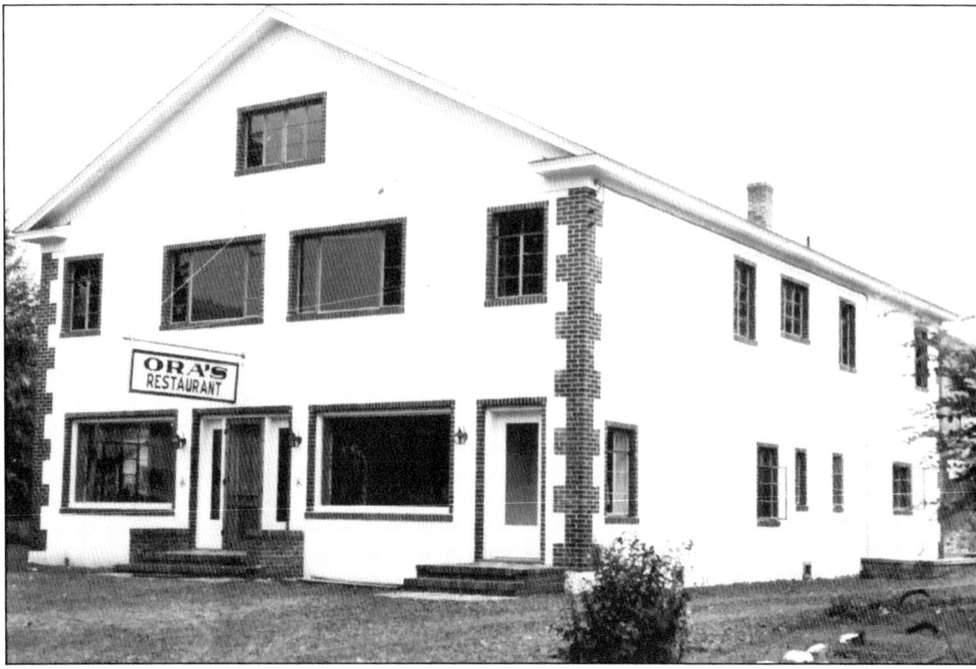

Ora Scheller's restaurant stood on the same side of the road as the Corner House, about the fifth building up from the blinker light. She operated the restaurant from 1948 to 1952. After that, various other businesses occupied the building. The building was leveled after the federal government acquired it for the Tocks Island Dam project.

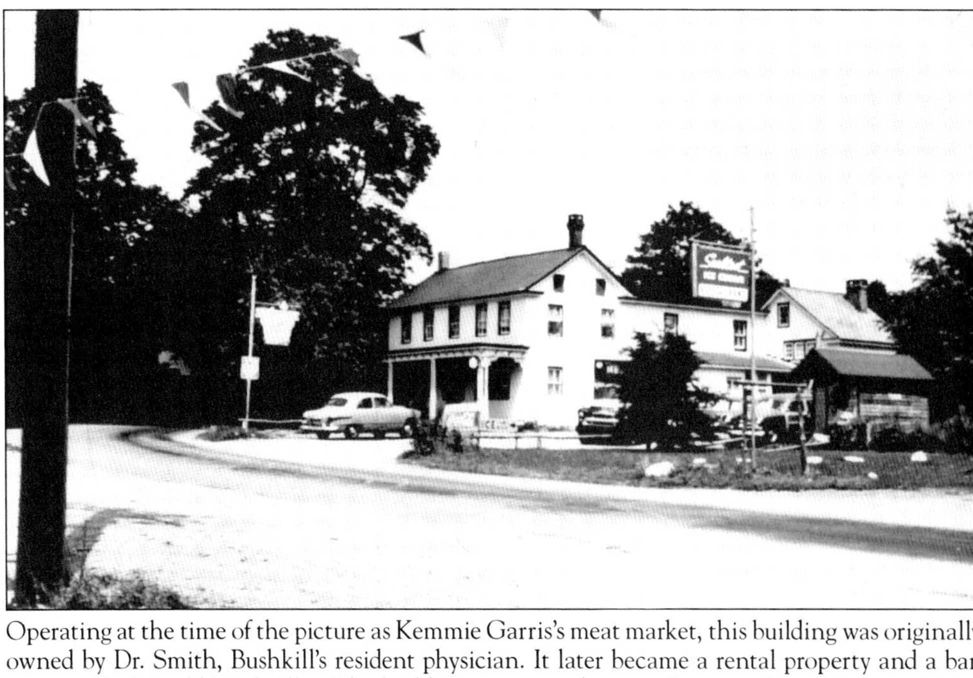

Operating at the time of the picture as Kemmie Garris's meat market, this building was originally owned by Dr. Smith, Bushkill's resident physician. It later became a rental property and a bar, operated by Harold Riedmiller. The building once stood across the street from Carpenter's Bar and the former post office, which still stands. This property was razed for the Tocks project.

Schlaefer's Bakery stood several doors down from the firehouse and five buildings from the corner store. Pictured are Mr. and Mrs. Fred Schlaefer. Kemmie Garris and Andy Lewis had a meat market there in the 1950s. It was seized by the government for the Tocks project and was demolished. (Photograph courtesy of Kemmie Garris.)

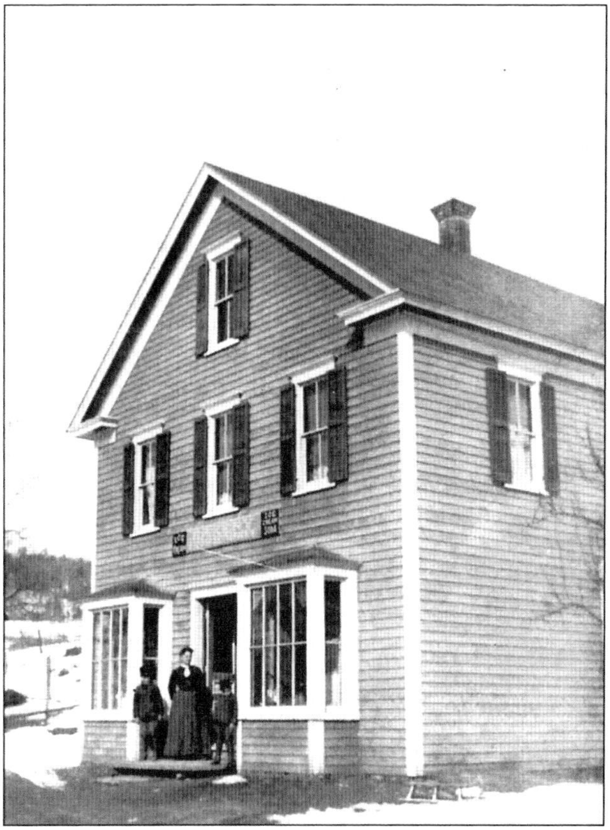

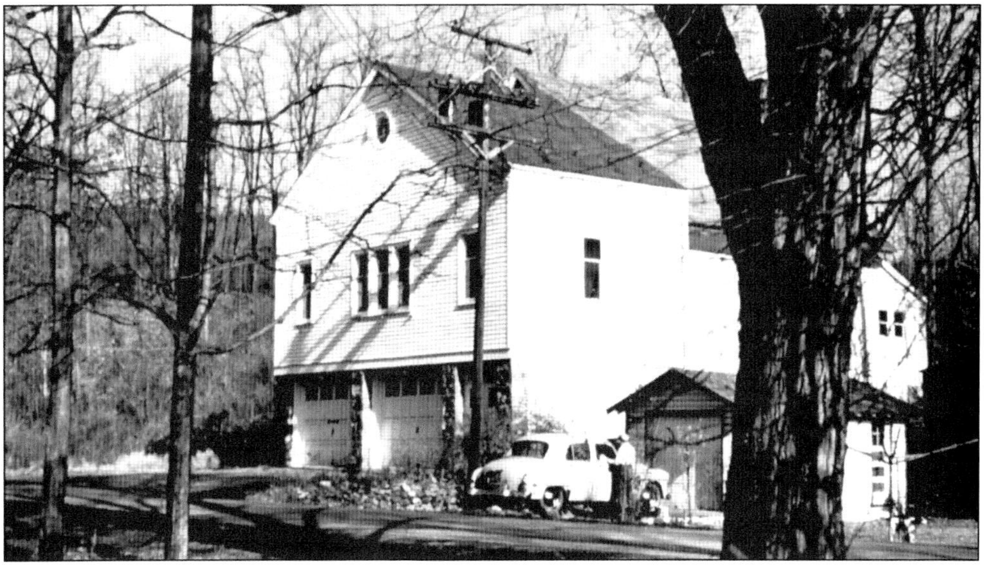

The old Bushkill firehouse has served many purposes over the years. When the Pine Ridge Church near Bushkill Falls ceased to operate, the building was moved down the hill and placed in this location, where in 1923 it served as a school. The old church was later raised up and built underneath to become the firehouse. Today it serves as one of the park service's administrative buildings.

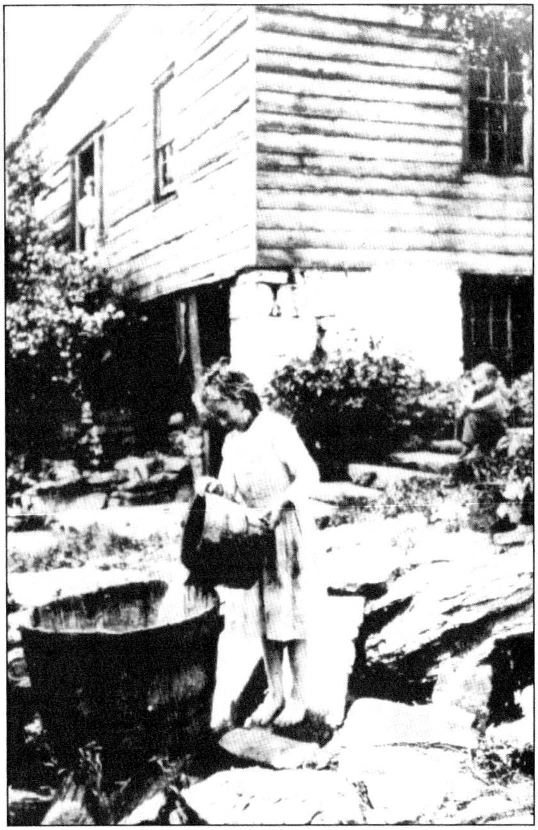

Josephine Smith is pictured pouring a bucket of water from the running water source on her right. G. Newman Smith, sitting on the stone steps nearby, was killed in action in World War I. Known as the Smith and Costello House, the building is one of the oldest in the county, originally owned by David Smith, a War of 1812 veteran. The house has been placed on the National Register of Historic Places.

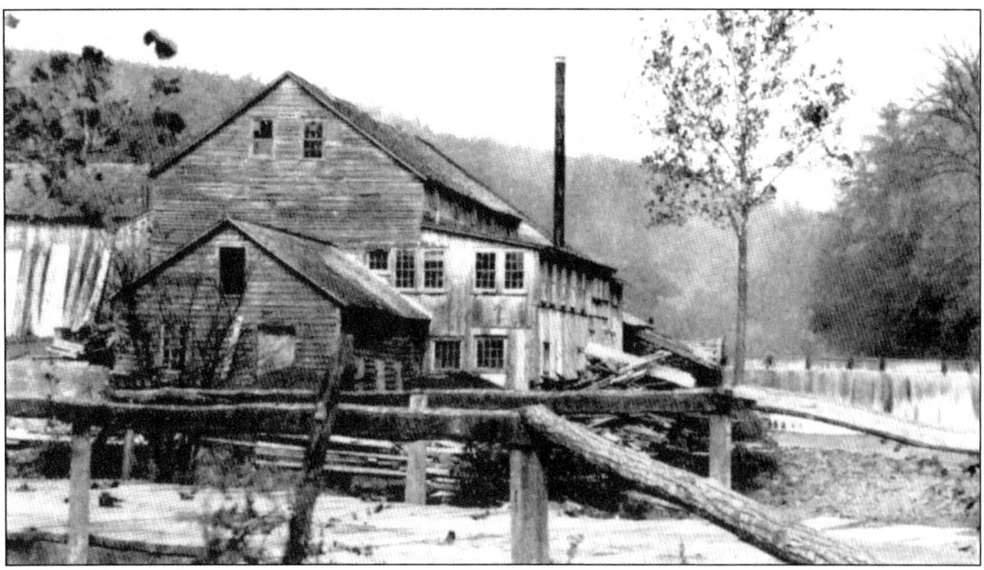

John Heller built this tannery on the Little Bushkill Creek at the juncture of the road leading up to Sugar Mountain. Here he tanned leather by using the oak tanning process. In 1880, Frank Denegri purchased the property, fully operating it with 20 vats. Later purchased by Mr. Hemingway, the building was then converted to a sawmill and cider press. The artist Frank Schoonover kept a studio on one of its levels. (Photograph courtesy of PCHA.)

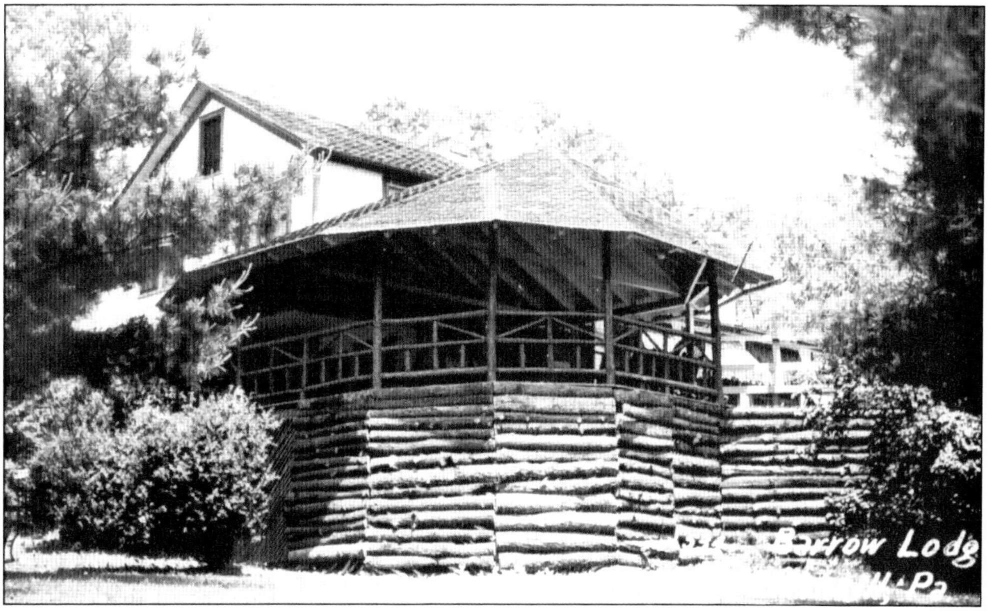

Samuel Press opened his Bushkill View Camp as a youth hostel. Across the road and down a small hill, the Work Projects Administration built a swimming pool in 1936, fed by a small spring and the Little Bushkill Creek. Morton and Ruth Barrow purchased the property in 1948, renaming it Barrow Lodge and adding two swimming pools near the main house. The resort closed in 1967, another casualty of the Tocks Island Dam project.

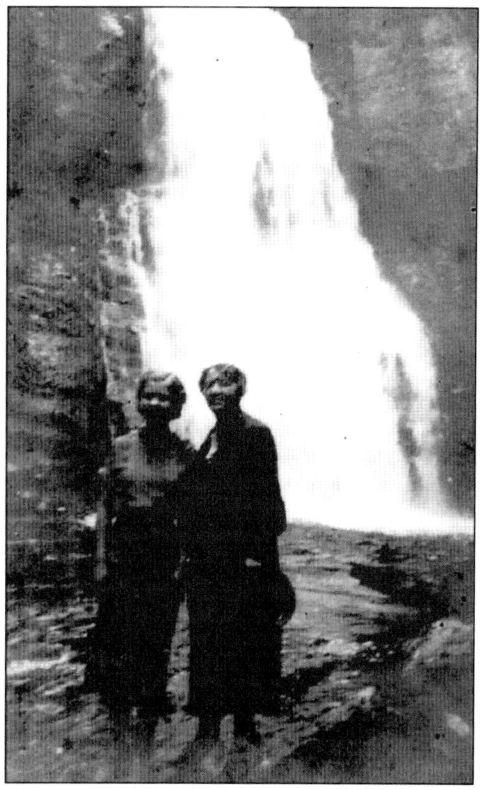

Riedmiller sisters, Rose and Elizabeth, are pictured before Bushkill Falls in this 1920s photograph. The falls had been a tourist attraction since the 1870s. The Peters family bought the falls and surrounding land at a public sale in 1882. Charles Peters, an astute businessman, further developed the falls in 1904, promoting it as the "Niagara of Pennsylvania." (Photograph courtesy of Katie Riedmiller Angle.)

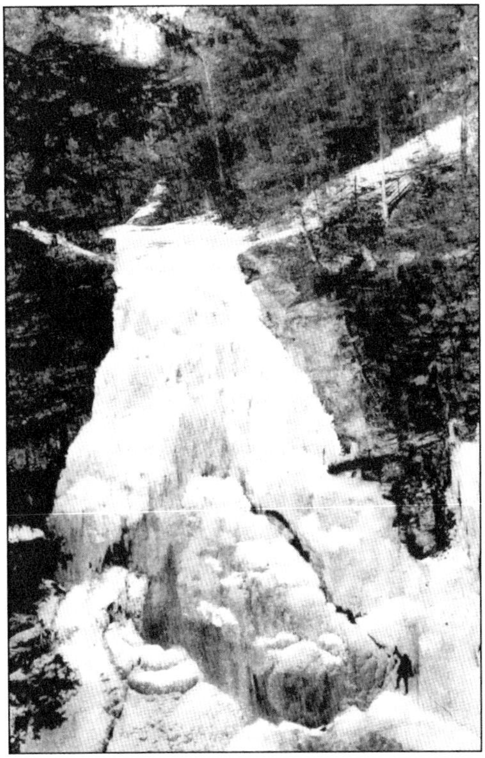

This view of the Bushkill Falls covered with an icy mantle presents an almost surreal picture. Evergreen trees of hemlock and rhododendron stand out in stark contrast to the glacial cascade. The rugged terrain surrounding the falls ices over as well. It must have been indeed a slippery slope for the photographer to follow in capturing this scene.

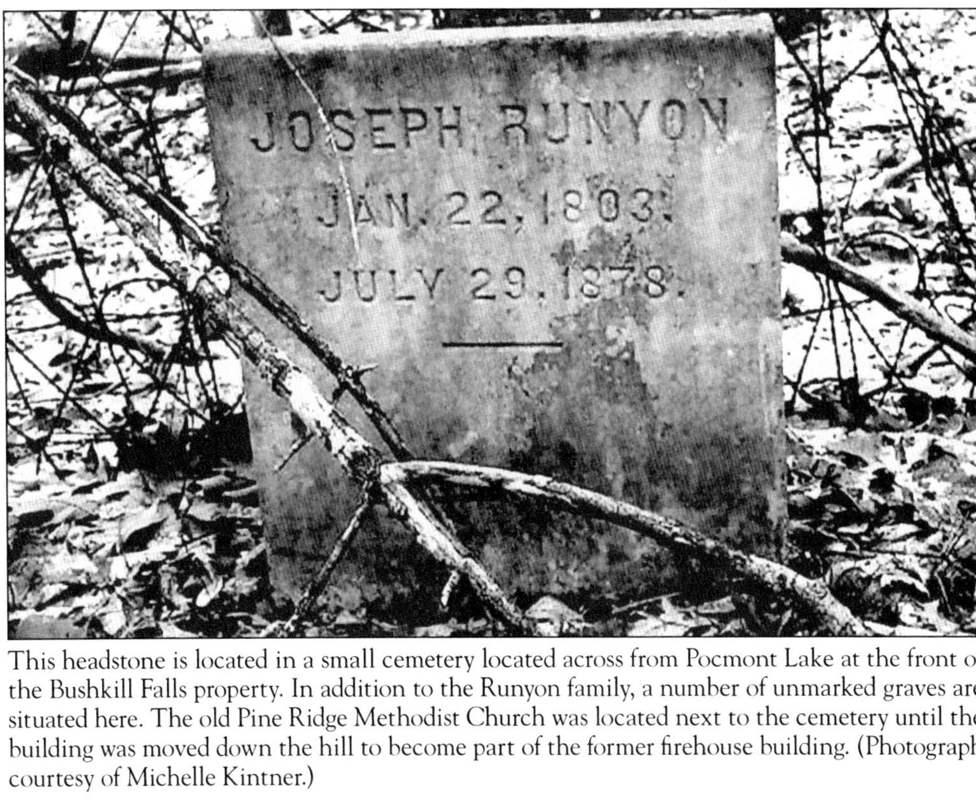

This headstone is located in a small cemetery located across from Pocmont Lake at the front of the Bushkill Falls property. In addition to the Runyon family, a number of unmarked graves are situated here. The old Pine Ridge Methodist Church was located next to the cemetery until the building was moved down the hill to become part of the former firehouse building. (Photograph courtesy of Michelle Kintner.)

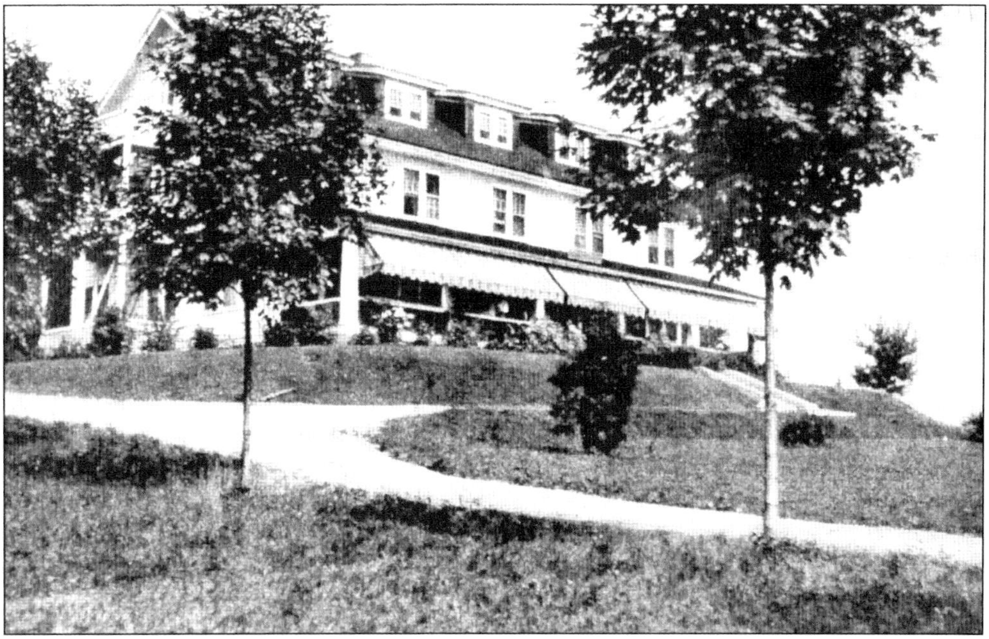

The Friedman brothers opened the Bushkill Falls House a short distance away from Bushkill Falls in the mid-1920s. They later operated the old Peters House in Bushkill under the name Country Villa.

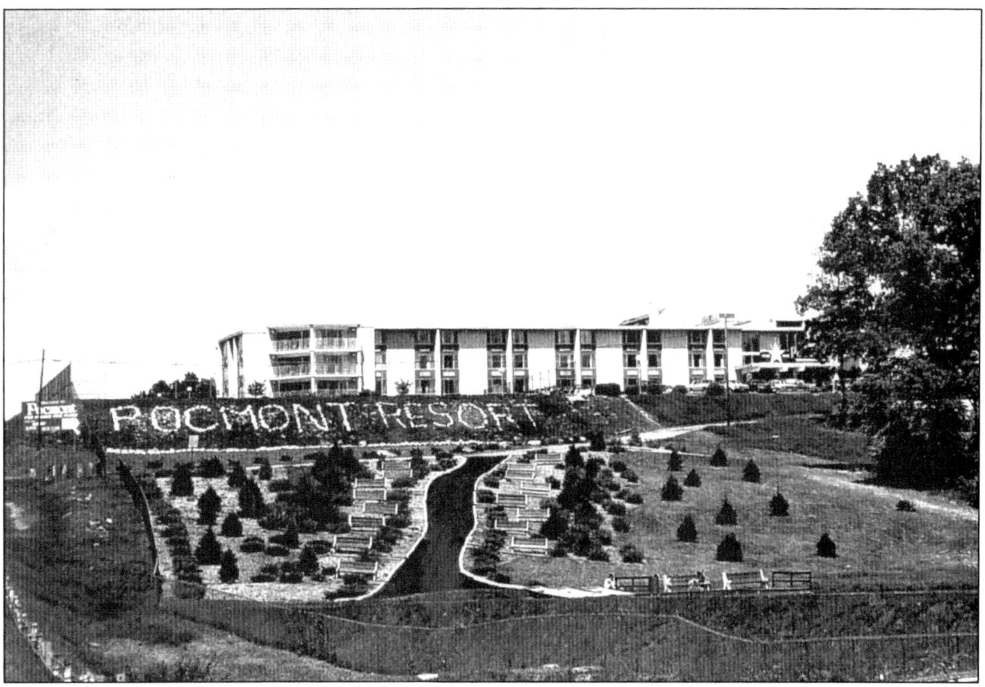

Darvey (Dave) Artzt, a former Atlantic City nightclub singer and beauty supply businessman, purchased Friedman's Bushkill Falls House in 1946 and renamed it Pocmont. He enlarged the main building and turned it into a larger resort. A March 1996 electrical fire destroyed most of the main building. It took over $11 million and over two years to rebuild it.

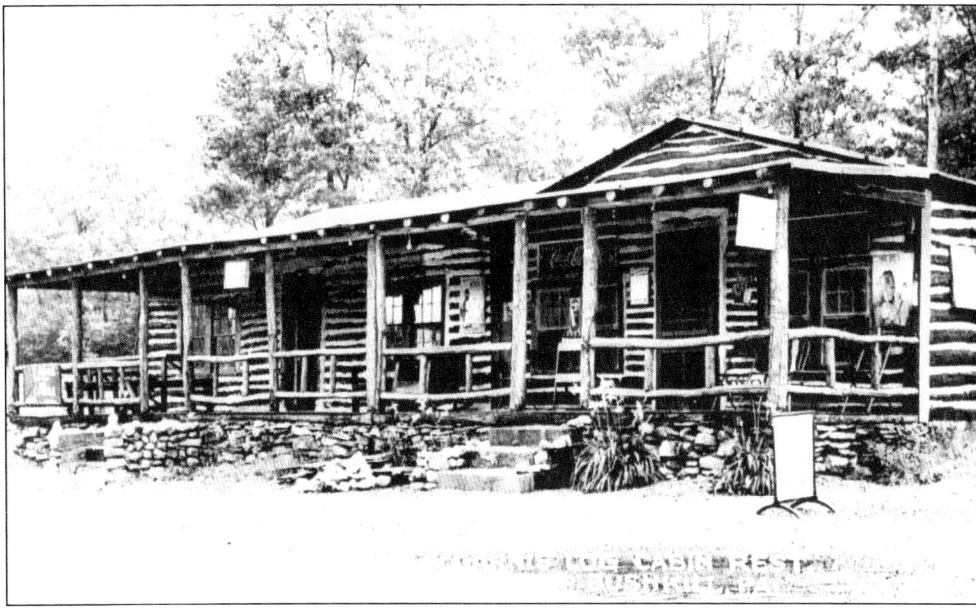

Upon his return from the U.S. Navy after World War II, Arthur Garris built this log tavern and restaurant. Surrounded by log cabins, its rustic charm attracted a host of clientele from all walks of life. The tavern and cabins were all constructed from trees hauled from the surrounding forest. Among other luminaries, actress Betty Garrett stayed here in the late 1940s. The main building was razed in 1983.

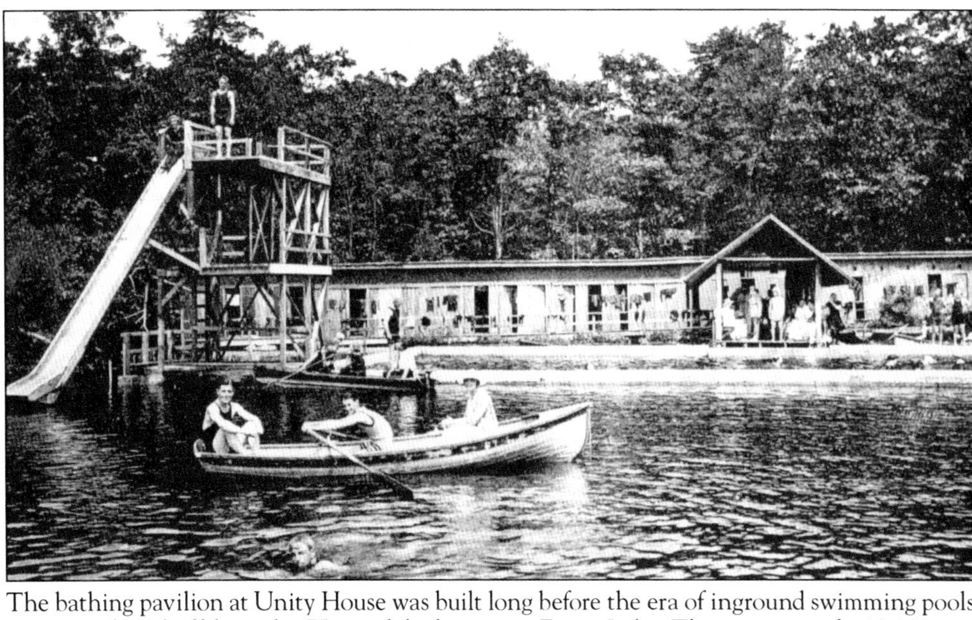

The bathing pavilion at Unity House was built long before the era of inground swimming pools. It was cordoned off from the 75-acre lake known as Forest Lake. This was part of a 12,000-acre tract of land purchased in 1892 by Mr. Otterheimer, later owned by Jacob Lederer, his son-in-law. Later purchased by the International Ladies Garment Workers Union, the property is now the Mountain Laurel Center for the Arts.

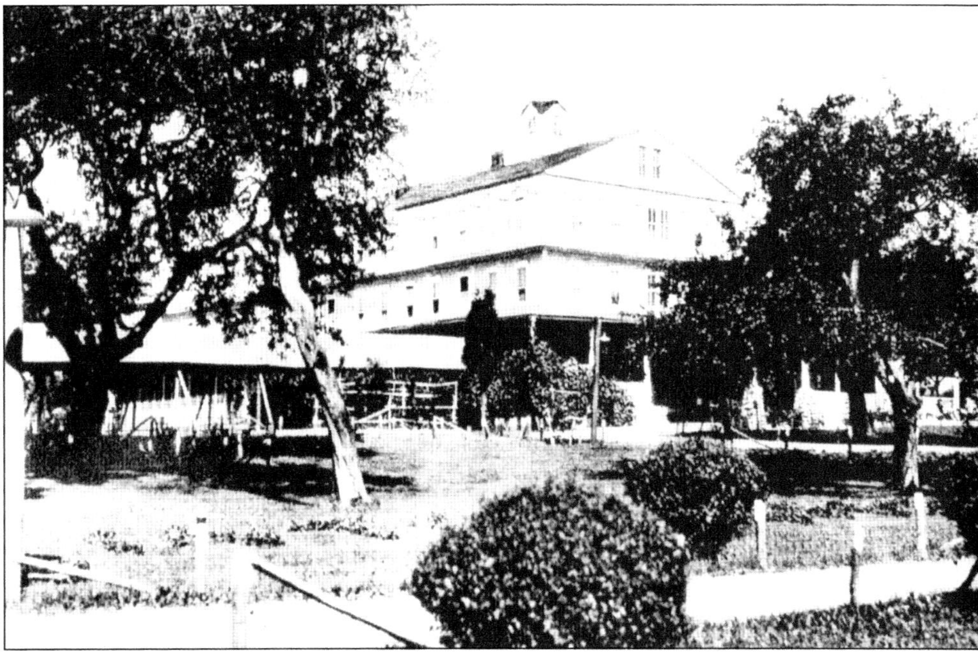

The main building at Unity House, seen in 1929, was part of a major 1919 purchase by two locals of the International Ladies Garment Workers Union from then owner Arthur Lederer. The locals later sold to the "International," which provided an affordable luxury vacation to its workers and their families. This main building burned in 1934, and a newer one replaced it.

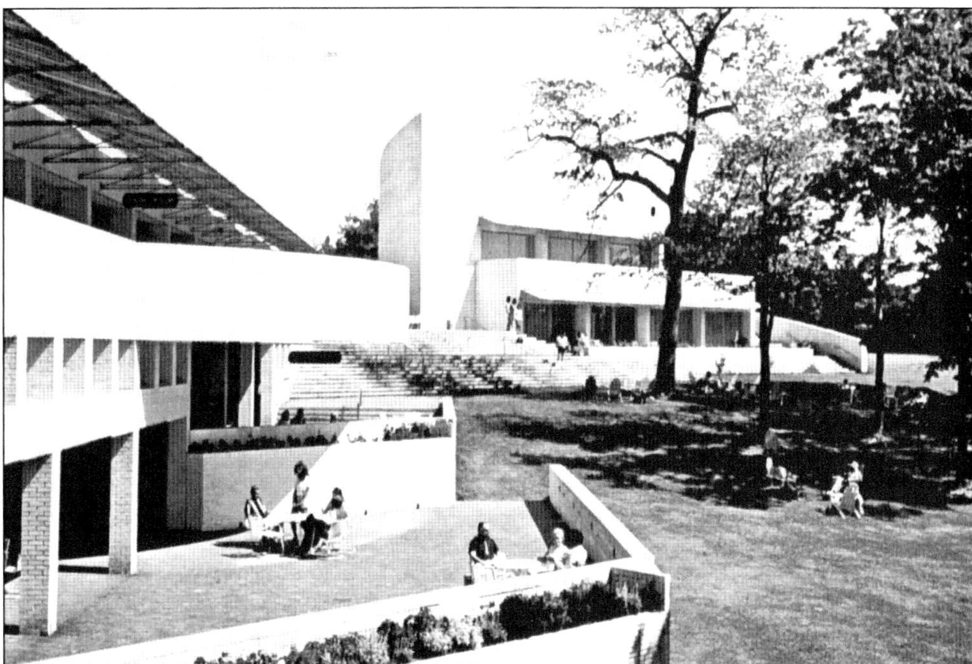

A new administration building replaced the main building lost in the 1934 fire and was in turn destroyed by a February 1969 fire, along with 13 Diego Rivera paintings donated by John D. Rockefeller. This new, ultramodern administration building was erected in place of the 1930s building.

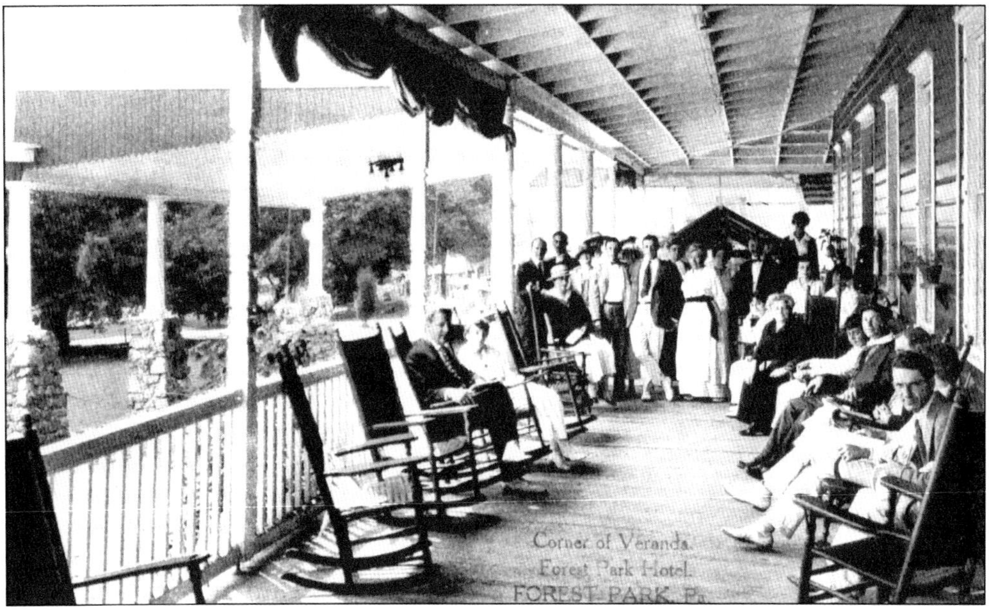

Guests of Forest Park lounge on the veranda of Forest Park, no doubt resting after a tasty dinner in the dining hall. Owner Arthur Lederer set a nice table, with filet mignon and spring duck offered, along with many other delicacies. Aside from lounging about the veranda, the resort provided many other amusements such as music, lawn bowling, billiards, cricket, boating, and archery.

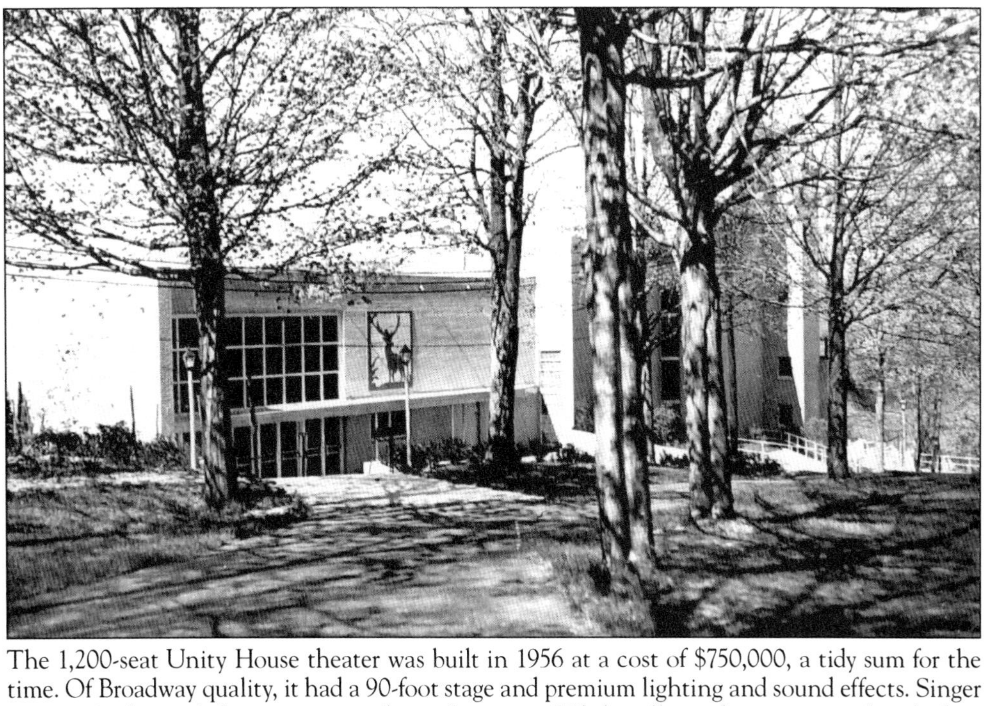

The 1,200-seat Unity House theater was built in 1956 at a cost of $750,000, a tidy sum for the time. Of Broadway quality, it had a 90-foot stage and premium lighting and sound effects. Singer Marian Anderson led its opening night performance. While still standing, it was replaced when the Mountain Laurel Center for the Performing Arts purchased the property and built the Tom Ridge Pavilion.

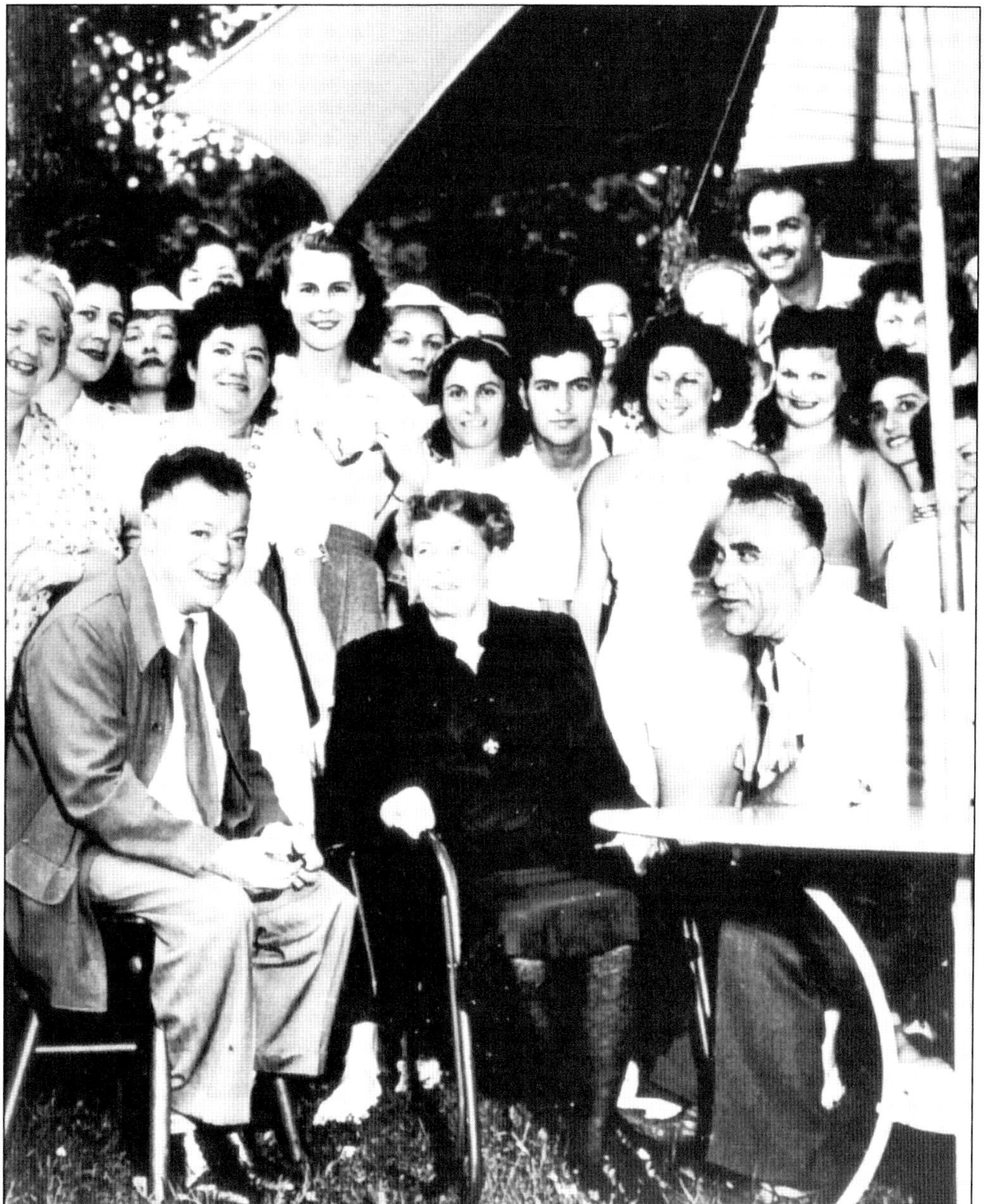

On June 15, 1945, recently widowed Eleanor Roosevelt paid a visit to Unity House. The occasion was a bond rally for the war effort. Of her visit she later wrote in her diary, "I want to speak of two things today which especially impressed me at the International Ladies' Garment Workers' Union vacation camp. It seemed to me worthy of comment that the bond drive rally was started by calling for contributions from individuals. As I sat there and saw young women and young men, fathers of families, older men and women, all get up one after the other and pledge to buy anything from a $100 bond up to a $1000 bond, I could not help thinking, 'Thank God for the United States.' The people of the United States, who work hard with their hands, who are now making enough to save and, at the same time, to help their country and their fighting men." (Photograph courtesy of Cornell University.)

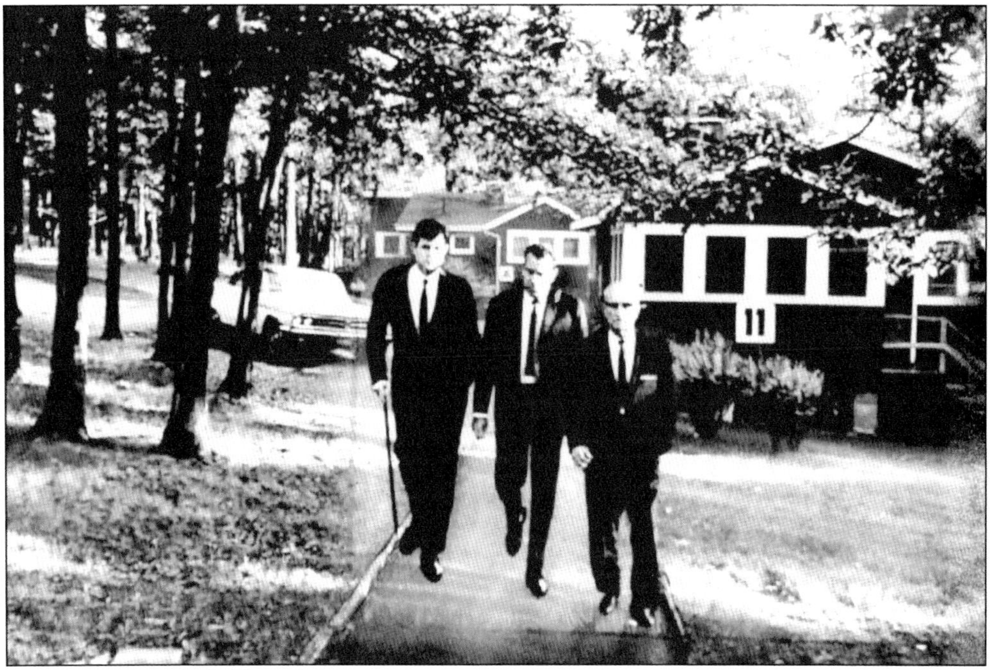

Sen. Ted Kennedy (left) paid a visit to Unity House on July 1, 1965. He is pictured here in front of one of the cottages with Sol C. Chaikin (center) and David Gingold.

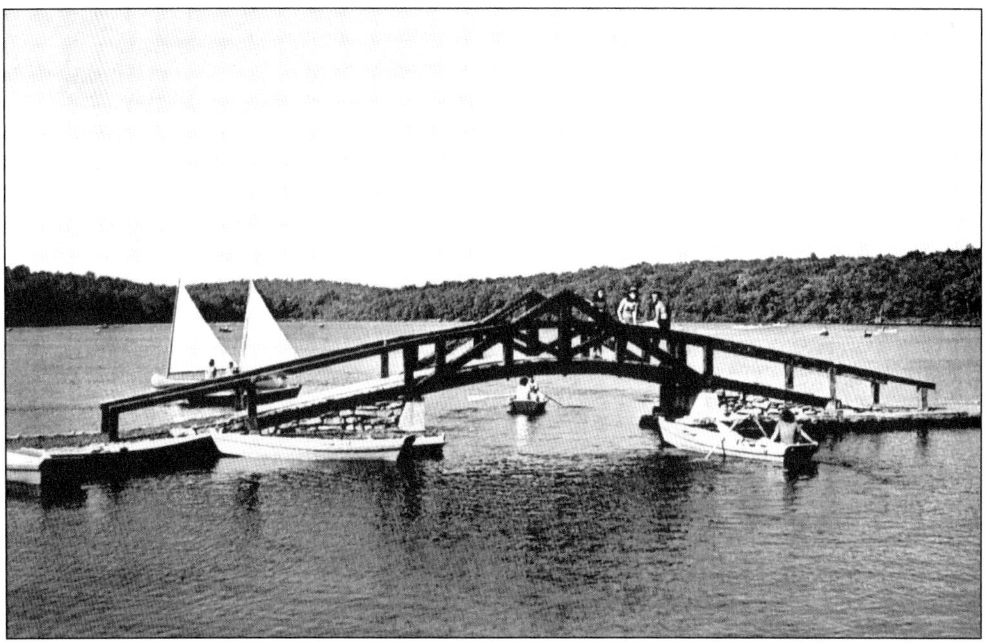

Tamiment Lake, with its solid rock bottom, covers 100 acres. Over the years, it has provided water recreation of all types—rowboating, powerboating, sailing, ice-skating, and ice-fishing. It was traditionally called the Second Pond or Tamiment Lake. When the People's Educational Camp Society, a socialist group, bought the property, it was named for the lake. Camp Tamiment opened on July 1, 1921.

The new Tamiment Playhouse was built by the Riedmiller family of Bushkill, as were most of the Tamiment buildings. Between 1921 and 1960, this theater gave rise to many future entertainers, including Imogene Coca, Danny Kaye, Jerome Robbins, Carol Burnett, Betty Garrett, and scores of others. Writers Neil Simon and Woody Allen began their careers there. Its educational quality was such that it was called the "Broadway of the Poconos."

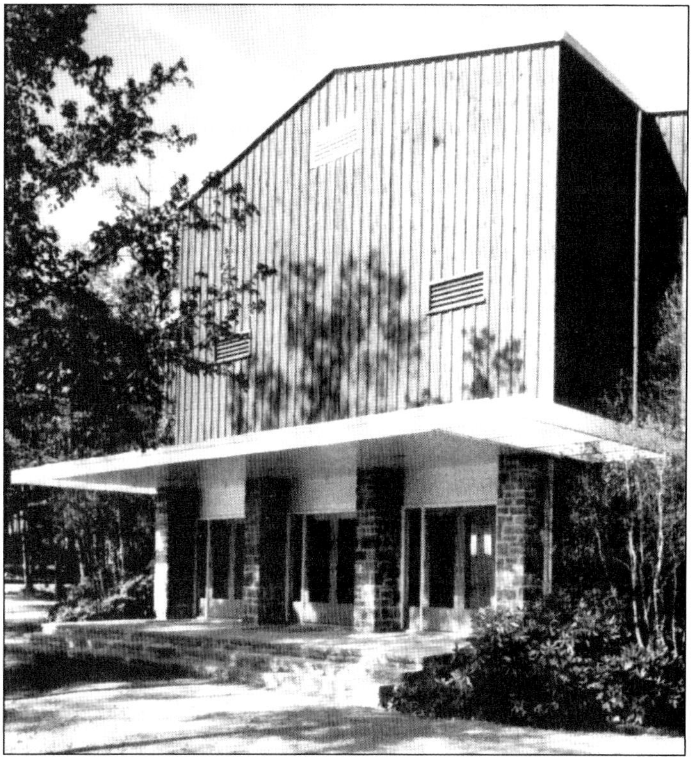

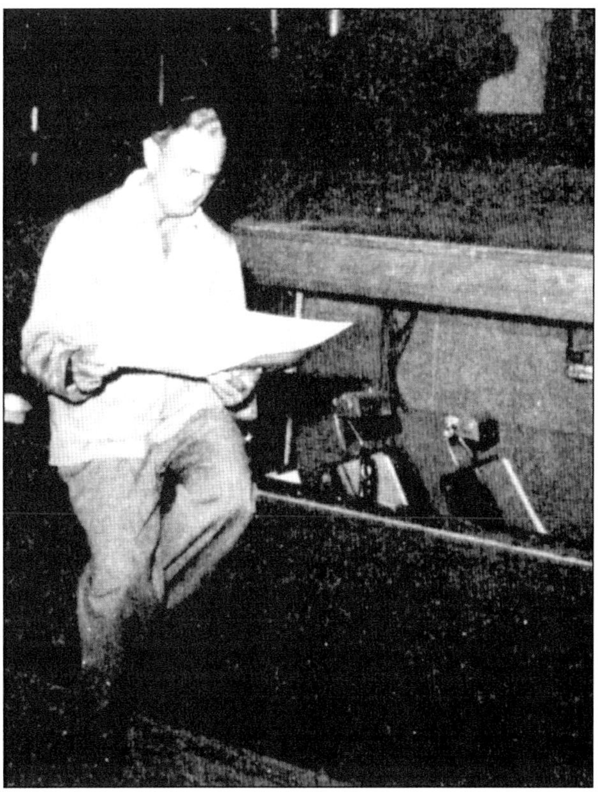

The genius of Max Liebman, Tamiment producer and director, was the driving force behind the Tamiment's success over the years. Liebman, responsible for the success of many later stars, arrived on the Tamiment scene in 1933 and stayed until 1949. From then on, his own career soared as he produced *Your Show of Shows*, based on the Tamiment productions, in 1950. (Photograph courtesy of Lew Goren.)

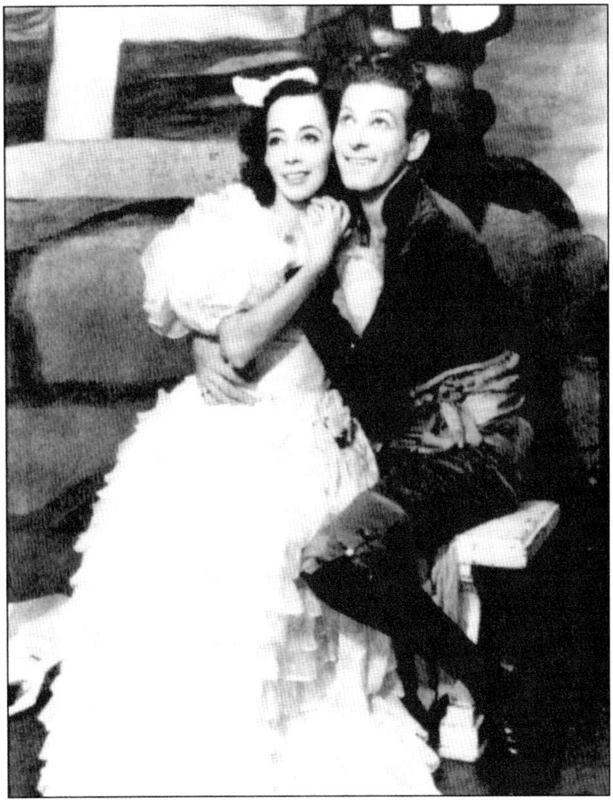

Imogene Coca and Danny Kaye are shown in a 1939 scene from *The Straw Hat Revue*, a Tamiment production that Max Liebman carried over to Broadway. Imogene performed at Tamiment in the 1930s and 1940s. Max Liebman summoned her in 1950 to perform on television, where she later starred in NBC's *Your Show of Shows*, with a four-year run. Kaye met his future wife, Sylvia Fine, at Tamiment. (Photograph from private collection.)

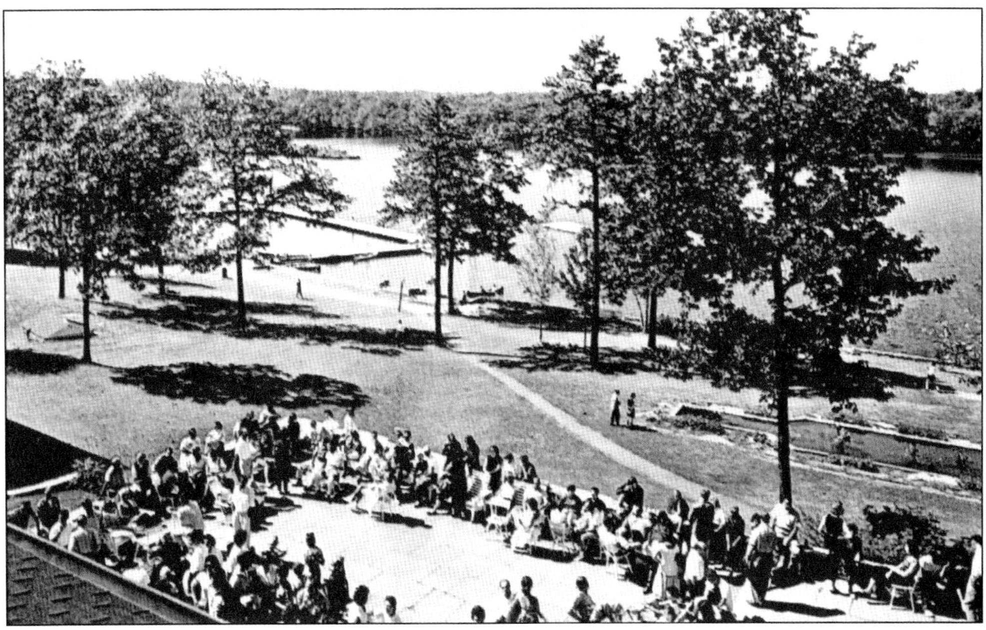

Tamiment's dining room terrace was a popular place to gather after feasting on the haute cuisine the resort's chefs had prepared. The terrace provided a delightful place for sunning, conversing, or taking part in al fresco cocktail parties, while enjoying the view and the gentle breeze drifting off Lake Tamiment.

Eight

River Road North

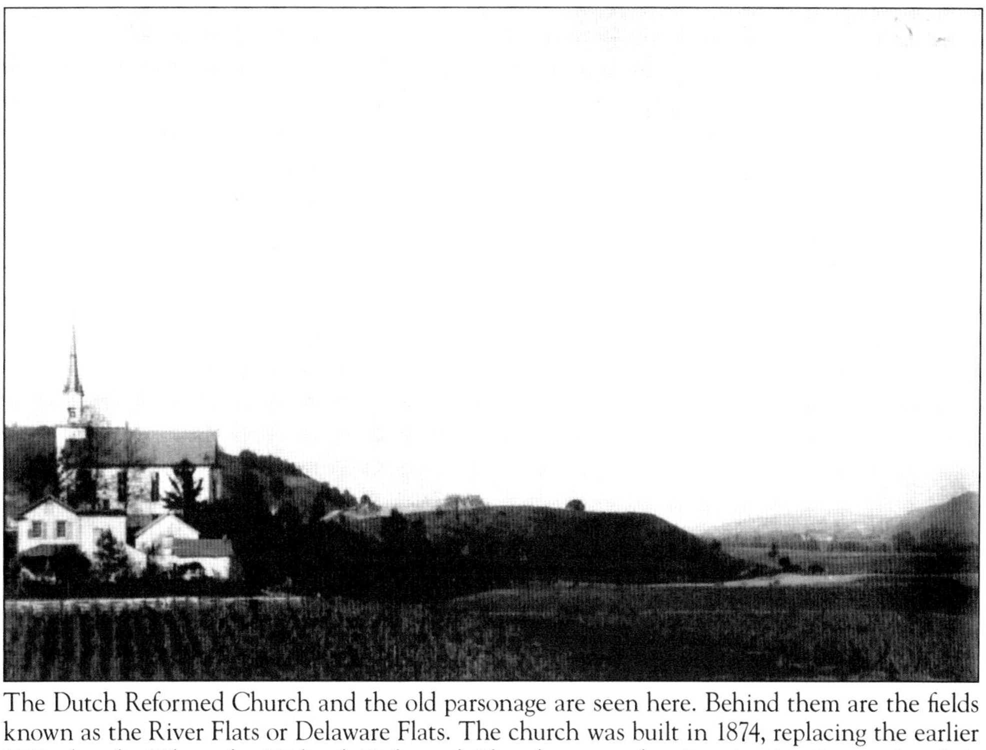

The Dutch Reformed Church and the old parsonage are seen here. Behind them are the fields known as the River Flats or Delaware Flats. The church was built in 1874, replacing the earlier 1832 church. When the Walpack Reformed Church across the river in New Jersey closed, it turned its records over to this church, and they were reportedly destroyed when some of the buildings burned. During the French and Indian War, the farmland along the Delaware River was subject to numerous Indian attacks. The river flats behind the church were the site of the kidnapping of Elizabeth Gonzalez, one of early settler Manuel Gonzalez's daughters. She was taken to Canada, where her father finally located her, 32 years later, and brought her back. The front of the church faces Route 209, which replaced a previous stage road and an even earlier road built in the 1750s between Bushkill and Milford.

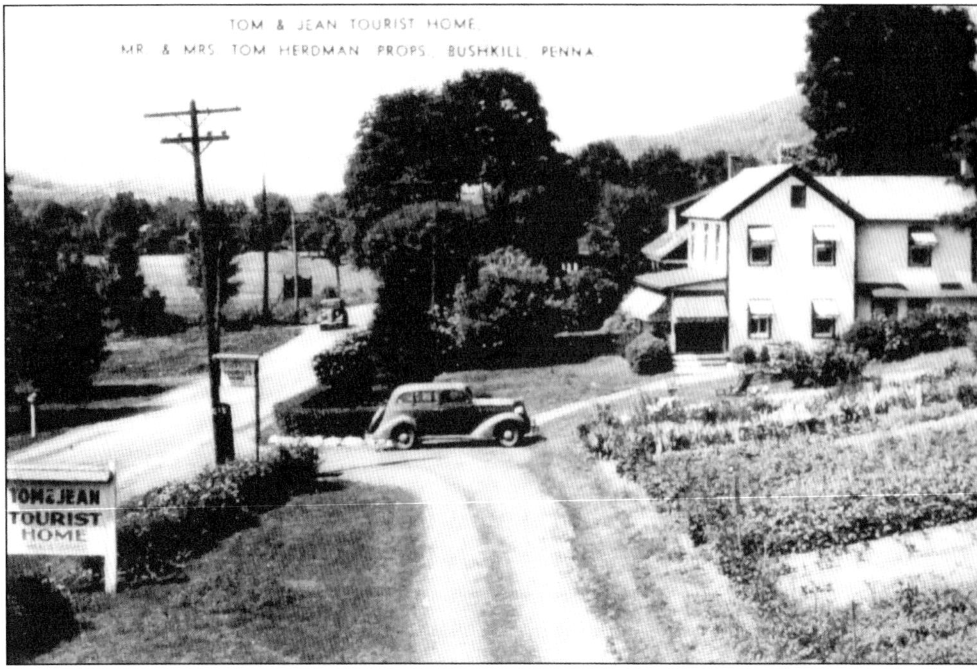

Tom and Jean Herdman originally came from Scotland and worked at Peter's House. Having familiarized themselves with the area and the tourism trade, they bought Bennett's house and turned it into a tourist home in the 1930s. It was located about a mile up from the Dutch Reformed Church and was destroyed during the course of the Tocks Island Dam project.

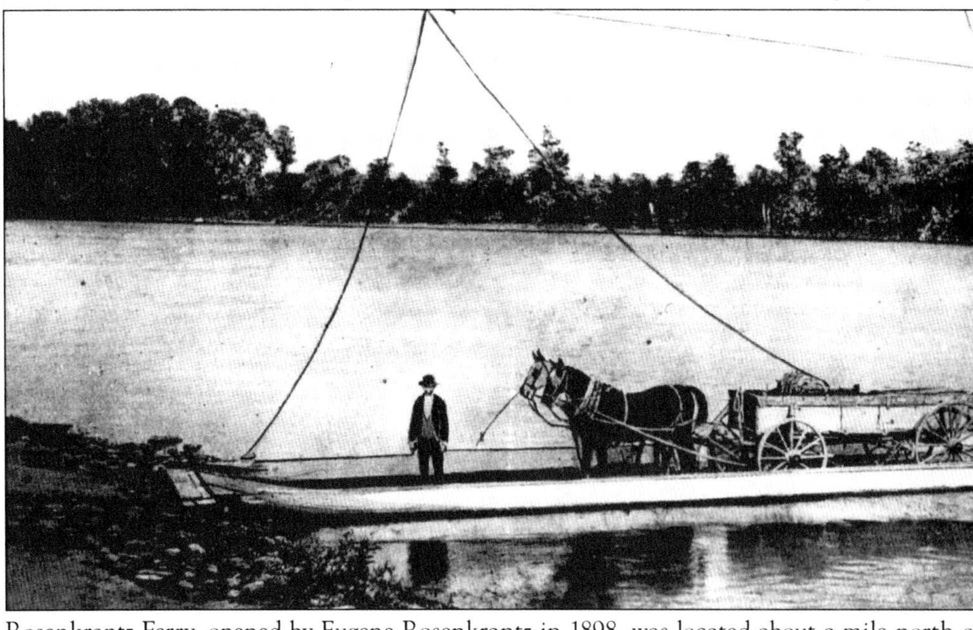

Rosenkrantz Ferry, opened by Eugene Rosenkrantz in 1898, was located about a mile north of the village of Bushkill. Traveling across the river, the ferry provided a convenient means for New Jersey folks to shop in Stroudsburg, a distance of 12 miles on the Pennsylvania side or 36 miles down the Jersey side. In early years, the ferry was poled across the river. Later the overhead crossing cable moved the ferry along.

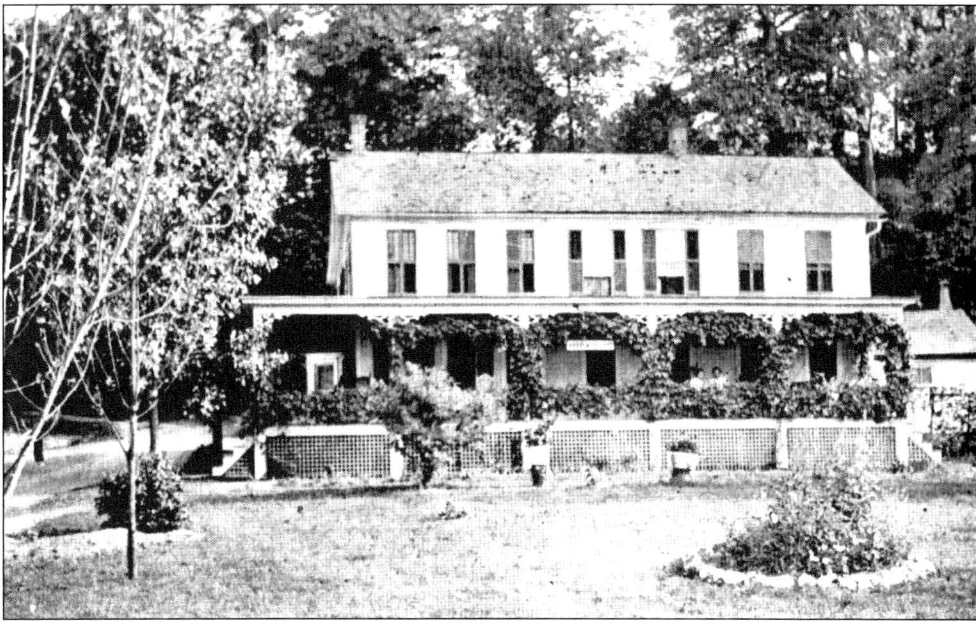

Daniel Brodhead operated his popular boardinghouse, known as Brookwood Farm. It was located on the river road, standing opposite to the lane leading to Rosenkrantz Ferry. Brodhead's daughter Lulu taught at the Brodhead School. It was taken for use of the Tocks Island Dam project.

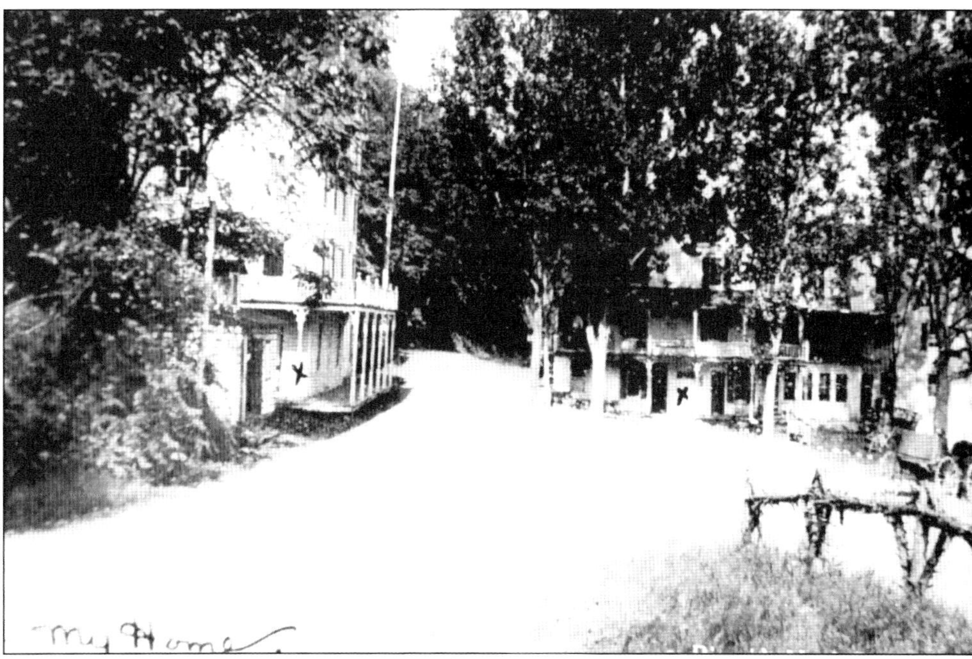

In 1838, William Place built the Cove, later known as the Riverside. In the heyday of rafting, its tavern was a popular stop for raftsmen. In 1902, Martin Bach, later the owner of the Maplehurst in East Stroudsburg, owned the place, followed by Paul Shannon in 1909 and John Cook in 1912. As seen in the photograph, the hotel annex stood across the road from the main house.

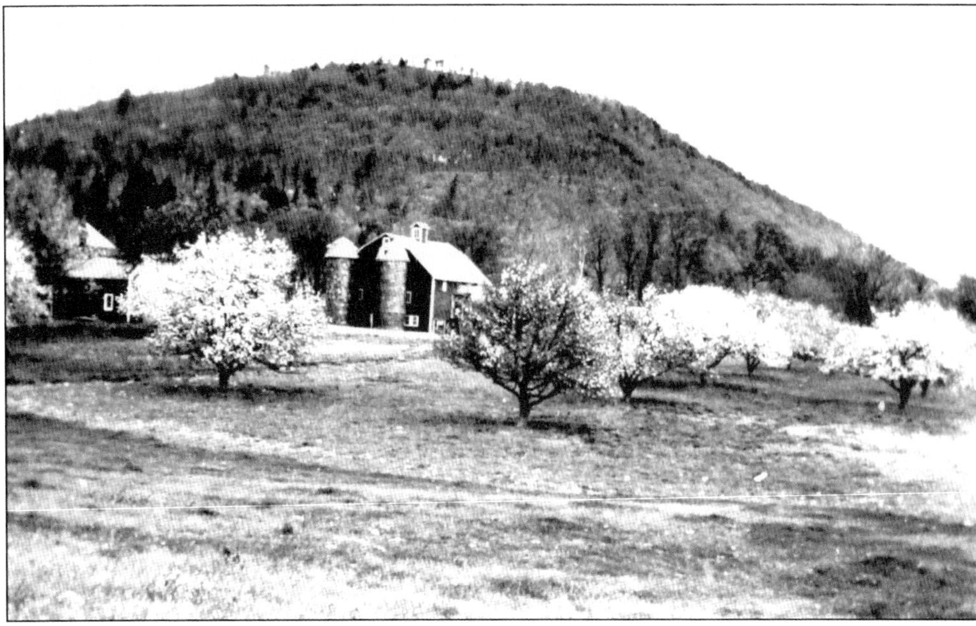

This farm at Egypt Mills was part of a very large land purchase William Nyce made during the Revolutionary War. His three sons built a gristmill along Toms Creek, the only one in the area. Many settlers came to the mill to buy flour and meal. The surrounding area became known as Egypt Mills, a biblical reference to famine-stricken travelers to Egypt in search of bread. (Photograph courtesy of Sylvia Miller.)

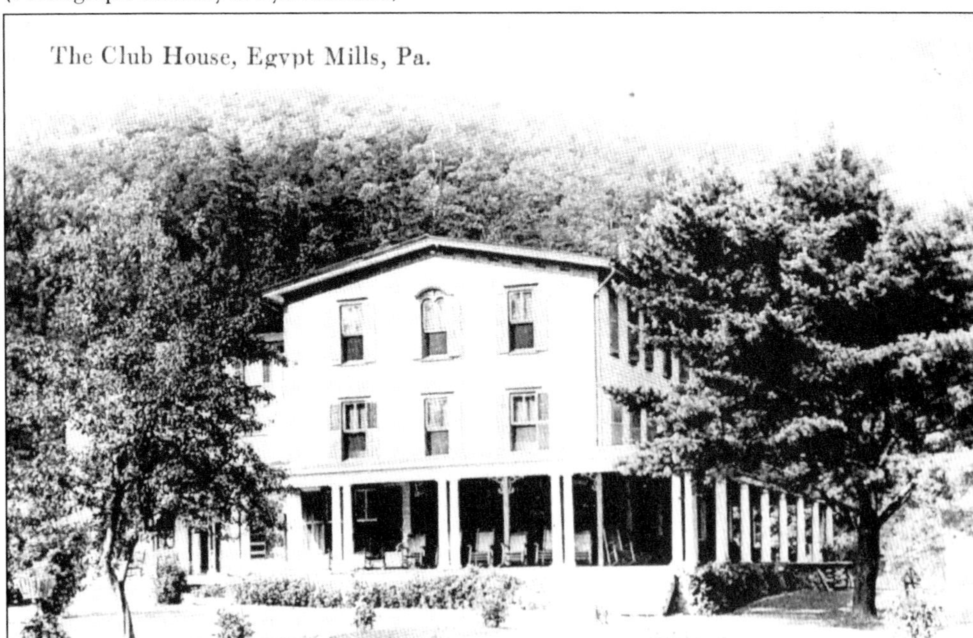

A group of sportsmen organized as the Egypt Mills Club and bought a portion of the Nyce property. The location, with an abundance of trout in nearby Toms Creek and game in the scenic surrounding woodlands, was ideal for their purpose. The property was sold in 1973 for the Tocks project, and the clubhouse and adjacent buildings were torn down.

The Egypt Mills Chapel also served the community as a meeting hall. Members of the local Egypt Mills Grange are pictured, along with their families. They were no doubt impressed with the automobile, for it was, indeed, an impressive sight. To date, the car has not been identified by make, model, or year; that will be left to auto experts to determine. (Photograph courtesy of Rita Laubner.)

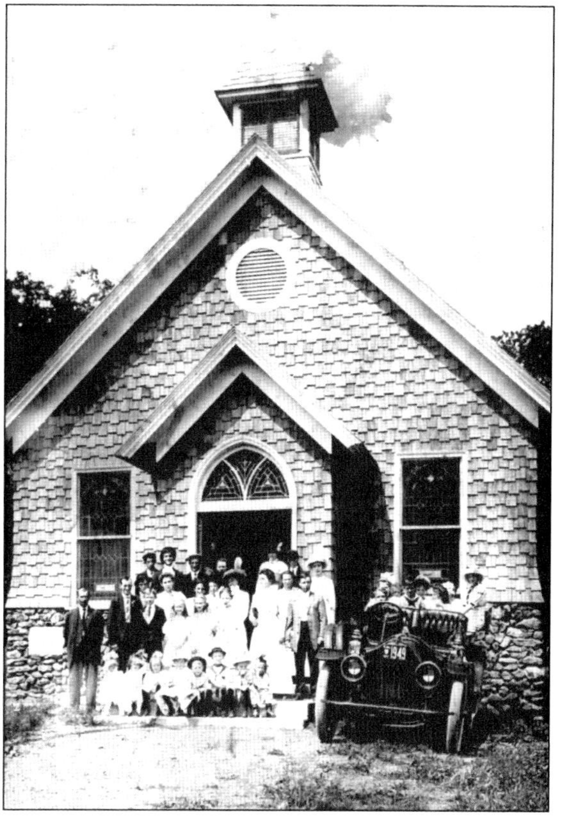

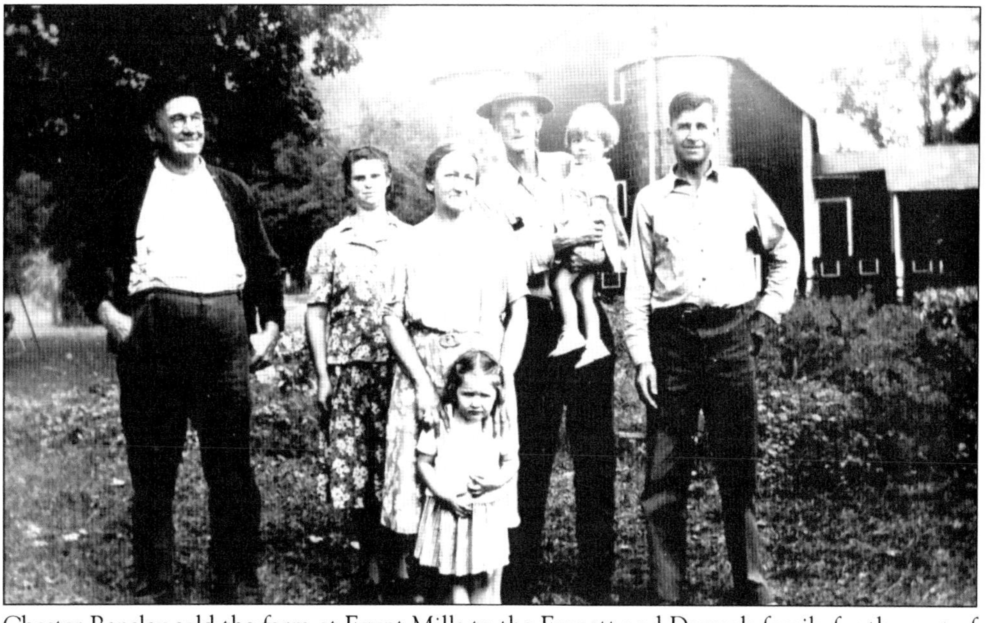

Chester Bensley sold the farm at Egypt Mills to the Faucett and Darragh family for the cost of the mortgage. Pictured, from left to right, are Chester Bensley, an unidentified farmworker, Edna Darragh, Sylvia Faucett (little girl in front), George Darragh (holding an unidentified neighbor child), and Cornell Faucett. (Photograph courtesy of Sylvia Miller.)

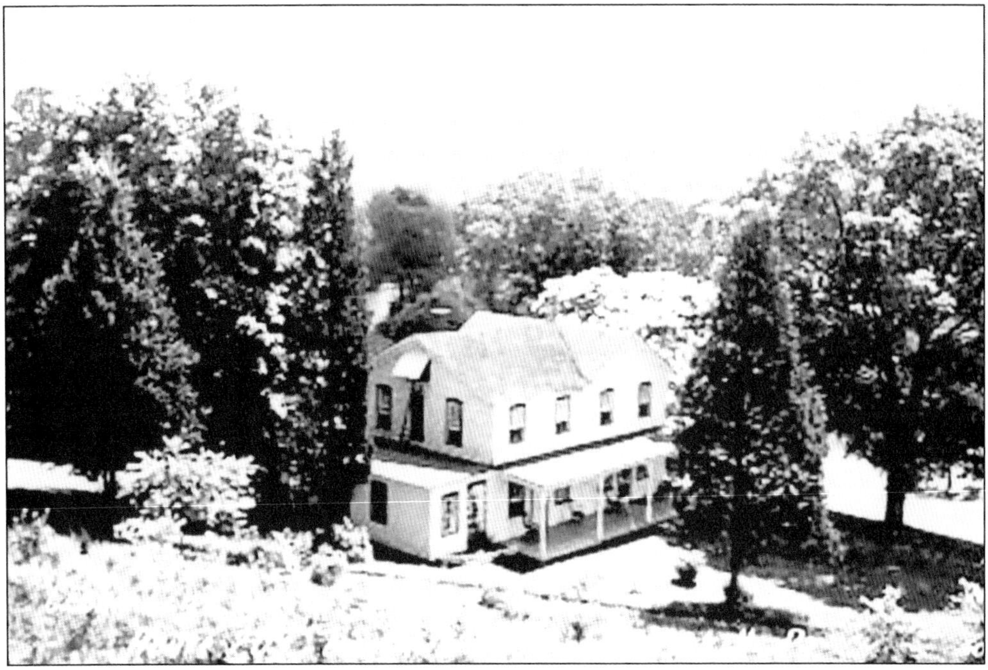

Albert Schoonover purchased Cedar Cliff Lodge in 1948, continuing to run it as a boardinghouse. It was open year-round to the summer trade and to hunters. The lodge and surrounding buildings were seized by eminent domain for the Tocks Island project. The family moved in 1970, and the buildings were subsequently destroyed.

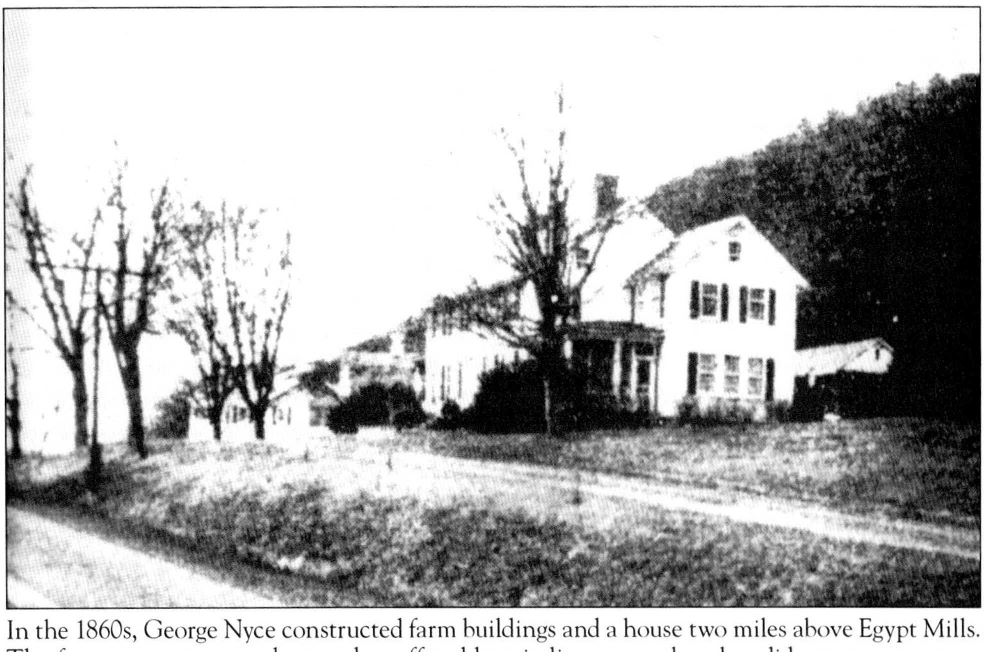

In the 1860s, George Nyce constructed farm buildings and a house two miles above Egypt Mills. The farm was a stagecoach stop that offered hospitality to travelers, but did not operate as an inn. J. Russell Eshback bought the farm with its 530 acres in 1948. The image shows the old stage road that passed in front of the house. The house was destroyed by a fire after Tocks Island purchased the land.

This picture of J. Russell Eshback was taken for his 1958 campaign for the Pennsylvania House of Representatives. Russell, often called the "gentleman farmer," devoted much of his life to public service in both the Pike County Courthouse and the Pennsylvania General Assembly. In his youth, he served as a model for artist Frank Schoonover, whose expert eye selected Eshback's rugged individualism as an ideal subject for his world war portraits. (Photograph courtesy of Jonathon Mark.)

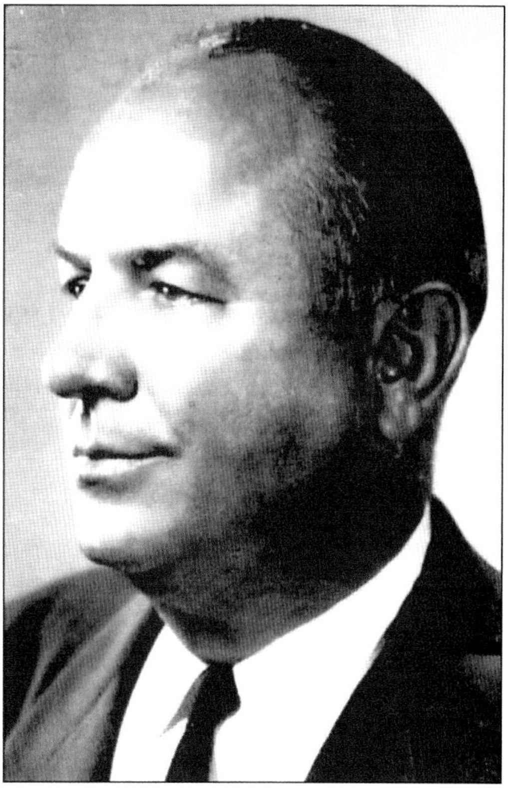

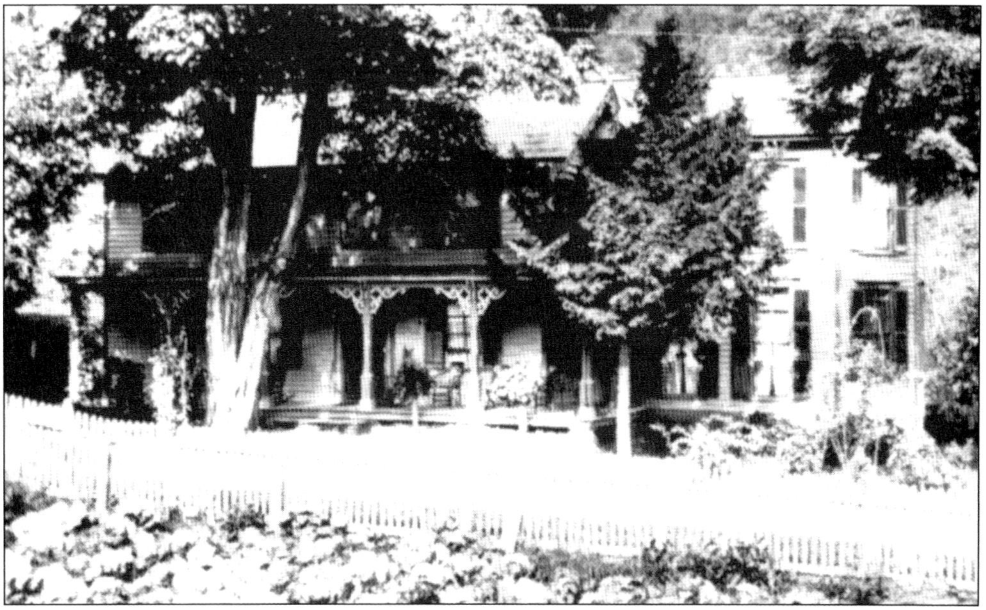

The Moses W. Van Gordon House stood along the River Road above Wheat Plains. The old stage road ran between the cabbage garden and the house. Van Gordon's daughter Savanna and her husband later owned the property. They moved, and during Prohibition, government agents found a two-story still in a subsequent occupant's barn. The "Revenuers" demolished it, to the dismay of some neighbors. (Photograph courtesy of PCHA.)

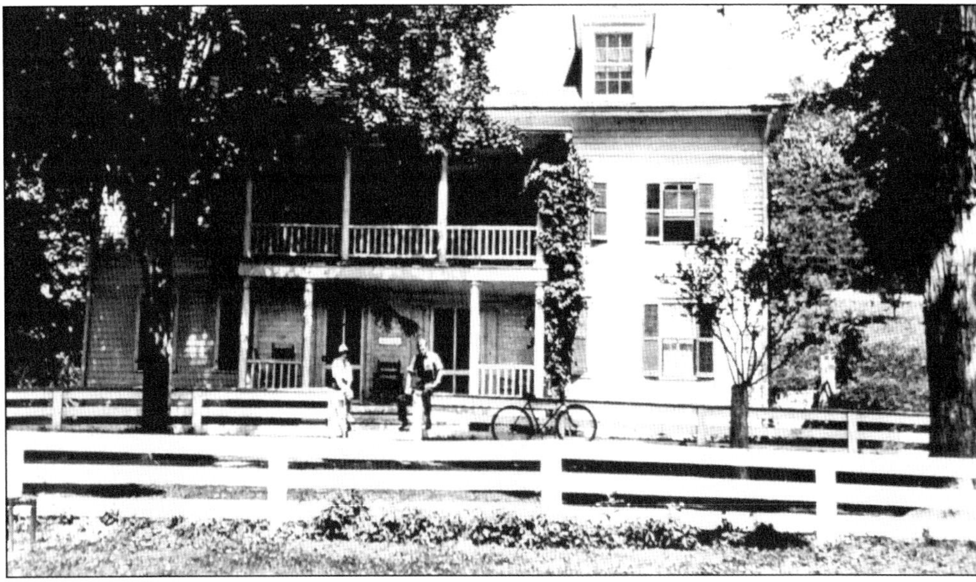

Garret Brodhead, a Revolutionary War soldier, established Wheat Plains shortly after the war. Cornelius Swartwood bought the property in 1871, owning it for 23 years. In 1874, Robert Packer Brodhead purchased the tract, bringing it back to the family. Six generations of the Brodhead family lived on Wheat Plains and farmed the rich flatlands soil. The old stage road passed close by the house about where the fence was located. (Photograph courtesy of PCHA.)

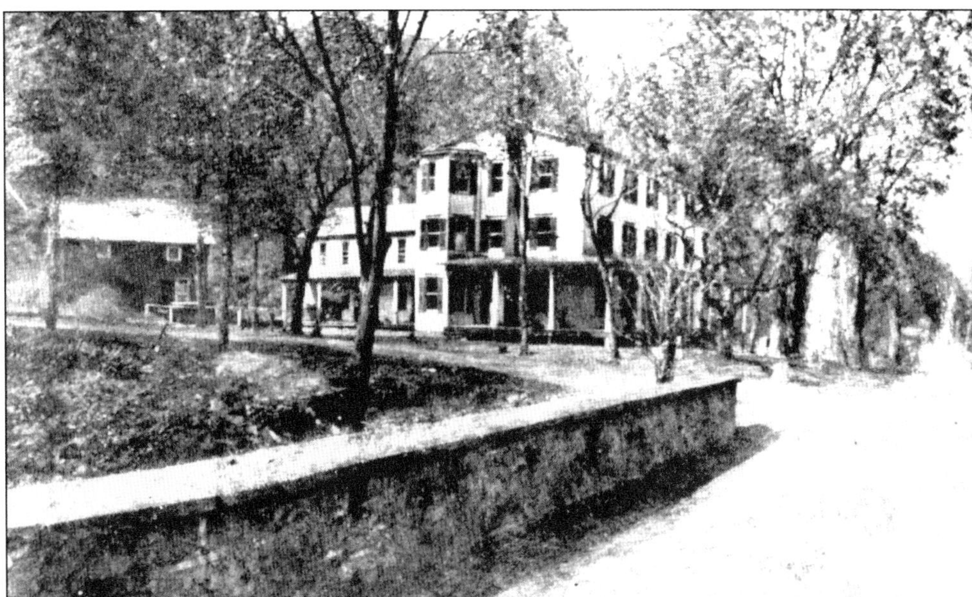

Moses Van Gordon Brisco owned the Brisco House, shown along the old stage road, at the time of the photograph. It was known as the Halfway House due to its location halfway between Port Jervis and Stroudsburg. Moses's father, James D. Brisco, was the previous owner and the only person in Lehman Township possessing a liquor license in 1869. James also served as postmaster when the area was called Delaware. (Photograph courtesy of PCHA.)

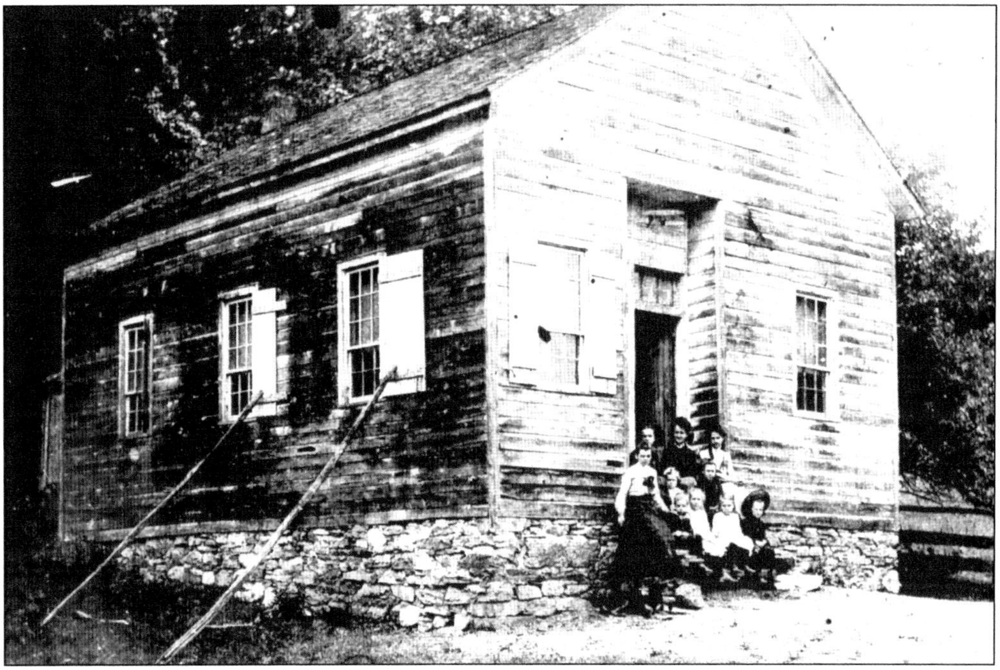

A 1904 photograph shows a group of students at the Brodhead School with their teacher, Lulu Brodhead. The school was located along the river road just below Brisco's. The one-room school opened before the mid-1800s and closed in 1925. (Photograph courtesy of PCHA.)

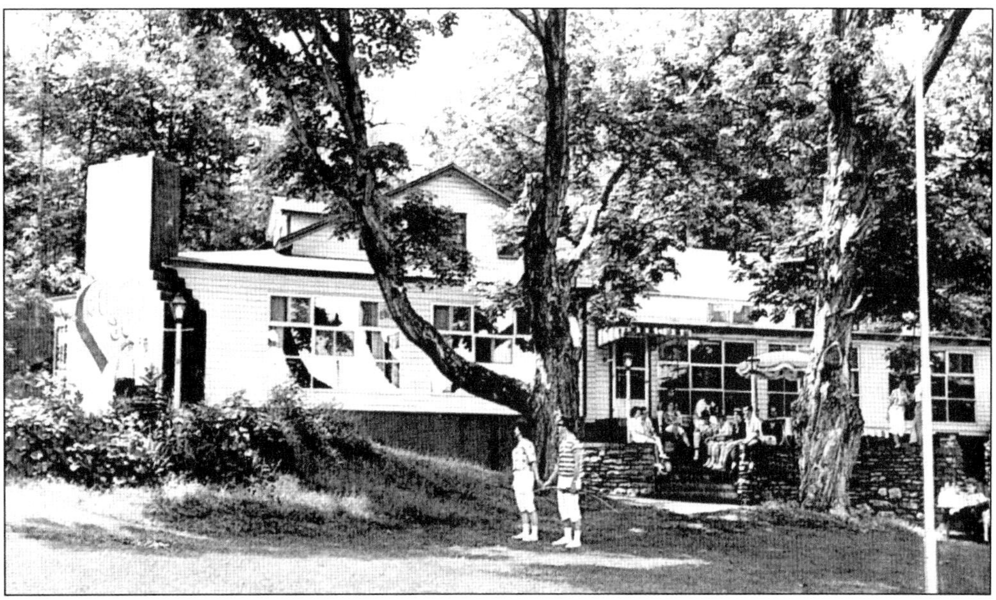

Ed and Claudine Glauser catered to newlyweds at Honeymoon Haven. They initiated the sunken Roman tubs, or tubs for two, that became the forerunner of the later heart-shaped tubs of other resorts in the Poconos. The former resort is now the home of the Pocono Environmental Center.

ACKNOWLEDGMENTS

We would like to thank the following individuals and organizations who have lent us their valued pictures, offered use of their facilities, and have given their time to supply information. For this, we are most grateful. Special thanks go to Katherine Riedmiller Angle; Lawrence and Margaret Butz; Dutot Museum; Charles Garris; Kemmie Garris; Roger Hartmann; Howard "Ike" Hineline; Robert Huffman; Russell Irwin; Michele Jacabella; Doug Kenney; Al Koster, Kirk, Summa, and Company, LLP, (CPA); Lucy Kosmerl; Middle Smithfield Township; Michelle Kintner; Susan Kopczynski, National Park Service, DWGNRA; Rita Schoonover Laubner; Marge Law; David MacDonough; Jonathon Mark; Sylvia Faucett Miller; Monroe County Historic Association; Penn State, Fred Waring Archives, especially Peter Kiefer; Pike County Historic Society; Jessica Mosier Sidlosky; Helen Sirola; Shawnee Inn, especially Monica Restrepo; Smithfield Township; Dixie Waring Wilson; and Walter Wyckoff.